OECD DOCUMENTS

EVALUATING INNOVATION IN ENVIRONMENTAL EDUCATION

PUBLISHER'S NOTE

The following texts have been left in their original form to permit faster distribution at lower cost.

ORGANISATION FOR ECONOMIC CO-OPERATION AND DEVELOPMENT

ORGANISATION FOR ECONOMIC CO-OPERATION AND DEVELOPMENT

Pursuant to Article 1 of the Convention signed in Paris on 14th December 1960, and which came into force on 30th September 1961, the Organisation for Economic Co-operation and Development (OECD) shall promote policies designed:

— to achieve the highest sustainable economic growth and employment and a rising standard of living in Member countries, while maintaining financial stability, and thus to contribute to the development of the world economy;

— to contribute to sound economic expansion in Member as well as non-member countries in the process of economic development; and

— to contribute to the expansion of world trade on a multilateral, non-discriminatory basis in accordance with international obligations.

The original Member countries of the OECD are Austria, Belgium, Canada, Denmark, France, Germany, Greece, Iceland, Ireland, Italy, Luxembourg, the Netherlands, Norway, Portugal, Spain, Sweden, Switzerland, Turkey, the United Kingdom and the United States. The following countries became Members subsequently through accession at the dates indicated hereafter: Japan (28th April 1964), Finland (28th January 1969), Australia (7th June 1971), New Zealand (29th May 1973) and Mexico (18th May 1994). The Commission of the European Communities takes part in the work of the OECD (Article 13 of the OECD Convention).

The Centre for Educational Research and Innovation was created in June 1968 by the Council of the Organisation for Economic Co-operation and Development and all Member countries of the OECD are participants.

The main objectives of the Centre are as follows:

— *to promote and support the development of research activities in education and undertake such research activities where appropriate;*

— *to promote and support pilot experiments with a view to introducing and testing innovations in the educational system;*

— *to promote the development of co-operation between Member countries in the field of educational research and innovation.*

The Centre functions within the Organisation for Economic Co-operation and Development in accordance with the decisions of the Council of the Organisation, under the authority of the Secretary-General. It is supervised by a Governing Board composed of one national expert in its field of competence from each of the countries participating in its programme of work.

Publié en français sous le titre :
ÉVALUER L'INNOVATION
DANS L'ÉDUCATION A L'ENVIRONNEMENT

ERRATUM

Evaluating Innovation in Environmental Education

(96 94 04 1) - ISBN 92-64-14211-8

The following text cancels and replaces the Foreword on page 3.

FOREWORD

Over the last seven years, teachers and pupils, university researchers and civil servants in many OECD countries have worked together with CERI (Centre for Educational Research and Innovation) to mobilise an innovatory programme in environmental education. This book is about innovation in education and its evaluation viewed through the experience of the OECD/CERI study, Environment and School initiatives (ENSI). In Part One we have drawn together some key papers which explore the main concepts, aspirations and practices of the ENSI study. Part Two of the book is derived from the evaluation conference for ENSI participants, which took place in Cromer, England, in June 1991, and was hosted by the Centre for Applied Research in Education (CARE), University of East Anglia, Norwich.

All the papers in this book are informed by the ideas and actions of many people across the globe, some of whom participated in the Cromer Conference. Particular acknowledgements are extended to May Pettigrew and Bridget Somekh, for their work in preparing and organising the contributions in this volume. Without their efforts this book would not have been published. Many others have also supported the production of this book, in particular Laura Tickner, Anne McKee, Lucila Recart, Catherine Beattie, Barry MacDonald and ENSI's head of study at the OECD, Kathleen Kelley-Lainé.

This book is published on the responsibility of the Secretary-General of the OECD.

Foreword

Over the last seven years teachers and pupils, university researchers and ministry administrators in many OECD countries have worked together with the Centre for Educational Research and Innovation (CERI) to mobilise an innovatory programme in environmental education. This book is about innovation in education and its evaluation viewed through the experience of this OECD/CERI study, Environment and School Initiatives (ENSI). In Part One we have drawn together some key papers which explore the main concepts, aspirations and practices of the ENSI study. Part 2 of the book is derived from the evaluation conference for ENSI participants, which took place in Cromer, United Kingdom, in June 1991, and was hosted by the Centre for Applied Research in Education (CARE), University of East Anglia, Norwich.

All the papers in this book are informed by the ideas and actions of many people across the globe, some of whom participated in the Cromer Conference. We would like first to acknowledge their influence on us as we shaped the presentations and discussions of the Cromer Conference into the papers that appear in Part 2. Many others have given us direct support in the production of this book, in particular Laura Tickner, Anne McKee, Lucila Recart, Barry MacDonald and ENSI's head of study at OECD, Kathleen Kelley. We are indebted to them for their kind support and advice.

Table of Contents

Part One
AN INTERNATIONAL STUDY IN ENVIRONMENTAL EDUCATION

Chapter 1
The study "environment and school initiatives": phase one

Peter Posch

Chapter 2
Developing community-focused environmental education through action-research

John Elliott

Chapter 3
Networking in environmental education

Peter Posch

Chapter 4
Evaluating the outcomes of environment and school initiatives

Michela Mayer

Part Two
EVALUATION PERSPECTIVES FROM THE CROMER CONFERENCE

Chapter 5
Values, power and strategy in evaluating design -- Some preliminary considerations

Barry MacDonald

Chapter 6
Evaluating action-research projects

Bridget Somekh

Chapter 7
The content of programme evaluation

Saville Kushner

Chapter 8
The conduct of evaluation

May Pettigrew and Barry MacDonald

Document 1
The inter policy evaluation -- Principles and procedures

Barry MacDonald and Ian Stronach

Chapter 9
Interviewing in case study evaluation

Barry MacDonald

Chapter 10
Making the most of judgement data

Nigel Norris

Chapter 11
Reporting evaluations

Bridget Somekh, Richard Davies and Maggie MacLure

Introduction

by

May Pettigrew and *Bridget Somekh*
Centre for Applied Research in Education
University of East Anglia, Norwich, UK

This book is about an approach to curriculum development and evaluation in which teachers and students worked with parents, local communities, politicians and a major international organisation, to carry out research and bring about improvements. Their focus was not some simulation game, but the concerns about the environment which are perhaps the major pre-occupation of our age. They were working in the Environment and Schools Initiative (ENSI), a major international curriculum development programme sponsored by CERI of the OECD.

This book is primarily about an approach to evaluation. Its genesis was a conference at Cromer in Norfolk, UK, in June 1990, led by Barry MacDonald and his colleagues at the Centre for Applied Research in Education of the University of East Anglia. Over a period of more than twenty years CARE had developed a methodology for evaluation which seemed to Kathleen Kelley, Head of the ENSI study at CERI, to be particularly suited to a multi-national project of this kind. The conference had the purpose of preparing those leading ENSI in all the participating countries to carry out an evaluation of their national projects. Throughout the week, the presentations drew upon examples of evaluations carried out by CARE, and these were continually compared and contrasted with the needs of ENSI -- in each country and at all levels. We have tried to retain this balance. Here is a book which presents a particular evaluation methodology, but since common -- and not-so-common -- methodological challenges and their resolution can only be described satisfactorily in context, the book also presents an overview of the work of the ENSI programme.

ENSI is an international curriculum development programme which starts from the premise that schooling offers a unique opportunity to address problems facing global society. Our planet, we are reminded daily, is under grave threat from the accumulated effects of human activities and technologies. The problems demand action at all levels in society: at the macro levels of politics and economics and the micro levels of individual citizens and their local communities. ENSI works at each of these levels. It carries political weight through its appeal to the imperative for states to be seen to be doing something about the environment. Whether or not such legitimation for ENSI is symbolic (as in the case, for example, of England and Wales which have chosen observer status rather than full participation in the project), or motivated by a genuine will to change, ENSI derives support through this political expediency. The focus of the project, though, is its work at the local level.

Aims and principles of ENSI

ENSI teachers and students aspire to work through their local community in improving the quality of the environment. In this sense the project has the capacity to bring the school into the community and the community into the school. Environmental issues are defined, analyzed and actively tackled. The aim is not just learning about the environment but generating usable knowledge in a meaningful problem context. The notion that schools can be producers of knowledge has a radical ring to it. But yet, there is something of a contemporary political flavour to this language. ENSI could be described as a project which develops entrepreneurial qualities in students through challenging them to acquire knowledge for a real purpose and use it in the service of the community.

Briefly, curriculum development in ENSI stems from two main aims:

i)   the promotion of environmental awareness;
ii) the promotion of dynamic qualities.

There are four principles informed by these overall aims. Students should:

i)   experience the environment as a sphere of personal experience;
ii)   examine the environment as a subject of inter-disciplinary learning and research;
iii) shape the environment as a sphere of socially important action;
iv)   accept the environment as a challenge for initiative, independence and responsible action.

These principles and aims incorporate a theory of teaching and learning inspired by the process model of the curriculum developed by Lawrence Stenhouse, the founder and first Director of CARE. In common with other curriculum theorists, such as Jerome Bruner, Stenhouse believed that the curriculum consisted not in specifications of learning outcomes set out on paper, but in students' cognitive and social processes. These processes depended more than anything else on the traditional practices of teachers, embedded in the cultural assumptions of, for example, their locality, nationality and social class. So, in order to change the curriculum it was important to involve teachers in researching their own practice, and in specifying a new curriculum in terms of practices which could be tested by other teachers in their own classrooms. Two essential principles of this approach to curriculum development can be seen in ENSI's aims and principles. Firstly, there is an assumption that the curriculum will be created through teachers' and students' action and not through developing a set of pre-specified objectives. Secondly, there is an emphasis on teachers and students engaging in an exploration of the environment which can be construed as a form of research. The cyclical process of research, reflection, planning, action, evaluation, question raising, research ... and so on ... can be applied to both environmental problems and the problems of bringing about changes in teaching methods: pupils engage in active enquiry and action in the environment and teachers research the educational strategies that they employ.

The origins and development of ENSI

In 1985 ministers of education from the OECD countries convened in Paris. Economic issues and their relationship to education were generally the main focus of discussion at this forum but this time the agenda was punctuated by a plea from the Austrian minister, Herbert Moritz, that environmental education must be taken much more seriously by member states. As a result this Ministerial committee agreed to include environmental education among other areas that called for further work.

The rationale for promoting dynamic learning qualities in students is persuasive. It centres on the argument that our increasingly complex world demands that pupils acquire qualities of responsibility, initiative and entrepreneurship, skills of problem posing and problem solving, and a capacity for synthetic and holistic thinking. New demands have been placed upon societies through changing work patterns, ever enlarging social institutions and the increasing inability and reluctance of governments to assume control of socio-economic institutions and processes. Relatively static economies in the past relied on educational systems to incorporate values of order, discipline, diligence and duty. Now there are demands that all citizens should be responsible and adaptable, not just the few at the top of industrial and administrative

12

hierarchies. Static, transmissive modes of schooling will be unable to meet these changing demands. And so there is a need for teaching and learning premised upon investigative experience, reflection and responsible action. The environment offers the potential to develop a curriculum in which students acquire dynamic learning qualities in a meaningful and challenging problem context.

Phase 1 of ENSI began in 1986 as an 'Innovation and Exchange activity'. This kind of initiative is relatively low-budget and small-scale. Eleven member countries participated: Austria, Belgium, Denmark, the Federal Republic of Germany, Finland, Italy, the Netherlands, Norway, Portugal, Sweden and Switzerland. Each country appointed a national coordinator to develop an infrastructure of local support and international collaboration. The number of schools formally involved in each country varied from one in Portugal to nine in Austria. These schools tended to act as network centres for others in their country. In addition, several countries chose to work alongside the project as observers. The first phase concluded with a conference at Linz, in 1988, where 350 participants included 150 students and 120 teachers. The success of the initiative, already apparent, was reinforced by the work presented at the conference (see Elliott, 1989). The governing board, decided on the basics of the report of the conference to include ENSI on the main programme of work.

"when the event was reported to the governing board of CERI the members were practically unanimous in their decision to continue the activity as an integral part of the main programme" (Kelley, 1992).

Phase II of ENSI was an extension of phase I in both scope and aspiration. Twenty member countries were involved: Australia, Austria, Belgium, Canada, Denmark, Eire, Federal Republic of Germany, Finland, France, Italy, Japan, Netherlands, Norway, Portugal, Spain, Sweden, United States, Turkey, Scotland, and Yugoslavia. Hungary later joined as one of the observer countries. In addition to the expansion of the number of schools involved, PHASE II was organised on an innovative basis, with the appointment of pedagogical support persons, to work alongside teachers, and in particular to facilitate their action research activities. Phase II aims to integrate the work in schools with the development of coherent national policies for environmental education: this will be represented in the country evaluation reports and through the in-depth policy reviews which are being carried out in six member countries.

The role of CERI in international curriculum development

The Centre for Educational Research and Innovation (CERI) of the OECD, as an international organisation, was ideally positioned to co-ordinate a multi-national education programme. As Kathleen Kelley (1992) says:

"ENSI ... is, I think, true to the original ambitions of the Centre: to combine questions of the teaching/learning process, with questions of educational policy and to assist member governments in reflecting upon their policy developments by providing them with relevant international data."

However, in some senses ENSI constituted a new kind of initiative for CERI. Generally, CERI works at the 'expert level' in relation to projects, which involves coordination of national representatives, commissioning of papers, the organisation of conferences and the writing of official reports. CERI's work with ENSI includes all of this, but in addition there is a more direct orientation towards supporting grass roots development carried out by teachers and students in classrooms and local communities.

There are particular challenges and opportunities for an international curriculum development project. Curriculum is an expression of the culture of a society and embodies its values: it follows that in an international study such as ENSI, each participant country develops its own unique approach. But, at the same time, there is an opportunity to make comparisons and exchange ideas: as a result, it is no longer possible to rely upon so many assumptions about 'the right way' of doing things. Environmental education raises value-issues in a particularly direct way, because damage to the environment is a result of life styles and technologies, and possible solutions to environmental problems usually have financial implications. Environmental education encourages young people to ask questions about basic human endeavours such as agriculture, manufacturing industry and trade; questions which challenge the maintenance of existing power and resources, for example in the relationship between developed and under-developed countries. Of course, environmental education can be construed as a more technical, information-based endeavour, in which students are taught a 'received' approach rather than being encouraged to pose problems. However, given the nature and scale of international debate on environmental issues during the period of ENSI's funding -- a period which included the 'Earth Summit' in Rio in 1992 -- it was not possible for any country to take such an approach without it being, de facto, contentious.

There is a sense in which ENSI became a different project in each country, as a result of either overt political control or incipient cultural reproduction. The governments of some nations, such as Austria, openly encouraged young people to raise awareness of environmental issues in their communities; others, such as the British government, declined to fund a national initiative at all. Through decisions on whether to fund or not, on the scale of funding, and on the selection of personnel, national projects were shaped by administrators equally, through existing traditions of curriculum and schooling, national projects were shaped by teachers, parents and the students themselves. At the opposite ends of extremes, some national projects were centred on the activities of students and teachers (for example, in developing local initiatives such as a community scheme to re-cycle waste), whereas others were centred on the development of materials and technology (for example, in developing an electronic network and national data base of information on the environment).

These differences in cultural values were reflected in the extent to which ENSI became an action research project in different countries. Action research as a methodology which encourages a student-centred, exploratory approach to curriculum development, fits well, as we have already said, with the values of environmental education officially espoused by ENSI: those countries where such values were politically acceptable and such educational practices feasible in the schools, engaged in action research on a large scale; in other countries where teachers had traditionally depended upon a text book-based curriculum, developed other ways of working which did not create cultural strain. It is true to say that these differences in working methods caused some problems when different national groups attempted to collaborate, but one of the strengths of ENSI was that it set up an infrastructure which enabled collaboration between willing partners without imposing it upon all.

ENSI phase II began in 1989 and was planned as a development project, incorporating evaluation within its overall action research methodology. In addition, there were to be a series of national policy reviews, carried out by consultants, which would ensure that its work in environmental education was disseminated effectively at the political level. This option of an additional policy review was taken up by six countries and funded from national budgets. While this was an important part of the OECD's strategy to disseminate the project's work in environmental education, it did not meet the OECD's need to demonstrate that ENSI had worked effectively; and by 1990 Kathleen Kelley had taken the decision to require each national project to produce an evaluation report, in addition to reporting on the research and development work in individual schools. For those countries which were engaged in action research on a large scale this additional requirement caused some problems: there appeared to be conflicting demands in both facilitating action research in schools and working in a more detached manner to evaluate the work of those same schools. For other countries the requirement was uncontentious. However, for all the national teams, the need to produce a report, which both coherently and adequately represented the work of a large number of divergent activities, presented a challenge.

An important feature of ENSI, during both its first and second phases, was a series of intensive conferences which drew together the co-ordinators, pedagogic support people and relevant experts from participating countries. These conferences were the foundation of successful, international collaboration

14

between a significant proportion of countries, particularly those who had taken up full member, rather than observer, status. They provided a forum for discussion of national infrastructures and teaching strategies, and did a great deal to break down any misunderstandings deriving from the differences in cultural values which have already been described. Since the Linz conference in 1988, there have been a number of other important project conferences and seminars in phase 2. Seminar themes so far, or planned, include: Action Research, Evaluation, Networking, Values, Complexity, Teaching for Sustainable Development and Environmental Economics in the curriculum.

An invitation to Cromer

This book puts forward a methodology for evaluation grounded in the need to understand the relationship between individual action and political and social systems. We have said that the ENSI Programme provides the context without which it would be very difficult to give flesh to the ideas. But there is another important context: partly because it was where 35 individuals came together without whom we would not have been able to write this book; but mainly because it symbolises our theme of the importance of international debate focused on researching and understanding the consequences of human action.

Cromer, 6-12th June 1991. A pretty if unremarkable little holiday town by the margins of the North Sea in East Anglia. Certainly an unusual place for an international conference on evaluation hosted by the Centre for Applied Research in Education and addressed to representatives of the OECD Environment and School Initiatives study.

CARE's role at this conference was to articulate a theory and practice of evaluation that would assist ENSI participants in formulating evaluation strategies. These should be appropriate to the political demands for accountability of the project at state and international levels and to inform debate at all levels in terms coherent with the values and spirit of the initiative. The CARE model of evaluation embodies a set of values congruent with ENSI aspirations; it is process in its orientation and participatory in its style. But it is also a political model which negotiates with power and politics in the evaluation context.

And so, is a ENSI, challenging programme in environmental education, a successful venture in international collaboration, and an active agent of reflective teaching and learning. It is sometimes easy to fall prey to suggestions that our attempts to realise educational values show little learning curve; that we invent, deploy and in cycles return to where we started from years before. Pessimists doubt that reform which is genuinely educational can be sustained. They might have suspected that ENSI would become an historical oddity, a kind of educational archaeopteryx that got off the ground but ended nowhere. This is not the case. The secret lies, we think, in a unique combination of political will and individual agency.

ENSI is unusual both for its size and its longevity. As an international collaboration in curriculum development, it is unique in a period when educational innovation in many countries is a matter of political dictate. The acknowledged importance of its focus on the environment, at a time when there is no longer any doubt of the inter-relationship between the activities and technologies of human beings and the ecology of the Earth, has provided the political will to secure funding for two phases of work over a nine-year period. We know from the research into educational innovation carried out over the past thirty years that all of these factors are essential enabling conditions for successful large scale curriculum development: without them there is simply not the time, scope for experimentation or resources to bring about any sustained educational change. But in themselves they are not enough. In addition, ENSI has been led by a team with a thorough knowledge of the conditions which, we know from this research, facilitate effective improvement in practice; individuals and organisations with experience of supporting change and development stretching back over a long period. The kind of in-depth preoccupation with the evaluation of ENSI which all of us at CARE experienced during the week of the Cromer conference had the fascination of peering into a n extensive, wild nature reserve. What flora and fauna were there? We had many glimpses and many travellers' tales, but no opportunity to explore. If you enjoy reading this book, we recommend that you also get hold of the evaluation reports from each participating country which will soon be published. They are sure to make interesting reading.

References

ELLIOTT, J. (1989), *Environmental Education in Europe: Innovation, Marginalisation, or Assimilation?* Report on ENSI commissioned by OECD/CERI, Paris.

KELLEY, K. 1992, *Environment and School Initiatives,* Paper presented to the AERA, San Francisco April 1992, San Francisco.

PART ONE

AN INTERNATIONAL STUDY IN ENVIRONMENTAL EDUCATION

EDITORIAL

by

Bridget Somekh *and* **May Pettigrew**
Centre for Applied Research in Education
University of East Anglia, Norwich, UK

The four chapters in Part One represent the Environment in Schools Initiative from the point of view of some of those who have been most closely involved in conceptualising its purposes, designing its infrastructure and supporting its implementation.

We have included here some of the most significant papers to emerge from the project since 1986. In relation to the book as a whole they serve two purposes: first, they provide an account of the project's aspirations and working methods, as well as an analysis of the problems and issues which have preoccupied participants; second, they trace the research and development of an approach to innovation, from theories and beliefs to educational practices across many national boundaries.

In the first chapter, Peter Posch, develops a philosophy for environmental education in the late twentieth century. He describes how, at its inception, ENSI Phase I, adopted two aims which served to harness the energy of potentially disparate ideologies: by a commitment to promoting environmental awareness it appealed to "a conservationist spirit and hostility towards economic and technological development", and by a commitment to promoting "dynamic qualities such as initiative, independence, commitment, the readiness to accept responsibility" it appealed to technologists and entrepreneurs. Thus, the strength of ENSI, from the beginning, was its recognition of the creative tension between the need for human beings to adopt earth-friendly life styles and the need for them to ensure the economic security, born of technological development, upon which these life style often, paradoxically depend.

In the enactment of these aims, the ENSI Study has adopted the methodology of action research and refined and reconstituted it to suit national cultures and an inter-disciplinary curriculum. Teachers and students spear-headed curriculum development by carrying out research and action in their schools and local communities. The chapter by John Elliott provides a closely-argued rationale for action research, as a methodology especially suited to promoting the values and aims of ENSI. He argues that, through its focus on constructing knowledge through practice, action research supports exactly the kind of exploration and risk-taking which develops dynamic qualities integrally with developing environmental awareness. The central section of the chapter focuses on the teacher competencies needed to enable students to learn in this way, and on action research as a means of developing these competencies. The chapter ends with a detailed description of techniques and methods which can be used by teachers and students carrying out action research. It is a long chapter, but we have included it in its entirety because it emphasises, through its range and balance, the importance of seeing action research as both a practical and a philosophical

19

endeavour. Action research is a "practical theory", in the sense that in carrying it out, the use of rigorous research procedures is allied with the development of understanding, and both are crucial to the improvement of the curriculum in schools.

Peter Posch's second paper in this section serves as a marker of the ENSI project's development over a period of five years and it invites comparison with his opening chapter. There is now a confidence of tone which reflects the considerable success of ENSI by the time Phase II was fully established. Here is a project in which, as he says, environmental initiatives "are self-initiated by teachers and students" as a response to "the growing pressures exerted both by external societal changes and by growing discontent inside school." In the rest of the chapter he develops and extends this theme. As in chapter one, space is devoted to describing a number of projects designed and carried out by students, with the support of their teachers: many of these involve the education of the local community through the initiatives of their own children. But these are not merely examples of children influencing their parents through a commitment and enthusiasm which is unexpectedly quaint. Whether it's the defence of an area of waterland threatened by sewage as a result of industrialisation in Italy; or the establishment in association with a nature conservancy association of "meadows for butterflies and hedges for birds" in Austria; or the collection and dissemination of information about water pollution to galvanise community action to challenge the local water company in Australia; these initiative have a political purpose and exert political leverage. Peter Posch argues for a reconceptualisation of systems and structures as a means of tackling the pressing problems of our age. He sees a need to reject the underlying tenets of technical rationalism in western society, in which everything from knowledge to social organisation has been constructed on hierarchical lines. Instead he argues for dynamic networks which harness the creative energy of individuals to exert political influence and bring about change. The international ENSI study is an example of what he calls a "broker-mediated dynamic network", in which an infrastructure of national co-ordinators and pedagogic support people, linked through CERI of the OECD, enables communication between the multiple nodes of the network. ENSI has been effective in bringing about change. Drawing upon the research of Schön and House he demonstrates that this is no grandiose, unrealistic scheme, but an important proposition to counteract the institutional inertia endemic in traditional western patterns of organisation. By such means we could begin to take action to create better living conditions for all which would, of course, entail devoting considerable cognitive energy and commitment to nurturing "Mitwelt" -- our "fellow world" of the environment.

Michela Mayer's paper is the final chapter in this section. By introducing the theme of evaluation, which is the main focus of the book, Michela Mayer reinforces the conceptual and structural coherence that link innovation, action research and evaluation in education. If Part One, as a whole, provides the contextualisation necessary to a full understanding of Part Two, this chapter has the added function of acting as a counter-point to the evaluation methodology advocated later in the book. It reflects the same desire to integrate conflicting ideologies which was a feature of chapter 1. Mayer's concept of "quality indicators" incorporates the notion that evaluation is a "theory-laden operation, full of values" but it pre-supposes a need to measure and compare initiatives to determine their quality, using a number of qualitative and quantitative procedures. Once again, it is environmental education which acts as the unifying catalyst: this is a field of human endeavour in which the cognitive can only be judged alongside the affective. Mayer's paper argues convincingly for quality indicators as a means of "describing the educational strategy of the projects ... from a cognitive point of view ... and also from an affective point of view ... in other words, describing the relationships and the interactions that the projects set up." Her chapter concludes with a useful review of techniques and methods which can be used by project participants to carry out this kind of evaluation.

Chapter 1

THE STUDY "ENVIRONMENT AND SCHOOL INITIATIVES": PHASE ONE[1]

by

Peter Posch
University of Klagenfurt
Austria

Following the meeting in Paris in 1985, at which Herbert Moritz, the Austrian Minister of Education won support, in principle, for an initiative on environmental education, a draft proposal was written, which I, in my capacity as the Austrian representative, presented to the Governing Board of CERI.

Guiding principles and organisational framework

Not long afterwards a position paper was prepared, which contained the following guiding principles (CERI 1986). The ENSI study was to supply findings concerning two relatively new school requirements, which are not normally related to each other:

-- the promotion of environmental awareness, and;
-- the promotion of "dynamic qualities", such as initiative, independence, commitment, the readiness to accept responsibility etc.

The former of the two is often regarded as telling of a conservationist spirit and hostility towards economic and technological development. The latter is interpreted, rather differently, as stimulating change and a positive attitude towards economic and technological development. The study, however, is based on the assumption that environmental awareness and dynamic qualities can be regarded as closely interrelated. It is assumed that environment offers the future potential for the development of human creativity, intelligence and organisational skills. Thus it is a challenge to initiative and entrepreneurial ideas. On the other hand, the development of these dynamic qualities has also become crucial due to the increasing complexity of work and of public and private life. However, these qualities can only be promoted where they are needed, and where every age-group finds opportunities to become active. The environment offers these opportunities.

Does such a joint promotion of environmental sensitivity and dynamic qualities provide the basis for an extended understanding of the teaching-learning process at school? This was the question raised by the study. It was self-evident that the experiences of those involved in the initiative, i.e. of teachers and pupils, were of decisive importance in this respect. Thus, we had to find schools and teachers, ready to

---

1.   A version of this paper is published as Posch Peter (90) "The project Environment and School Initiatives". In ARGE Umwetterziehune Vienne ESIP - series No 10.

document their work and present it at an international conference. By way of discussions of their experiences, and comparative analysis, their pioneer work was to be examined, and strategies were to be developed in order to benefit the further development of education.

Examples of project activities

I want now to illustrate the four target dimensions of the study by some examples of school-projects. The dimensions concern four different aspects of the two guiding principles:

-- to experience the environment as a sphere of personal experience;
-- to examine the environment as a subject of interdisciplinary learning and research;
-- to shape the environment as a sphere of socially important action;
-- to accept the environment as a challenge to initiative, independence and responsible action.

Many school projects incorporate all four dimensions, if at varying degrees of intensity.

The environment as a sphere of personal experience

This dimension is designed to convey the message, that environmental awareness presupposes a minimum degree of personal involvement and emotional commitment. The term "environment" (and the corresponding German word "Umwelt") -- "that which surrounds" -- gives evidence for an anthropocentric way of thinking: the idea that the environment is related to man in a functional way only, and may thus be considered from a technical, rational point of view and manipulated at will, having no "significance value" as described by Tenbruck (Tenbruck 1975; cf. also Fischer 1985), but only "utility value". If man is regarded as a part of the environment and as an element in a complex system, then his attitudes towards himself and towards the environment cannot be separated from each other. In order to underline this idea in German a new term for the environment, namely "Mitwelt" -- "fellow world" -- has been suggested.

Many projects stress this point of view. I would like to cite one example (Cicatelli and Schirru 1989): In the vicinity of Serre, a small town south of Salerno, Italy, one can find the Oasis of Serre, a wetland area that was formed 50 years ago when the river Sele was dammed up. This wetland is a conservation area managed by the World Wide Fund for Nature (WWF). After the last earthquake in 1980, the dire economic situation of the region led to the location of industries near the wetland, and the oasis was threatened by the expected sewage.

The primary school of Serre, two teachers and 40 nine-to-ten-year-old pupils made it their task to preserve the conservation area. They conducted an opinion poll on the population's attitude regarding the protection of the oasis. They carried out interviews with former workers involved in building the dam, and by means of historical sources studied dam-construction and its agricultural and economic implications. They examined the geographical and geomorphological situation in a conversation with a geologist. In excursions and discussions with experts they studied the river itself, its sources, the characteristics of the water, the degree of industrialisation, the impact of pollution on the natural equilibrium and on agriculture, etc. Supported by the WWF they visited the oasis, talked about its fauna and flora and carried out minor activities themselves (e.g. animal censuses). The conversations, interviews and personal experiences were compiled into a small brochure for the information of the public, which was written by the pupils and edited by the teachers. A further step was the translation of the pupils' experiences into a play. They staged the play for the population, presented their activities in an exhibition and invited experts to make their contributions. Finally, in an open letter to the competent authorities, the children pointed out the importance of the oasis and asked for a withdrawal of the industrialisation scheme in exchange for a stronger support of agriculture and tourism. The letter was a combination of a sober description of facts and an expression of the children's emotional attitudes.

22

What was the outcome of it all? It seems that the school's activities contributed -- not to an abandoning of the plans for industrialisation -- but to the construction of a channel in order to direct the sewage around the oasis. This was regarded as an incredible success by many people, but the children considered it rather a failure, because they had committed themselves to a much more comprehensive aim. Nonetheless, the example shows that children are able to create awareness in an initially sceptical and resigned population, and that strong emotions supported by solid facts play an important part in that process.

The environment as a place of interdisciplinary learning and research

This dimension concerns the fact that the environment offers an ideal opportunity to acquire knowledge on complex issues and interconnect various disciplines. The systematic arrangement of knowledge is one of the great achievements of science, which above all facilitates clarity and easy access to knowledge. The price to pay for this organisation is the fact that knowledge becomes sterile: useful, but no longer meaningful. Its incomplete and preliminary character is masked, and finally its utility value also decreases. The study of 'real' situations offers an opportunity to identify problem areas. This is difficult to achieve in systematic instruction, because textbook knowledge predominantly concerns problems that are already solved. It might well be the case, however, that the identification and definition of problems will be one of the few activities that a computer will not be able to carry out, while it is often better equipped than man to solve clearly defined problems.

In many projects the environment allows for interdisciplinary learning and research. Again one example (Fjortoft 1988): Two comprehensive schools and five teachers from Middle-Norway participated in the project "Archaeology at School". The incentives for the project were new archaeological discoveries in the community area and a revival of an interest in the past. In co-operation with archaeologists of the University of Trondheim and the local museum, the teachers developed an approach which allowed their 15-year-old pupils direct access to early history. It comprised a plurality of activities. The pupils participated in the excavations, documented discoveries, mapped the changes in the landscape since the Iron Age, reconstructed Stone Age methods, wrote small brochures on early local history and wrote a play based on a scientific paper concerning the living conditions during the Iron Age. They also staged the play, held early-history classes for younger pupils, etc. The pupils' work constituted a contribution to the formation of historical awareness in the community. It was integrated into science instruction, civics, history and language classes and was carried on over a period of one year. Most of the field studies and excursions were carried out in spring and autumn.

This example clearly shows the holistic, interdisciplinary potential of environmental activities and the close connection between learning and research, when pupils concern themselves with complex and realistic tasks. It also illustrates that school-geared environmental activities can be a service appreciated by the community.

The environment as a sphere of socially important action

At school, learning predominantly means acquiring a stock of knowledge and skills, because we trust in their later applicability, and because society is interested in perpetuating its cultural assets. For the pupils the meaning of what they learn is predominantly based on predictions and lies in the acquisition of qualifications. Thus they trade their performance for grades. They lack the immediate experience of the meaning of learning. Exceptions to this situation are opportunities where they can make use of their knowledge in order to help modify social processes. This point of view becomes apparent in several projects.

One example is the waste project of a vocational secondary school in Oberwart in Eastern Austria (Schweitzer 1990, and personal communication). At this school a geography teacher, together with 60 of his pupils, aged 15-17, mapped and made photographs of illegal waste dumps in the surrounding communities, listed them and put the results at the disposal of the communities concerned. This led to conflicts, because the communities had tolerated the waste dumps up to that date and reacted against the pupils' interference. After talks with local politicians the pupils increased their activities, organised letter campaigns and found support in the press. After a training seminar they held numerous, informative lectures on waste problems in general and on their findings in particular in schools and institutions of adult education. Finally the waste association joined their ranks and with the approval of the communities started to clear the illegal waste dumps. In the process several jobs were created. The greater part of the pupils' activities was carried out in their leisure time.

During projects of this kind pupils experience several things:

-- that they are capable of achievements that are appreciated by society;
-- that information and a readiness to stand up for one's interests can indeed lead to changes and;
-- that argumentation skills, knowledge and courage are prerequisites of human progress in a democracy.

The environment as a challenge to initiative, independence and responsible action

The growing claims on the schools to offer the pupils incentives and opportunities to develop dynamic qualities, such as independence, flexibility, entrepreneurial initiative etc., will probably lead to a profound restructuring of education. This change is promoted by several large-scale social developments:

-- due to micro-electronics the structure of work becomes increasingly complex, because routine activities are taken over by machines;
-- the state and big organisations increasingly lose their ability to solve problems for the citizens (old-age pensions, security, quality of the environment, etc.);
-- the reduction of working hours increases the amount of unstructured time, the meaningful use of which is left to the individual.

The man in the street (and not only the member of social elites) is increasingly forced to cope with insecurity and complex situations. This puts more pressure on the school, which up to now has confined itself to the promotion of static qualities (industriousness, discipline, a sense of order, etc.) and largely neglected dynamic qualities. Therefore a new balance of static and dynamic qualities, both important for the survival of society, will have to be found.

The environment also offers many opportunities for the promotion of dynamic qualities. This becomes evident in several projects. One of them is the water-analysis project (Sutti 1989), carried out jointly by four secondary vocational schools in Mantova, Italy. Within the framework of normal teaching these schools examine the water quality of sewage drains and waters in the various communes of Mantova. After negotiations with the authorities, the 15-19-year-old pupils were commissioned to take samples, carry out a preliminary analysis and a discussion of the findings on site, make detailed chemical and bacteriological analyses and a microplankton analysis at the schools, and submit comprehensive reports to the district administration and the parties concerned. The research is carried out according to a precise scheme and are co-ordinated by a teacher-pupil group. After a detailed division of tasks the pupils work autonomously and have to make independent decisions at various levels:

-- at the social level, e.g. when contacting authorities and other parties, before and after the sampling, as well as during discussions of results;

24

-- at the technical level, e.g. when determining the site and type of sampling;
-- at the scientific level, e.g. when processing the data.

As the pupils' results are published and could lead to administrative measures against polluters, the pupils also assume considerable responsibility as regards the exactitude of their work.

More than 350 pupils and 16 teachers have participated in the project which has been going on for several years. 225 to 360 samples undergo 5-10.000 chemical analyses, 100-120 samples undergo 300-600 bacteriological analyses, and 75-90 samples are analyzed for micro-plankton annually.

This example clearly shows how a school succeeded in creating a socially recognised field of action, in which pupils can independently accomplish complex tasks and assume responsibility for their work.

The quality of environmental projects probably depends on a balanced relationship among the four dimensions cited above. If, for example, the first dimension (personal involvement) is too dominant, this could mean a "retreat to inwardness", if the third dimension (shaping the environment) is overly stressed the result might be action just for action's sake.

Environment-oriented project work: crossing borders

A common denominator of all projects is the crossing of the traditional borders of school-related activities. Borders have been crossed in both directions. From the outside to the inside, because the environment is brought to the schools, from the inside to the outside, because pupils and teachers left their familiar structures and made the environment their sphere of learning and action.

An example of an inward crossing (Schlager 1990): At a secondary commercial school north of Vienna, pupils worked on "Energy and the Environment", and during a project week they found the opportunity to talk to numerous experts invited to the school.

An example of an outward crossing (Mair 1990): At a secondary school in the Austrian province of Tirol, pupils, together with their teacher, worked out a design for a municipal park as an alternative to the already existing municipal design. After many meetings with local politicians, public information events, and with the help of experts and the press, they were finally authorised by the community to design the park according to their ideas and to supervise the construction.

Both types of border-crossings, but especially the outward-bound type, offer favourable conditions for the promotion of dynamic qualities:

-- Ill-structured situations, i.e. situations in which the problems to be solved have yet to be defined. They considerably differ from standard teaching situations, in which pupils are offered pre-structured and systematic information.

-- Realistic situations, i.e. situations which require a holistic approach and thus stimulate intellectual, creative and organisational skills. Again, these situations are not normally part of teaching traditions, which are mainly concerned with the primarily intellectual acquisition of a stock of knowledge.

In ill-structured realistic situations it is nearly impossible to present the pupils with pre-defined instructions. And this is precisely the leeway needed for the development of dynamic qualities: self-reliance in the definition and treatment of problems and in evaluating the outcomes.

Problems and perspectives

Environmental projects also give rise to problems:

-- There is a tendency to push activities of this kind towards the margin of school activities and into the leisure time of pupils and teachers. How can their integration into "normal" teaching be promoted, and how meaningful is their promotion?

-- Many project teachers report little understanding for their activities on the part of their colleagues. What are the reasons, and how can these attitudes be changed?

-- In the course of initiatives, pupils and teachers are sometimes involved in public controversies and conflicts. To what extent are they inevitable, and how can the schools' potential to cope with these conflicts be increased?

In some schools environment projects have become part and parcel of teaching. They have thus led to a transformation of normal teaching. The water-analysis project of the four schools in Mantova is an impressive example of this process. It is completely integrated into normal teaching and thus has a stable institutional basis. In other schools (or school systems) there are structures that at least favour activities of that kind. In most cases however, environmental project work is an extra-curricular activity, resting on the shoulders of especially committed teachers. Most of them are strong personalities, "who do not feel the urge to be loved by everybody" (J Elliott).

Project work requires a lot of time, energy and stamina. Being regarded as "not normal", it continuously risks being marginalised by normality. The problems encountered in normal teaching are considered to be normal. Problems encountered in project work confirm its abnormal character and justify its rejection.

This field of tension is easier to understand, if we start from the assumption that due to its open structure, its uncertainties and turbulences, project teaching cannot be located at the centre of our notion of "school", but belongs instead to its periphery. Centre and periphery are mutually dependent on each other (Strohmeier 1987). The centre provides stability for the periphery, and the periphery provides the centre with innovations. However, the centre can only be stable if it protects itself from peripheral turbulences.

Teachers who participate in environmental projects are, metaphorically speaking, sitting on the fence at the periphery of the school system. They are both part of it and part of other systems. Communication between centre and periphery is conflict-prone, because it jeopardises the stability of the centre, and thus the functioning of the whole system. On the one hand a certain destabilisation is a prerequisite to the incorporation of new developments. On the other hand, a certain vigilance and scepticism are crucial for the survival of the centre, since not each and every peripheral activity is apt to promote the evolution of the system.

At present these tensions are particularly threatening, because due to societal changes the schools will probably be confronted with more profound changes than ever before. The existing paradigm of learning at school will presumably become less dominant. It is based on the classical separation of insight and action and on the imparting of knowledge for future action. In its place we see the formation of an extended concept of learning: learning not only from the teaching by those who know of those who don't know, but learning also as a process of joint seeking, joint experimenting and a joint formation of awareness for possible futures (Fischer 1987). Teachers who take on this duty need to communicate with each other and need external support (through co-operation with non-school institutions, national and international projects, meetings, networks, etc.).

This, however, is not enough. I would like briefly to outline a further aspect. When teachers no longer content themselves with imparting systematic knowledge, but exceed the limits set by the school and are prepared to cope with ill-structured situations, they increasingly need to be aware of what they do; they need a kind of systematic reflection on their own actions, in order to keep a check on the risks connected with environmental projects, and in order to facilitate communication and further development. Therefore we want to encourage and help project teachers (and their students) to evaluate their work themselves and to write about it. What are pupils' experiences? What do they learn, what don't they learn? Which pupils learn what, and which don't? What is the impact of links between school and external institutions on the social role of the school, and on the hierarchical structures in which it lies embedded?

Studies of that kind have provided us with interesting experiences. One teacher, for example, studied the question why it was almost exclusively girls who participated in his project (Schweitzer 1990). Another studied the impact of pupils' initiatives on their parents (Haas 1990). Another analyzed an unexpected conflict which broke out in his class in the course of the project (Schindler 1990).

I think that this aspect of "research" as a sort of systematic reflection on one's own actions, in order to improve them, will become increasingly important; it is not only apt to contribute to the building up of a stock of practical professional knowledge, but will also improve the social status and the autonomy of the teaching profession. (On the theoretical background cf. Ebbutt/Elliott 1985; Elliott 1985; Altrichter 1988; Altrichter/Posch/Somekh 1993).

As regards the further development of environmental project teaching, I personally attach particular importance to three perspectives:

-- the improvement of teacher-teacher communication and the integration of a greater number of teachers/schools into this exchange of experiences;

-- the production of knowledge on environmental project teaching by the teachers themselves, and finally;

-- a more dynamic and innovative design of infrastructural conditions for this sphere of work.

These are ambitious and long-term targets, and the project Environment and School Initiatives can only be one step towards their implementation.

References

ALTRICHTER, H. POSCH, P. and SOMEKH, B. (1993), *Teachers Investigate their Work, An Introduction to the Methods of Action Research,* Routledge, London.

ALTRICHTER, H. (1990), *Ist das noch Wissenscheft, Darstellung und wissenschaftstheoretische, Diskussion einer von Lehrern befriebenen Aktions/orschung, Profil, Munchen.*

CICATELLI, A. und SCHIRRU, G. (1989), L'Oase di Serre-Persano -- un' esperienza di educazione ambientale, In: MAYER, M. (ed.): Una scuola per l'ambiente -- Risultati, di una ricerca ambientale dall'OCSE., CEDE, Frascati, pp. 407-416, Frascati.

EBBUTT, D. and ELLIOTT, J. (1985), Why should teachers do research? In: ds. (ed.): *Issues in Teaching for Understanding,* Longman, London.

ELLIOTT, J. (1985), Teachers as Researchers, In: HUSEN, T. and POSTLETHWAITE, T. (eds.): *International Encyclopedia of Education,* vol. 9, Pergamon, Oxford , pp. 5042-5045, UK.

EULEFIELD, G. (1988), *Environment and School Initiatives -- National Report: Federal Republic of Germany,* CERI, Paris.

FISCHER, R. (1987), Vernetzung und Widerspruch -- Systemisches Denken und Handeln als didaktisches Problem (Eine Projektskizze). *In: Interuniversità res Institut für Fernstudien: Projekte für Niederösterreich,* IFF, Klagenfurt.

FJORTOFT, I. (1988), *Environment and School Initiatives -- National Report: Norway,* CERI, Paris.

HAAS, K. (1990), *Engagement für die Umwelt -- Chance für die Schulpartnerschaft,* Arge Umwelterziehung, Wien, USI-Reihe Nr. 5, Vienna.

MAIR, G. (1990), *Eine Probelehrerin lernt den Projektunterricht kennen,* Arge Umwelterziehung, Wien USI-Reihe Nr. 2, Vienna.

OECD/CERI, (1986), *Environment and School Initiatives -- Proposal by the Austrian Authorities,* Doc.Nr. CERI/CD(86)11, Paris.

PECCEI, A. (Hrsg.) (1979), *Das menschliche Dilemma -- Zukunft und Lernen -- Berichte des Club of Rome für die Achtziger Jahre...* Molden, Wien.

PFAFFENWIMMER, G. (1988), *Environment and School Initiatives -- National Report: Austria,* CERI, Paris

POSCH, P. (1990), *Dynamic Qualities and Environmental Sensitivity in Education,* Arge Umwelterziehung, Vienna, ESI-Series, No. 10, Vienna.

SCHINDLER, G. (1990), *The Conflict,* Arge Umwelterziehung, Vienna, ESI-Series, No. 6, Vienna.

SCHLAGER, M. (1990), *Experiences with Interdisciplinary Project Instruction*, Arge Umwelterziehung, Vienna, ESI-Series no 7, Vienna.

SCHWEITZER, K. (1990), *Emancipation through Environmental Projects?* Arge Umwelterziehung, Vienna, ESI-Series, No. 4, Vienna.

STROHMEIER, G. (1987), Gedanken zur Projektidee "Vernetztes Denken" von Roland Fischer, In: *Interuniversitä res Institut für Fernstudien: Projekte für Niederösterreich,* IFF, Klagenfurt MS.

SUTTI, S. (1989), WAP -- un modello alternativo d'indagine ambientale, In: Michaela Mayer (ed.): *Una scuola per l'ambiente -- Risultati di una ricerca promossa dall'OCSE*, CEDE, Frascati, pp. 407-416, Frascati.

TENBRUCK, F. (1975), Der Fortschritt der Wissenschaft als Trivialisierungsprozess, In: N. Steer und R. König (Hrg.): *Wissenschaftssoziologie,* Kölner Zeitschrift für Soziologie und Sozialpsychologie, Sonderheft 18, pp. 19-47.

Chapter 2

DEVELOPING COMMUNITY-FOCUSED ENVIRONMENTAL EDUCATION THROUGH ACTION-RESEARCH

by

John Elliott
Centre for Applied Research in Education
University of East Anglia
Norwich, United Kingdom

Introduction

From 1986-88 eleven member countries of the OECD participated in Phase 1 of the "Environment and School Initiatives" Project (ENSI). All participating countries were European. The project itself constituted an innovation within the OECD context in as much as it aspired to more than the customary international "information exchange". It was designed as a piece of cross-national curriculum development in which schools developed environmental education curricula that were consistent with two basic aims and four guiding principles. The aims were:

i) to help students develop an understanding of the complex relationships between human beings and their environment through inter-disciplinary inquiry;

ii) to foster a learning process which requires students to develop "dynamic" rather than "passive" qualities, e.g. "exercising initiative", "accepting responsibility" and "taking action" to resolve real environmental problems within their locality.

The four guiding principles derived from these aims were:

i) students should experience the environment as a sphere of personal experience, i.e. by identifying problems and issues within their local environment;

ii) students should examine the environment as a subject for inter-disciplinary learning and research;

iii) students should have opportunities to shape the environment as a sphere of socially important action;

iv) students should accept the environment as a challenge for initiative, independence and responsible action.

Together, these aims and principles specify a theory of learning in which the development of "environmental awareness\understanding" occurs through an active engagement in finding and implementing solutions to real life problems that fall within the sphere of students' personal experience. "Developing" and "applying" understanding are viewed as interacting rather than separate processes. Environmental understanding is presumed to develop via a process of continuously reflecting about its applications in practice. The aims and principles of the project establish a perspective from which learning about the environment can be viewed as a form of action-research.

It was anticipated by the project's designers that a teaching-learning process which conformed to all the principles outlined above would involve teachers making significant changes to their customary practice. The assumption was that customary practice in most of the participating countries would tend to share the following characteristics:

-- that it would emphasise knowledge-acquisition in forms which dissociated it from its practical usefulness;

-- that in doing so it tends to disconnect the development of environmental awareness from the value-issues which transactions between human beings and their natural, physical, and social environment raise in societies;

-- that the acquisition of knowledge in the form of discrete and tightly bounded subject-parcels reinforces the dissociation of knowledge acquisition from its use, and thereby promotes passive qualities in students e.g. intellectual dependence on authority, conformist attitudes, and a belief that one is powerless to significantly affect events.

Evidence indicating that these assumptions are largely justified was contained in the forty case studies produced by phase 1 teachers which reported their attempts to realise the aims and principles of the project in classrooms and schools. They also met to share their experience at the end of the Phase 1 conference in Linz, Austria. The key problems which emerged from their experience were as follows:

i)   implementing inter-disciplinary inquiry in schools where the curriculum is predominantly organised in terms of discrete subjects;

ii)   handling the value-issues which emerge from students' active involvement in improving the environment in their local communities;

iii) handling the complexity of evidence about the effects of human beings' interactions with their environment;

iv)   linking local with global environmental concerns;

v)   identifying and assessing the development of the dynamic qualities fostered by an active learning process.

It is clear that such problems would only emerge in the experience of teachers who were attempting to realise the kinds of pedagogical principles specified by the project. They would not have emerged within the framework of assumptions which underpin customary practice, and are therefore indicative of genuine attempts by participating teachers to change their practice in the direction of the project's aims and principles. It is only when students examine the environment as a subject for inter-disciplinary learning (principle 2 above) that their teachers experience the problem of handling complexity in fostering understanding. When students explore the environment as a sphere of personal experience (principle 1 above) teachers confront the educational problem of how they help students to create linkages between their local concerns and more global ones. If students are given opportunities to shape the environment through social action (principle 3 above), such actions are bound to raise controversy in the local community, and thereby present teachers with the problem of how they professionally handle, in a publicly defensible manner, a learning process which poses value-issues. When students are given opportunities to exercise initiative, independence, and responsibility (principle 4 above) teachers are faced with the problem of how they identify and assess the capacities which are activated and developed in this context.

The successful transition to a pedagogy which supports the learning process proposed by the ENSI project will depend on the extent to which teachers operating in Phase 2 can effectively resolve the problems identified at Phase 1. The reports of Phase 1 teachers enabled a range of pedagogical problems to be identified but provided little detailed analysis of their nature or evidence concerning how they might be resolved in practice. The time-scale was too short to develop the support system teachers need to enable them to develop problem-solutions on the basis of systematic reflection. Phase 2 was planned to support a professional learning process which builds on the agenda of problems generated at Phase 1 and is problem-focused, reflective, and action oriented.

Such a learning process can also be characterised as action-research. This form of research therefore operates at least at two levels within the ENSI Project: at the levels of both student and teacher learning. Students undertake action-research into how to improve the quality of their environment (level 1), while teachers undertake action-research into how to pedagogically improve the quality of students' curricular experiences (level 2). However, there is also a third level of action-research which focuses on the problems of providing support for the professional learning of teachers. At this third level, action-research constitutes the means by which a support system is developed by those responsible for providing it. It involves those in pedagogical support roles gathering evidence about their own practices to identify, clarify and resolve the problems they experience in facilitating teachers' action-research at the second level.

Systematic support for pedagogical development through teachers' action-research was provided in very few of the participating Phase 1 countries. Austria in particular provided high quality support for school based action-research. This was not surprising given the fact that the project is this country's "brain-child", and that school based curriculum development through teachers' action-research was an important feature of the proposal the Austrian Ministry submitted to the OECD. The quality of the Austrian support was clearly evidenced in the quality of the case study reports produced by Austrian teachers. In the light of this the Phase 2 planning recommended the establishment of pedagogical support units to help teachers undertake action-research into the kinds of problems listed above. Participating countries were asked to nominate support personnel, in addition to National Co-ordinators. In June 1990 a conference on action-research approaches to curriculum and pedagogical development was organised for the support personnel and co-ordinators.

Action-research as a form of practice is essentially linked to the problems of bringing about change in those practices. Not all practical problems necessitate an action-research approach. Problems emerge during the course of customary practice for which solutions are available from the common stock of professional knowledge, developed from repeated experience over time. Responses to such problems become routinised and habitual and part of established practice. Even when new problems emerge they tend to be viewed as merely calling for some fine-tuning rather than any fundamental departure from customary practice. It is only when people experience a need for more profound change and novel solutions that they adopt an action-research stance towards their practice.

Although different groups of participants have primary responsibility for action-research at each of the levels described previously, their members may be involved in the action-research process at more than one level. For example, pedagogical support persons may find that collaborating with teachers in data gathering and analysis activities at the second level constitutes an effective third level support strategy. Similarly, teachers may discover that collaborative inquiry with students at the first level is an effective second level strategy for improving students' learning. Finally, teachers may discover that involving students in the collection and analysis of data about their pedagogical and curriculum strategies is a good level two strategy for bringing about significant curriculum and pedagogical change. The rest of this paper will be primarily concerned with the principles and methods of action research at levels two and three, although much of it can also be applied to student-based action research...

Guiding principles for supporting school based action-research

    i)   Participation in the project should be voluntary, and involve schools and teachers who are either:

        -- already engaged in a form of environmental education, which broadly reflects the aims and key principles of the ENSI project, or;

        -- wish to initiate changes in curriculum and pedagogy in line with the project's aims and principles.

Schools and Teachers are unlikely to be motivated to undertake action-research into the problems of realising the aims and principles of the project if they are coerced rather than committed. Even where participation is voluntary, it is important to avoid involvement that is out of step with the project's aims and principles -- otherwise these will suffer and pedagogical support for change through action-research will be unable to operate effectively.

    ii)   Participating teachers should play a major role in identifying and clarifying the problems of realising the aims and principles of the project in action, and in the development of curriculum and pedagogical strategies for resolving them.

Action-research focuses on the problems practitioners experience in realising their aims and values in practice. Such problems are basically experienced at the level of feelings, e.g. of powerlessness, frustration, anxiety, fear, and anger. They may remain unarticulated or even when they are articulated they may be inappropriately defined.

One of the important functions of A-R facilitators is to develop strategies which enable individual practitioners to reflect about feelings which persist and recur in certain practical contexts. Such "patterns of feeling" are likely to be indicative of salient problems within an individual's practice. The articulation of appropriate problem-definitions will depend on the quality of the individual's self-reflection.

    iii)   Participating teachers should be given opportunities to share their problem-definitions, and the experiential evidence from which they are inferred, with each other.

Although the process of problem-definition must be grounded in individual self-reflection it is by no means an individualised process. Sharing problem-definitions, and the experiential evidence from which they are inferred, with peers who are trying to realise similar aims and values, is an important safeguard against self-deception and bias. Such collaborative peer discussion is an important feature of the action-research process. It enables individuals to compare and contrast each other's experience and in doing so to identify and define problems they have in common. This can be immensely reassuring for individuals, who if left to reflect in isolation, would tend to view the problematic aspects of their practices in largely idiosyncratic terms. This enhances feelings of guilt and damages self-esteem. The discovery of a common problematic generates a non-threatening, safe and mutually supporting climate in which individuals can begin to collaborate in the search for solutions.

iv)   Individual teachers should exercise control over which aspects of other people's problem-agendas are incorporated into their own.

Any consensus about problem-definitions should emerge from individuals reflecting about each other's data in dialogue with each other. External facilitators must be careful to avoid manipulating a false consensus amongst the group(s) they are supporting in favour of a particular view. Judgements about which problem-definitions are significant for practice should be the ultimate responsibility of individual practitioners. This does not imply the impossibility of consensus. Rather that genuine consensus emerges from mutually negotiated agendas in a context of free and open dialogue. Facilitators must also avoid manipulating a consensus in favour of an externally derived agenda such as the problem-definitions specified at Phase 1 of the ENSI project.

v)   Access to externally derived problem-agendas should facilitate rather than suppress or constrain individual self-reflection and the free and open sharing of experience between peers.

One of the situations pedagogical support persons will need to address is the relationship between the problem-definitions generated by Phase 2 teachers and those which emerged from Phase 1 of the project (see 1-5 in previous section). It is important that the latter are not used impositionally to pre-structure teachers' thinking about their practices. Rather their generalisability should be tested by Phase 2 teachers in the light of their independent self-reflection and dialogue with each other about their practical experiences. Through such testing, the Phase 1 agenda of problem-definitions can be accommodated within the personal agendas of individuals and the common agendas which emerge from peer dialogue. Access to external agendas can, given certain conditions, support rather than constrain self-reflection and dialogue. Developing strategies which establish such conditions is a task for Level 3 action-research by support persons.

vi)   Individuals and groups should control which externally derived problem-definitions are judged to be significant for their practice.

The principle presupposes a context of self-reflection and peer dialogue. In this context, "control" does not mean that pre-existing, personal and group problem agendas are assimilated by external agendas. The former are challenged, tested and reconstructed by accommodating (rather than assimilating) elements of the external agenda. Similarly with the externally derived agenda. It gets tested, extended and reconstructed in interaction with the problem-definitions of teachers under conditions of self-reflection and peer dialogue. ENSI support persons should avoid treating the Phase 1 problem-definitions as fixed and unalterable foci for action-research. To do so would be to foster a distorted understanding of the action-research process, and indeed place the development of teachers' insights into the problems of pedagogical change in jeopardy.

vii)   Teachers should be helped to develop their understanding of the practical situations they confront in classrooms and schools through the use of comparative case study methods.

Through action research a form of understanding is developed which is best described as "situational" and "practical". It is "situational" because it comprehends a particular set of circumstances rather than abstract ideas or theories. It is "practical" because it involves discerning and discriminating practically rather than just theoretically significant features of the situation. The research methods appropriate to this form of understanding will differ from those which are concerned with discriminating generalisable aspects in terms of their significance for abstract theory. The former are concerned with gathering EVIDENCE in order to interpret or "read" the situation as a whole. The latter are concerned with the gathering of DATA in order to abstract the general from the particular. Case Study is a form of inquiry which involves gathering and assembling evidence about particulars as a basis for understanding them. Not all such understandings involve judgements of practical significance for future action in the situation. It follows that not all case studies occur in the context of action-research. People may wish to study particulars of different kinds and for different purposes. The study of practical situations is not the only type of case study. All I wish to argue here is that it constitutes one type. Although action-research is concerned with developing situational and practical understanding it does not imply the irrelevance of comparison. Although no two practical situations are the same in all respects they may well be similar in some respects, and these similarities may be practically significant in the sense that they can inform intelligent action in both situations. In other words the discernment of similarities between one or more situations can illuminate each for those who have to act in them. Similarly with the discernment of differences. Grasping what makes one situation significantly different from another informs the situational understanding of the agents in each.

The development of situational understanding is not best served by teachers reflecting about their situations in isolation from one another. Hence the importance of the peer-discourse cited in principle 3 (above). It is the responsibility of the action-research facilitator to structure this discourse in ways which enable teachers to progressively discriminate similarities and differences between their practical situations on the basis of case evidence they share with each other.

The process of developing situational understanding has no fixed end point. It can always be improved on. In this sense case reports are always provisional accounts of an ongoing process rather than end-products. The action-research facilitator should avoid distorting the process of comparative case study by dividing it into two discrete phases:

    a) the production of case reports, to be followed by;
    b) the comparison of such reports.

The development of situational understanding is best served by a process which involves the constant comparison of case evidence assembled in report form. The mapping of similarities and differences is a process which interacts with the continuing construction and reconstruction of the case report.

    viii)   Teachers should be given access to a range and variety of case study research methods which are appropriate to an action-research context as opposed to one in which social research as a process is dissociated from social practice.

Facilitators of action research, especially those located in academic institutions of higher education, are often prone to methodological dogmatism in their relations to teachers. They tend to impose on teachers methodological requirements which promote and legitimate the latter's intellectual dependence on outside expertise. These requirements stem from research traditions which dissociate social inquiry from social practice, and social researchers from social practitioners. In this context the role of the action research facilitator becomes distorted. Instead of supporting a form of inquiry in which research becomes an integral dimension of practice, and methodological competence becomes inseparable from practical competence, the "facilitator" promotes dependence on methods which stem from alien traditions of inquiry. The role of the authentic action research facilitator is to give practitioners access to research methods which conform to the methodological canons of a distinctive form of "Insider Research" aimed at the development of situational understanding. These canons might be summarised as follows:

    --   The situation must be comprehensively described. No information about the case can be dismissed a priori as irrelevant to understanding it. All is potential evidence and should be regarded as bearing possibilities of significance. Which aspects of the case are significant should not be judged in advance of the research, and the use of pre-ordinate categories should be avoided.

The implication here is that no single kind of information or method of information gathering can meet the requirement of comprehensiveness. What is required to capture the complexity of the situation is a range and variety of methods.

-- Since the researcher is an active agent in the situation information must be processed naturalistically, i.e. as events "naturally" unfold within the flow of everyday experience. What are required are unobtrusive methods which enhance rather than disrupt the practitioner-researcher's capacity to act intelligently and responsibly in the situation.

The methods employed by outsiders, who dissociate themselves from the responsibilities of agents in the situation, are often ill-matched to the requirements of insider action-research.

-- Organising one's experience of the situation in terms of categories should be a matter of "progressive focusing". Since information is processed naturalistically, discriminations of practically significant features in the situation progressively emerge.

Methods which are used to gather pre-coded information (e.g. structured questionnaires and interviews and observation schedules) can inhibit the development of a comprehensive understanding by trapping reflection in sets of pre-judgements about the situational significance of some elements rather than others.

-- As an active agent in the situation the researcher's methods should enhance reflexive capacity i.e. the ability to reflect about the quality of one's actions and transactions and the ways in which these influence and shape events.

The attempt to dissociate the situation from the self in order to achieve a spurious objectivity is self-defeating because it involves the distorted view of the situation it sought to avoid. Objectivity in the context of action-research is achieved not by the researcher dissociating the situation from the practical biases which shape his/her interventions but by adopting a stance of critical reflexivity through which they are continually brought to awareness, and then modified and reconstructed rather than eliminated. There is an important sense in which we can describe the development of situational understanding as the progressive reconstruction of one's biases through a self-transcending reflexivity, in contrast to a self-dissociating objectivism.

-- In action-research the validity of one's understanding does not rest on how accurately it represents the situation as it is, because the situation is not a fixed and stable entity but an ever-changing scenario. The validity of one's understanding as an active agent resides in its ability to open up new possibilities for future action in the situation. This alternative account of validity presupposes the inherent instability of the human situations which provide the focus for action-research.

Through a self-dissociating objectivism some researchers attempt to arrive at a fixed and definitive account of the situation. Action-research, grounded in a self-transcending reflexivity, has no end-state. Because the understandings it generates are always provisional so are the actions they shape. From an action-research perspective the situation is a continuously changing object of inquiry.

In short, research methods which rest on the assumption that they validate understandings in terms of fixed and stable meanings inherent in situations are ill-matched to the requirements of action-research.

Action-research and the development of practical competence

Underpinning the methodological canons cited above (under 8) is a particular conception of practical competence. In action-research methodological and practical competence are not different things but the same.

Practical competence is often reduced to mere technical competence in producing pre-specified states of affairs construed as "objectives" or "targets". For example, competence at driving a car might be viewed as the ability to use such a vehicle to arrive at one's intended destination. Such a view is mistaken. Driving competence consists of more than the technical skills involved in moving from A to B. Such an objective could be accomplished in a most undesirable manner, e.g. without consideration for other road users or without care for the safety of pedestrians.

Practical competence embraces the manner as well as the objectives of performance. In the context of a teacher's performance it embraces not only techniques of information and skill transmission but the manner in which they are selected and employed in any given situation. For example, there is a world of difference between using didactic techniques of information transmission in a manner which stifles critical thinking about certain topics and using them in a manner which activates and develops this power. Whereas the objectives of teaching specify the knowledge, skills, and attitudes ("content") to be learned, the aims of education ("critical thinking", "autonomous learning", "creativity" etc.) specify the human powers and capacities which teachers qua educators have an obligation to protect by the manner in which they transmit content. Competence as an educator is not simply the ability to transmit content effectively. It also involves safeguarding educational values through the manner of transmission.

Practical competence as an educator subordinates the technical to the ethical. Its outcomes consist of wise judgements and decisions about how to realise human values in concrete and often complex social situations. In other words they are human acts which manifest the quality of "wisdom", a more ancient term for what I have called "situational understanding". Practical professional competence consists of the abilities involved in generating such acts. They are abilities which underpin the process of professional learning which I have characterised as action-research. It follows that the principles of support for action research, outlined in the previous section, define the conditions under which such abilities can be activated and developed in the context of the ENSI project.

So what are these abilities? What follows draws heavily on research carried out at Harvard by the Occupational Psychologist David McClelland (1973, 1976) and his associates (see Spencer 1979, Klemp 1977) at McBer & Company. This research has identified a number of "generic" abilities which characterise good practice in a variety of professional occupations involving judgement and discretion in complex social and inter-personal situations. What I have done (see Elliott 1991) is to articulate the relationship between these abilities and the process of developing situational understanding through action-research. The abilities are grouped into four clusters:

Cognitive abilities

-- synthesising different aspects of a complex and dynamic human situation into a coherent picture of that situation as a whole;

-- discerning thematic consistencies in diverse information and organising them in communicative forms;

-- understanding the controversial issues at stake in conflicts between people, and the different perspectives held by the conflicting parties.

38

Interpersonal abilities

-- empathy in accurately grasping the thoughts and feelings of others in a way which indicates to them that they are understood and that something will be done in a form they will understand;

-- promoting feelings of efficacy in others involving:

  a) positive regard for others;
  b) providing others with active support;
  c) controlling impulsive feelings of hostility or anger which, if released, would make another person feel powerless and ineffective.

Self-monitoring abilities

-- learning from reflection on experience by observing and analysing one's own behaviour in the context of the behaviour of others in the situation;

-- eliciting feed-back on one's own performance from peers, clients, and subordinates;

-- setting time-phased realistic goals;

-- taking moderate and deliberate risks in the situation in order to achieve something new and original.

Impacting abilities

-- *Cognitive initiative:* the ability to act in the belief that one has the power to influence events.

-- *Networking:* the ability to learn inter-personal influence networks.

-- *Goal-sharing:* the ability to influence others by sharing with them a super-ordinate goal.

-- *Political awareness:* the ability to identify influential groups with regard to both their level in the social hierarchy and their orientation to one's aims and values.

The items cited should not be viewed as isolated, independent elements. For example, with respect to those involved in actively influencing a situation -- impacting abilities -- cognitive initiative underpins all the other elements cited for that category; micro-political awareness depends on the ability to network and goal-sharing depends on both. Similarly, in the Interpersonal category the ability to create feelings of efficacy in others clearly depends on the ability to empathise with others.

The linkages are not confined to a particular category. The cognitive abilities cited can clearly be linked to the aim of action-research; namely, "situational understanding". They constitute powers of practical understanding, i.e. for developing insights into complex and dynamic human situations in order to act wisely in them. But this presupposes an awareness of the "self" as an active agent in the situation which is capable of influencing events in it. In other words the cognitive abilities linked to "situational understanding" presuppose the importance of the kinds of Impacting abilities cited. And since actively influencing situations is an integral dimension of the action- research process methodological competence involves the exercise of Impacting as well as Cognitive abilities.

"Situational understanding" depends upon the exercise of the Self-Monitoring abilities cited, since the inquirer is actively influencing the situation s(he) wants to understand. Such abilities are also constitutive elements of methodological competence to undertake action research. Finally, we must include the Interpersonal abilities as a dimension of that competence. As an active agent in the situations to be understood the inquirer has to interact with other people. In Self-Monitoring the impact of his/her behaviour on others s(he) will need to grasp their thoughts and feelings about the situation ("empathy") and will be unlikely to accomplish this if lacking in positive regard for others or unable to control negative and hostile feelings towards them. Moreover, people are unlikely to reveal their innermost thoughts and feelings to another agent in the situation if they feel that disclosure will elicit a negative reaction.

I have attempted to demonstrate how the clusters of abilities outlined above can be structurally linked to the idea of "situational understanding" in a way which illuminates the nature of methodological competence in action-research. In fostering such competence in teachers ,those in external support roles are not enabling them to develop a form of research expertise which is separate from their expertise as practitioners. The teacher who is methodologically competent to undertake action-research into his or her teaching is also competent to teach. This is why external facilitators of the action-research process are also functioning as teacher trainers.

Since the primary concern of pedagogical support personnel is to enable the professional development of teachers they have a responsibility to monitor, as a dimension of their level three action research, the quality of that development in individuals. Such monitoring provides a basis for diagnosing teachers' learning needs. In this context the framework of abilities outlined above can function as a specification of "quality indicators" to guide diagnostic appraisals and the construction of "professional profiles" which record the progress of individual teachers in developing practical competence. However, the validity of the framework as a definitive specification of "quality indicators" should not be taken for granted by pedagogical support personnel. The extent to which it accurately and adequately describes the elements of practical competence manifested in teachers' action- research needs to be addressed as a third level action- research task by the pedagogical support personnel. The framework may need to be continually revised by the support personnel in the light of evidence they collect via observations of pedagogical practices and interviews with relevant teachers, their professional peers and students.

At the level of the pedagogical support personnel themselves the framework specifies possible indicators of their competence as enablers of teachers' professional development. Pedagogical support personnel will not be competent at enabling the development of teachers' professional competence through action research if they themselves lack the abilities necessary for undertaking action-research into their own support strategies. And this implies that support personnel need to develop similar methodological and practical abilities to those advocated for teachers.

The abilities specified in the previous section do not simply describe elements of competence with respect to teachers and pedagogical support personnel. They are also activated and developed in students through their action-research into local environmental issues. At the student level the abilities specified may well describe the "dynamic qualities" of learning which the ENSI project aspires to foster, and which teachers are asked to identify and assess through their second-level action research. The framework outlined in the previous section could be treated by participating teachers as a specification of "quality indicators" for assessing students' personal development in the context of environmental education. It could equally be applied to other inter-disciplinary curriculum areas which focus on human situations that impinge on students' lives. In other words it has the potential of providing a basis for assessing the cross-curricular aspects of student learning. But teachers should beware of the fallacy of assuming that dynamic abilities developed in one curriculum context will inevitably transfer to others. For example, one cannot assume that people who are good at empathising with people in one kind of situation possess this quality in their dealings with others generally. Although intelligent judgement and decisions in a variety of human situations manifest similar human qualities such qualities may need to be developed in each type of situation.

40

I would also warn teachers not to adopt the framework uncritically, but to test its validity through action research. As they reflectively transform their pedagogy in line with the aims and principles of the ENSI project one might hypothesise that student learning will increasingly manifest the qualities specified in the framework. This hypothesis can be tested by gathering evidence on the extent to which the abilities specified in the framework are progressively manifested by their students. Reflection and discussion about this evidence may lead teachers to modify and refine the framework as a basis for profiling student development, and thereby make a significant contribution to our understanding of the dynamic qualities fostered in students through realising the pedagogical aims and principles of the ENSI project.

In this section I have suggested that the abilities involved in undertaking action-research competently at all levels of the ENSI project are structurally similar. This is because, as McClelland and his associates at McBer & Company have argued, intelligent judgement and decision-making in complex practical situations depends on generic qualities people bring to their roles and tasks and not simply on technical knowledge and skill which are role and task specific. The latter are a necessary but not sufficient condition of competence. Students, for example, need to acquire relevant knowledge about their environment, but such knowledge alone will not guarantee their "environmental competence". Similarly, teachers need to have a good knowledge and understanding of the subject-matters they teach but this alone does not guarantee pedagogical competence.

In this section I have attempted to show how the "generic" aspects of practical competence in complex human situations underpin the action-research process at all levels of the ENSI project: student learning, teacher development, and pedagogical support. Since action-research fuses action and reflection, practice and research, the distinction between practical competence in everyday life and methodological competence in research becomes redundant.

Collecting, analysing and reporting data in action-research: some methods and techniques

One of the reasons why I have dealt with the question of methodological competence in action-research in some detail is to guard readers against the fallacy of assuming that expertise in this field largely consists of mastering a body of highly specialised technical knowledge. Pedagogical support personnel should avoid a methodological dogmatism which defines action-research in terms of a definitive set of research techniques, and competence to undertake it in terms of their mastery. Such dogmatism is likely to alienate many teachers and even when it doesn't it will encourage them to view research as a separate activity to pedagogy.

What follows is an inventory of case study methods and techniques which action-researchers have used to develop and communicate their practical insights. It is not a definitive list and the applicability of particular items should depend upon practitioners' judgements about their appropriateness to the focus of their inquiry and their practical feasibility. In constructing this inventory I had the needs of teachers for practical support with research methods particularly in mind. Pedagogical support personnel may find it useful as a resource they can use in advising teachers about possible methods and helping them to explore their appropriateness and practical feasibility. The usefulness of the inventory as a source of pedagogical support could itself be explored through third level action-research by support personnel.

Triangulation

This is not so much a specific technique as a broad strategy of data collection and analysis within which a range and variety of techniques can be utilised for the purposes of Case Study.

Triangulation involves collecting data about the situation from the point of view of people occupying different roles and positions within it. The assumption here is that they will understand the situation rather differently according to the practical interests and concerns which guide their participation. Therefore any comprehensive view of a situation needs to take these multiple perspectives into account. Triangulation also furnishes evidence of the controversial issues which arise between people in a situation and create conflict about how to act appropriately within it.   The relevance of triangulation to the development of situational understanding as a basis for wise and intelligent action in a situation should be obvious.

Triangulation data can provide a basis for informed dialogue between people in different roles and positions aimed at increasing mutual understanding and a better appreciation of the issues at stake in the conflicts which emerge between them.

Although the term "triangulation" suggests collecting data from three perspectives I prefer to interpret the strategy as an expression of the basic principle that it is important to understand a situation from a multiplicity of perspectives. In the context of classroom action-research triangulation techniques have often been employed to collect pedagogical data from three points of view: of the teacher, his or her students, and an external observer. But in the context of the ENSI project the pedagogical situation may be far more complex, involving perhaps a team of teachers with different subject specialisms, members and representatives of the local community, as well as students and perhaps an external observer occasionally. In this situation the complexity of the role relationships will require the collection of data from a larger number of perspectives.

Triangulation involves both data collection and analysis. These two tasks interact with each other as part of the overall progressive focusing strategy referred to earlier. Analysis consists of discerning patterns in the data: themes and issues which clarify aspects of the situation and the nature of the problems which need to be addressed. These analyses constitute a framework for understanding the problematics of the situation. This framework evolves interactively with the data collection process rather than in retrospect. The analysis of one set of data indicates the need for more data and when this has also been collected and analyzed yet more data may be required to clarify the significant and salient features of the situation.

The analysis of triangulation data need not be an isolated activity on the part of the practitioner(s) undertaking the research. Support can be provided through at least three kinds of discussion about the data; namely:

    i)   With an outsider who cannot be associated with the system of social roles that directly impinge on the situation, e.g. with a higher education based teacher educator or educational researcher.

In the context of the ENSI project, the outsider's role would be the responsibility of the pedagogical support person.

    ii)   With a group of fellow practitioners undertaking action-research in different classroom, organisational and social settings to the one in which the data to be analyzed was collected.

In the context of the ENSI project this would involve discussion between individuals or groups of teachers operating in different classroom or school settings. Cross-classroom and school comparisons can illuminate a particular collection of triangulated case data in ways which would be impossible if it were analyzed in isolation.

Within the ENSI project there should be opportunities where possible for teacher-researchers to discuss their data with other teacher-researchers, both within and across schools. The pedagogical support person would have a particular responsibility for establishing the across school discussion context.

     iii)   With other participants in the situation whose understandings and experiences are evidenced in the data.

This kind of analytic discussion is relevant to questions about the validity of the emerging analysis. It is essentially a form of "respondent validation" in which all participants can influence the way in which their views and experiences are represented and made intelligible by the "researcher".

Initially, insider researchers may find it impossible to collect authentic data, and validate their analysis of it through free and open discussion with other participants (see iii above), if their role in the situation is treated with distrust and suspicion by other role partners. Thus teachers usually have great difficulty in eliciting students' authentic understandings and experiences of pedagogical situations because students are suspicious of how someone in the authority position of teacher will respond to them. In such circumstances an outside observer may have to initiate and manage the processes of data collection and analysis, but in a manner which increasingly enables the insider-researcher(s) to take over these responsibilities. And this involves the outsider in establishing conditions which create trust between those in insider research roles and other participants within the situation. In the context of the ENSI project, the pedagogical support personnel are perhaps in the best position to play this enabling role. However, it is very time consuming and they may need to co-opt others to assist them in their outsider role. The problem is, who qualifies for this status in the eyes of participants?

The term "outsider" carries two rather different meanings. Firstly, it may mean someone who enters the physical territory of another person or group which (s)he doesn't normally inhabit. In this sense an academic researcher or school inspector will be perceived as "outsider" by teachers who work in that physical territory known as the school.

Secondly, "outsider" status may be attributed to "the stranger", who not only enters unfamiliar physical territory but is unfamiliar with the beliefs, values, and customs of a social group.

It is in this cultural sense that ethnographic researchers in anthropology and sociology have primarily attributed "outsider" status to themselves. In order to theorise about the social practices of a social group, they first need to understand the cultural significance of those practices for the practitioners. Hence, the importance of "participant observation" as a research strategy for the study of unfamiliar cultures and sub-cultures. The "participant observer" attempts to participate sufficiently in the life of a social group to grasp the significance of situations and activities from their cultural perspective, while at the same time maintaining a sense of detachment. The dangers such an observer faces are two-fold. Too much involvement on the basis of inadequate understanding can disrupt the situations under study. Participation must be unobtrusive. On the other hand there is the danger of co-option into the culture so that the researcher loses his or her sense of detachment and outsider status. (S)he becomes an "insider" and loses the capacity for objectivity as this is defined from the perspective of the academic discipline.

The "outsider" as "stranger" may be perceived by members to be relatively free from the hierarchical system of social roles and relations which governs action in the situation. In this respect "insiders" may trust "outsiders" with information they would not be prepared to disclose to those they associate with hierarchical control for fear of the consequences.

The senses of "outsider" discussed above frequently overlap inasmuch as cultures and sub-cultures can be located in terms of a particular type of physical territory, and strangers to them do not occupy any role in a hierarchical system of control over the members of such cultures.

What are the strategies then which outside observers and other members of a pedagogical support network can employ to foster trust? The following suggestions are based on my own experience of helping teachers to collect and analyze triangulation data about their classroom situations. They constitute an ethical code of practice for observational support personnel:

-- Do not observe in classrooms or interview students if this is unacceptable to the teacher(s).

-- Involve the teacher(s) in decisions about the focus for the observations and interviews with students, e.g. teacher questioning strategies, student talk while engaged in learning tasks.

-- When observing classrooms collect low inference evidence about observable patterns of action and interaction. This can be done through tape and video recordings, photographs, and written notes in which highly interpretative accounts of participants' conduct (resting on inferences about their intentions, motives, and values) are separated from the record of observable patterns, e.g. by bracketing them in written notes to indicate their conjectural and challengeable status. (See the section below on "pattern analysis" as a technique for accomplishing this separation). The separation is not so important when written notes on observations are used in conjunction with other recording techniques that can be used to collect the low inference data (See below for an account of recording techniques).

The point of involving "outsiders" is that they are likely to be trusted in a situation where little trust exists within the system.

Researchers, once they have established credibility without having succumbed to co-option, may find it easier to secure the trust of teachers.

The "outsider" status of observers in education tends to be somewhat ambiguous. Academic researchers may be visitors to school sites and occupy no significant role in hierarchically controlling what teachers do in them. However, they will not be total strangers to the occupational culture. The vast majority will have spent years as students interacting with teachers in schools. Moreover, most educational researchers will have had earlier experience as school teachers. Many will tend to adopt a very non-participative stance to classroom observation, confident in their ability to describe pedagogical activities and events without recourse to how teachers and students define their meaning and significance. Teachers may view educational researchers rather differently as at least relative strangers, whose previous experience in schools is now largely redundant since "things are different now". They may want researchers to immerse themselves more in pedagogical activities, perhaps by doing some teaching or at least entering into conversations with them about the meaning and significance of such activities. This invitation to dialogue can easily be interpreted by researchers as an attempt to co-opt them into the teachers' point of view. That may be true, but this is no reason for retreating into an entirely non-participant observational role. The researchers, by virtue of their previous experience of schooling, will carry into their observations a "student's eye view" which biases their observations in the present. Such biases need to be made explicit, placed in "brackets", and tested against current realities. The means of accomplishing this process are conversations and interviews with teachers and students.

School inspectors may have a similar even enhanced, ambiguous status as "outsiders". It may be more difficult for inspectors to play a participant observation role because of a tendency to distrust people in hierarchical control systems.

However, there are usually particular individuals within the system who command respect and trust irrespective of their position and it is important for pedagogical support persons to identify these individuals and solicit their help in creating an observer network to support the collection and analysis of triangulation data in classrooms and schools.

The above strategies enable the observer's point of view to be presented as an aspect of the triangulation data that carries no greater authority than other aspects, e.g. the views of the teachers and students. They also enable the analysis of different points of view to be grounded in observational evidence. The overall intention behind such strategies is to minimise the extent to which the teacher(s) and students feel threatened by the presence of an observer and to maximise sufficient trust to enable them to freely participate with the observer in analytic discussions of triangulation data.

-- Interview the teacher(s) before and after an observation session, and prior to interviewing students. Prior access to student views is likely to make the teacher(s) feel over anxious.

-- Before interviewing students make it clear to both them and their teacher(s) that they have the right to control the extent to which the latter can have access to the views they express, either as a whole or in part. Such access should be negotiated with the students after the interview along with any conditions they may stipulate, e.g. that the teacher(s) discuss their reactions to the material with them.

This strategy is aimed at reducing students' anxieties about the consequences of teacher access to their views, and at enabling them to risk an honest expression of them. If the consequences are not what they feared then conditions of trust are established which enable teachers to elicit authentic views unmediated by the external observer.

The strategies outlined enable observers to perform a midwifery role in establishing trust within the data gathering and analysis process between teacher, students and him/herself. Once trust has been established the process can move into a second stage where the teacher(s) can successfully manage and control it. At this stage the observer's and students' views are elicited either by:

-- The teacher(s) who take responsibility for recording their own in some form, e.g. by keeping a diary or journal. The teacher(s) also accept more responsibility for recording the observable features of the situation, although they may seek technical assistance in this respect from the observer (e.g. in operating an audio or video recorder to gather information requested by the teacher(s).), or

-- A process of self-generation in which all the parties are involved in selecting observational data from the "record" to stimulate a reciprocal and exploratory exchange of views.

The more specific techniques which I shall now describe should not be viewed in isolation from the triangulation method outlined above. Some have already been alluded to, e.g. observational pattern analysis and interviewing techniques. In describing them I shall try to illustrate their usefulness to some aspect of the triangulation process.

Video and tape recordings

These are obvious techniques for collecting observational data. Video is difficult to operate without the assistance of an external observer, if it is to be used without creating too much disruption. There will be occasions when a video camera can be used by participants, e.g. a teacher recording a group of students working autonomously or a student recording a learning activity or episode of teacher-student interaction. Also, in the absence of an observer a fixed camera can be used. It has limitations because fixed positioning may not enable a lot of relevant data to be picked up, e.g. the non-verbal communications of people who are physically obscured from view. This is the advantage of having a skilled observer using a hand video-camera to record what (s)he selects as relevant.

Whether the camera is fixed or used as the external observer's "record", the data collected need not just serve as a resource for the teacher's reflection either in private or in the presence of an observer. Students can be involved as active partners in action-research by suggesting selections from the video record as a basis for a discussion in which different interpretations of data can be shared and explored by the different parties in the situation.

Such uses of the video record presume that a degree of trust and mutual respect prevails between the teacher(s), students, and external observer. Video is a very seductive medium. It has the power to make people believe that they are experiencing not so much a selective record of reality as the total reality of the situation itself. This power is considerably enhanced when video records are used as a basis for discussion in a context where participants deeply distrust each other. They will use the video record as "ammunition to fire at each other" rather than as a partial selection of data, which calls for a degree of tentativeness in drawing inferences and an exploratory reflective attitude in discussing them.

Constructive uses of video may only become feasible in many classrooms after the kinds of external observer interventions in initiating the triangulation process described earlier. At this stage the teacher(s) and students will play a more passive role as interviewees of the observer. However, even in the context of observer-led interviews the video record can be used in a way which allows the teacher(s) and students to play an initiating role. Rather than initiating questions for the interviewees to respond to, the observer may simply invite them to stop the recording at any point where things of personal significance are depicted and to talk about them. This simulated recall technique has in my experience proved a very effective means of developing trust in the external observer and therefore of eliciting authentic views. Interviewees are not continuously trying to guess at the "hidden agenda" they may feel to be implicit in the observer's interview questions.

Tape recording is a more flexible technique than video. In the absence of an observer it can be executed by the teacher(s) more easily and unobtrusively. And it can serve similar functions of stimulating recall and a grounded discussion of alternative interpretations of events and situations. As data the audio record is far more partial than a video record, containing largely linguistic data. It certainly needs to be supplemented by other kinds of observational data. However, it is precisely because tape recordings clearly constitute partial representations of a situation that they are, in my opinion, rather better than video recordings at stimulating tentative interpretations and reflective discussion about them. They are more difficult to use as an authoritative basis for punitive judgements about people's actions and for confidently projecting blame. They do not reinforce existing distrust to the extent video recordings can. Indeed they can often counteract it to a degree, which suggests that they may be may be a preferable technique to use at the initial stage of the triangulation process, leaving video for the later stage after sufficient trust has been established between the various parties involved in the action research process.

Transcripts

Transcripts of audio and video recordings are a valuable supplementary record because they assist data analysis in a number of respects. Firstly, they can be more easily circulated to others for comment, feed-back, and discussion. Secondly, when used in conjunction with an audio or video recording they enable one to move backwards and forwards through the data more easily than one can by having to exclusively rely on the technology; for example, by switching the tape backwards and forwards. Thirdly, the act of transcribing itself assists reflection about the data. Insights into the significance of the data can be generated in forms that may not emerge if one simply listens to or watches a recording. These reasons for transcribing apply equally to recordings of interviews.

The vast majority of teachers I have worked with testified to the value of transcription. However, it is extremely time-consuming for both teacher-researchers and external observers to undertake on a frequent basis. A full transcript produced very occasionally however, may prove to be well worth the effort with respect to the insights it yields. More frequently it may be possible to transcribe short episodes selected on the basis of a prior listening or watching. These episodic transcripts can then be used as a basis for deepening the analysis through either private reflection or an analytic discourse with others.

The feasibility of transcription is enormously enhanced by access to secretarial support. However, an exclusive reliance on secretarial transcription ignores the third reason cited above. It is important that those directly involved in the collection and analysis of data should undertake some transcribing tasks themselves, if only occasionally.

Transcripts are not only of value during the data collection and analysis phases of action research. They are valuable in the context of producing written reports, where there is an obligation to clearly demonstrate and display the evidential basis of inferences, interpretations, and judgements.

Conventions governing transcription need to be agreed, particularly when secretarial resources are employed, when observers are producing transcripts for use by participants, and when transcripts are being used as a basis for across classroom/school analysis and reporting by groups of teachers. Idiosyncratic transcription procedures may fail to take into account the information needs of all those involved in processing and reporting the data. For example, a teacher researcher may not need for the purpose of private reflection to incorporate contextual information about students, material resources, and classroom organisation that professional peers would find useful in discussing a transcript of a recording made in his/her classroom. Conventions need to be evolved to ensure that the best is obtained from transcripts across the variety of contexts in which they are likely to be used.

Photography

Photography can be used to collect visual data about situations and events for the following reasons:

-- When video-recording is unfeasible (e.g. the technology is not available or a skilled observer is not available to operate it).

-- When video or audio recording is undesirable (e.g. too obtrusive in a particular context).

-- When the practitioner researcher or external observer wants to collect visual data on a continuous basis in a form which can be speedily and economically processed.

-- When the practitioner researcher or external observer is at that stage in the research process where they are clear about the kinds of visual data they want to collect in advance .e.g. "which students frequently appear in queues at the teacher's desk?", or "what is the teacher's physical posture when (s)he moves around helping students with their learning tasks?" Such data may be much more economically processed through photography than through video-recording.

-- When an external observer wants to collect relatively non-threatening data as a basis for analytic discussion with the practitioner(s).

Photographs may be seen by practitioners to be more open to a wider range of interpretations, more obviously a subjective selection of data, than video data. They may therefore enhance their capacity to participate in genuinely reciprocal analytic discussions of the data with an observer.

-- when the practitioner researcher or external researcher wants a powerful stimulus to elicit the authentic views of others, together with the values and beliefs which underpin them, within an interview situation where trust needs to be established.

It is difficult for people, particularly young children, to think about their experience of some event or aspect of a situation in the absence of concrete representations. Photographs, by virtue of their obvious status as partial and subjective representations, are excellent "projective material" that evoke interpretations in which the general attitudes (values and attitudes) underpinning them are clearly manifested. People may display their general attitudes in this way with respect to photographs, compared with video recordings, because they feel relatively unconstrained by the presence of "objective" data.

Field notes, logs, journals and diaries

Anthropologists and naturalistic sociologists engaged in ethnographic inquiries tend to call written records of their observations "field notes". They are outsider researchers attempting to understand human conduct in particular societies and groups in terms of the cultural values, norms, and beliefs which underpin them. Ethnographic researchers produce "thick descriptions" which portray human acts in terms of the social meanings which insiders within the culture ascribe to them. These descriptions provide the data-base for a theoretical analysis of human acts which may explain how they function to promote and maintain certain conditions (e.g. gender or social class differences). Field note descriptions take a form that enable theoretical explanations of the conduct of insiders to be constructed and tested.

Insiders tend to record their activities in the form of logs, journals and diaries. The log is simply a basic record of events, and where and when they happened. The criteria governing what should be included in a log are usually commonly understood by practitioners as part of the framework of obligations which define their role and responsibilities. It enables the organisation to which they belong to monitor their activities and therefore serves an accountability function. The log largely contains "surface" descriptions compared with the "thick descriptions" contained in field notes.

The Log is not an inferior record to field notes, which may well also log events as a subordinate aspect of the record. It just satisfies the different purposes of people operating in different roles.

The insider's log is based on a need to monitor events as a basis for "answering to others" within the organisation. Once recorded, the meaning or significance of the activities may often be taken for granted by the recorder and other members of the organisation. In which case the log is regarded as a sufficient record for use by insiders.

The journal tends to be associated with the record of "the journey" by the traveller or soldier in foreign lands. Its purpose is to serve as a source of stories about the author's experience upon his or her return to the homeland. The journal record therefore tends to adopt a narrative form. It differs in form from the field note record. In the latter, description serves the primary purpose of theoretical analysis for academic peers. In the journal, description serves the purpose of narration within the vernacular of the people back at home. It differs from the log because there is no obligation for the author to record particular events. What is recorded is a matter of personal significance.

The diary is primarily a personal and private document in which the author not only documents life events and experiences but reflects about their emotional responses to them. Diaries are sometimes published after a period of time (e.g. after the death of their authors) and may even be written with an eye on eventual publication. However, the primary function of a diary is to support the individual's private reflections about their life experiences. It is this function which determines the form of description. In the diary the writer is primarily concerned with constructing a portrait of the self for the self from the data of experience. This is rather different to the functions of field notes, journals, and logs which are concerned with constructing accounts of observable happenings for an audience.

All of the methods outlined contain aspects which are useful in the context of action-research. But there will be other aspects which are dysfunctional. We as yet have to fully articulate a method of constructing written records which is distinctive to action research (but see Holly, 1989 and Winter, 1989).

The logging of classroom events in the form of lesson profiles using predetermined and agreed criteria is a useful exercise in the context of action- research (one basic format is illustrated below). However, the Log should only be a subordinate aspect in the construction of observational records in an action-research context. The problematic context of teaching and learning activities means that their relationship to this context needs to be described in some detail. In this respect the observational record will have certain things in common with an ethnographic researcher's field notes. It will include rich observational detail but whereas the ethnographer's observations are primarily guided by the theoretical perspective of his/her discipline, observation in the context of action-research is guided by the practitioner's practical perspective. Observational accounts in the context of action research should enable practitioners to improve their understanding of the complex and dilemma-ridden problems they confront in practice and possible solutions to them.

Example of a basic format for a Log taken from Walker and Adelman (1975):

Time	10 mins	20 mins	30 mins	40 mins
Teacher activity	Settling in; giving out books	Introduces experiment; gives directions asks questions	Moves round helping small groups working on experiments	Clearing up
Pupil activity	Finishing work from last lesson	Listening to teacher's directions; answering questions	Working on experiments	Write up results of experiments
Resources	Text books; pens; exercise books		Bunsen burners; tongs; foodstuffs; balances	Exercise books; pens

This difference in the form of description employed is a matter of emphasis. The action researcher may need to isolate a particular aspect of a problematic situation for detailed analysis from a particular disciplinary perspective. However, such analyses provide limited and partial understandings of the total situation. The practical usefulness of these understandings depends on the extent to which they can be synthesised into a picture of the problematic situation as a whole and thereby enhance the action researcher's capacity for wise and intelligent judgement in it. Observational support for action research involves helping practitioners to improve their understanding of the complex problems they confront in practice. Those operating in observational support roles should ideally be familiar with a variety of relevant theoretical perspectives which they can eclectically employ to discriminate relevant data. This data can then be used by practitioners as a basis for wide-ranging analyses that can subsequently be synthesised into more comprehensive pictures of practical problems.

Ethnographic researchers need to collect data in terms of its relevance to the problems participants perceive themselves to be addressing through their practices. But the second order constructs they subsequently employ to analyze this data are usually derived from a specific discipline with the result that the inquiry becomes increasingly abstracted and dissociated from the practical context of participants' lives. This is because the primary aim of the inquiry is the development of a theory to explain a particular aspect of practice. Such theories may subsequently prove useful to participants in informing intelligent practice but their practical utilisation falls outside the immediate scope of the inquiry. This is not the case in action-research where the development of an abstract theory is subordinated to the development of a holistic understanding of practical situations.

This difference will be reflected in the forms of description which observers use to record data. Whereas in an action-research context observational accounts will progressively move in the direction of synthesis and concreteness, the observational accounts of ethnographers will become increasingly abstract and analytic.

All this has implications for the observational records outsider observers make in the context of supporting teachers' action-research. Their "audience" is not a group of external researchers committed to a particular theoretical and disciplinary perspective, but a group of insider researchers who are attempting to clarify and resolve the complex and problematic practical situations they are engaged with as active agents. Such observers need not avoid using the formal theories of the behavioural and social sciences to guide their observations but they need to do so eclectically if they are to generate data which illuminates the complex practical problems teachers face in pedagogical situations. No single theoretical perspective or discipline can be sufficient as a basis for developing situational understanding. There will be times when observations need to be highly focused on understanding a single aspect of a problem and therefore employ a limited set of theoretical constructs to yield meaningful data about it. But such observations should never become too disassociated from the overall aim of helping the insider to develop a comprehensive understanding of the problem as a whole.

There is also a place for the narrative form in observational notes produced by or for insider researchers. But the purpose of such "stories" about pedagogical events is not so much to share unfamiliar experiences with one's fellows "back home", but to provide a concrete illustration of significant aspects of a situation to enable those who are familiar with similar situations to assess their significance for their own practice. In other words concrete narratives or stories can be used to communicate insights about a particular situation to others in a form which enables them to test the generalisability of such insights to their own experience. The production of narratives provides the basis for a process of sharing which enables teachers to learn from each other's experience. Such a process has been called "naturalistic generalisation" by way of contrast with the process of formal generalisation involved in the natural sciences.

Finally, there is an important role for aspects of "the diary" in the written records of both teacher-researchers and those in external observational support roles. Practical problems, which provide the focus for action-research, are essentially experienced at the level of feelings. Practitioners may experience situations and events as problematic without being able to articulate in language any understanding of the problematics. In this respect action-research differs markedly from research which is exclusively concerned with solving the theoretical problems which have emerged in the development of a particular discipline of knowledge. Such problems can by definition be articulated in advance of the research. In action-research "understanding what the problem is about" is one of the aims of the inquiry. The recording of feelings and reflection about them therefore plays an important role in the search for understanding. However, in the context of action-research such records have a very restricted use if they remain private. The aim of action-research is to improve a social practice for which individuals are accountable to others. In this sense the audience for self-accounts of practice can never simply be restricted to the "self".

The diary is essentially a method of self-development. Its primary audience is the "reflexive self". By reviewing entries over time individuals can monitor changes in the ways they respond and react to situations in the light of the person they want to be, and indeed clarify to themselves what sort of a person this is. On the basis of their diaries individuals not only learn about themselves but also continuously reconstruct themselves. The reflexive development of oneself is essentially a private enterprise conducted in private space, beyond the restrictions of public surveillance and control.

Of course, the enterprises of self-development and improving practice are not discrete. The former involves the latter and vice-versa. The private diary is not irrelevant to the task of improving a social practice. But the appropriate form for representing and explaining one's personal feelings to oneself is inappropriate for representing and describing them to others. This is partly because what one learns about oneself from studying the self in the context of a particular practical situation is not all equally relevant to understanding how it might be improved. Thus what constitutes relevant subjective data about feelings and emotions to record in action-research contexts may be far more selective than what constitutes relevant data for the overall purpose of self-development in general. At best relevant subjective data for action research purposes will constitute only a selection from the private diary record. And even here the form in which that data is represented will differ from the private diary form, because it is a representation aimed at making a practical situation intelligible to others and not merely to make oneself intelligible to oneself. The private diary may therefore serve as a useful basis on which to construct "personal data" for the purposes of action-research. But one should not confuse the difference between public and private personal records. At best "the diary" is a useful metaphor for articulating the reflexive aspect of action research methodology.

The written accounts of outsider and insider researchers can eclectically utilise aspects of the forms of commentary outlined above for the purpose of action-research. Notes can be organised in sections labelled "event log", "detailed observations", "stories", "personal reflections".

Interviewing techniques

Interview techniques for research purposes tend to be differentiated according to the degree of structure the interviewer imposes on the interviewee's responses. In "structured" interviews the interviewer controls the focus and sequence of responses, usually through an agenda of pre-set questions. In "unstructured" interviews the interviewee is given a considerable amount of freedom to select what they want to talk about within a broadly defined topic area. The focus and sequencing of responses is under their control. The role of the interviewer in the unstructured situation is to listen, and ask questions which seek clarifications, elaborations, explanations or justifications of responses. In between the extremes of "structured" and "unstructured" we can have "semi-structured" interviews in which there is room for both responding to pre-determined questions and free responses. In my view the best kind of semi-structured interview begins with the unstructured form because in this way many of the pre-set questions may get incidentally addressed by the interviewee without them having to be explicitly raised by the interviewer. Then towards the end of the interview the interviewer can raise any questions on his/her agenda that have not been addressed. This format is likely to impose less constraints on the expression of authentic views than one which moves from structured to unstructured responses, especially when interviewer and interviewee do not know each other well. The danger, in this context, of beginning an interview in a highly structured form is that the interviewee will tend to interpret questions as "exam type" ones, in which the interviewer has a pre-determined view of what constitutes a correct response. Beginning with the interviewee's free responses enables him/her to develop confidence and to assess the interviewer's capacity to listen with interest and empathy. It enables the interviewer to establish a climate in which the interviewee will feel able to respond authentically to the questions (s)he wants to raise.

All three types of interviewing have a role in action-research. Its major function in this context is to elicit experiences of situations and events within the overall triangulation strategy outlined previously. It is a context where the interviewer is likely to have had either direct or observational experience of the same situation or event. S(he) will therefore want to use the interview not simply to elicit the experiences of others, but to compare their own experience with that of others.

A concern for comparable data suggests the use of a structured interview format. However, this alone is not a sufficient basis on which to collect all relevant interview data. For example, an observer may want to know what a student felt about a certain teacher intervention to compare this with their own feelings about it. But the interviewer's selection of significant teacher interventions may not correspond fully with those which the student experienced as significant. If the main purpose of an interview is to allow the student an opportunity to talk about the full range of significant experiences for them, then this would suggest an unstructured format to be appropriate. In the context of action-research many interviews will need to serve both the purposes of comparison with the interviewer's perceptions and feelings about specific aspects of a situation and of understanding the range and variety of significant experience from the point of view of the interviewee. This suggests the general appropriateness of a semi-structured format. But as the action-research process develops and the parties involved achieve more consensus about what constitutes significant aspects of the situation to collect data about, then interviews can appropriately become increasingly structured, since they can focus on a common agenda of shared concerns.

Interviewing is best conducted on the basis of some concrete record of the situations or events to be talked about, e.g. a video or tape-recording or a set of photographs. Such evidence enhances recall and disciplines responses in a way which encourages authenticity of expression. This technique has been called "Instance Interviewing" because it focuses on a tangible representation of a situation or event. It is appropriate to all interviews in an action-research context. It is particularly useful in helping the interviewer to resist over-structuring in response to interviewee passivity. The material itself will tend to stimulate free responses to a greater degree than interviews which simply rely on memory as a basis for recalling experience.

Interviews can be conducted on an individual, pair or group basis. The problem with pairs and groups is with ensuring that individuals are able to express their individual views and are not inhibited from doing so by peer pressure or other dominant individuals. If these problems can be overcome by a skilful interviewer then pair and group interviews are an economical interview method. Of course one needs to set aside rather more time than with individual interviews if one is to achieve an in-depth exploration of people's thinking and experience, but overall a number of pair and group interviews will be less time consuming than a series of individual interviews.

The advantage of individual interviews is generally felt to lie in the absence of group pressures on individual self-disclosure and the provision of sufficient "space" for individuals to articulate their experience and views in depth. However, in an action- research context things are not so simple. The interviewer is likely to be a fellow participant in the situation under investigation and may indeed be in a super-ordinate role within that situation to the interviewees. This is certainly the case with a teacher interviewing students in his/her class. Even when the interviewer is an outsider the interviewees are aware that his/her aim is to elicit data from them which can be fed back to, and used by, other participants in the situation. Individuals may feel anxious about the consequences of interviews with other insiders, and indeed with outsiders, in an action-research context. This is why the terms and conditions under which the data will be subsequently used needs to be negotiated in advance with interviewees (See above under the discussion of triangulation for examples).

In an action-research context isolated individuals can feel reticent about self-disclosure, while in the presence of one or more peers that they trust they can feel more confident about expressing their authentic views and negotiating the terms and conditions under which this data can be subsequently used. The emotional support provided by peers in an interview situation can also be extended into the realm of consequences. If, for example, a teacher subsequently misuses the self-disclosure of a student and thereby abuses the latter's trust this will be clear to other students in the class who were involved in the interview. The student is therefore more likely to have the moral and active support of his/her peers in defending him/herself against later unfair treatment than an isolated interviewee might be able to command. The knowledge of this may also check any tendency the teacher might have to unfairly exploit the student's self-disclosures. For the interviewee there is a "safety in numbers" when the interviewer is in a position to subsequently use the data elicited to harm him or her.

In an interview situation it is possible to elicit the authentic views of others in an impersonal form by using the interviewee as a "reliable informant" about the views of other participants, without pressurising them to disclose the identities of the people who hold them. For example, a student who relates well to the majority of other students in the class is likely to know quite a lot about their perceptions of, and feelings about, the situation and events being researched. S(he) can then be selected for interview as a reliable informant. In such circumstances, given there is no pressure from the interviewer "to play spy" and disclose identities, the interviewee can faithfully report a variety and range of views. This is not only an economical interviewing technique but its depersonalised format enables the interviewees to report their own and other's views without too much fear of the consequences to themselves or others. Sometimes, however, in order to provide emotional support to interviewees and enable the interviewer to cross-check an individual's account, it may be better to interview informants in pairs or trio's.

Checklists, questionnaires, and inventories

Checklists in the context of action-research may be used to guide observations or the analysis of data such as recordings. They may take the form of action-hypotheses the action researcher intends to test as a means of resolving a practical problem or improving some aspect of a situation. Or they may cite problematic aspects of a situation which the researcher is attempting to resolve and which are listed as a means of monitoring the extent to which they recur.

An exclusive reliance on checklists, especially at an early stage in the action-research process, can be counter-productive inasmuch as they may blinker the researcher to salient and significant aspects of a situation which have not previously been noticed. Check-lists are most useful once the researcher has collected and analyzed sufficient data to feel reasonably confident that the significant aspects of the situation have been discriminated.

Questionnaires and inventories are normally employed in the context of survey research. The danger of "blinkering" perception also applies to the use of these instruments in the context of action-research. This is because judgements of salience and significance are presupposed in the design of a questionnaire or inventory. These judgements need to be determined in the light of more open and less structured data gathering techniques. One should not design a questionnaire before one has determined in the light of evidence gathered by other means (e.g. participant observation and interviews) which are the important questions to ask. One of the merits of an inventory of statements, to which people have to indicate the extent to which they agree or disagree with them, is that it can faithfully represent views expressed in earlier interviews with a small sample of people.

Questionnaires and inventories can be used to quantify issues which have been identified by other means, i.e. determining how many, and what kind, of people line up on each side of the issue. They are also useful at the "action phase" of the research when the researcher is attempting to bring about change to a situation. (S)he can use them to elicit quick feed-back from participants on the effects of the action-hypotheses (s)he is testing, or the extent to which they perceive previously identified problematic aspects of the situation to persist.

Pattern analysis

Observational data -- collected through audio or video recordings, photography, or in the form of descriptive notes -- can be analyzed in terms of actions and interactions which frequently recur during the period of observation. Such regularities constitute patterns which can be described at a low level of inference. In other words such descriptions do not refer to intentions and other mental states of participants which are manifested in their observable behaviour. They refer only to what can be directly observed. Examples of observable patterns are:

-- the teacher addresses boys by their surnames and girls by their first names;

-- teacher-student interaction takes the form: T-St-T-St-T;

-- when the teacher intervenes in a discussion to ask students if they agree with the views expressed by a previous contributor they respond with silence;

-- when teachers move around talking to students about their work, they stand above them looking down.

Discrimination of such patterns are not unbiased. They are inevitably conditioned by the values and concerns of the observer, e.g. that teachers should refrain from exerting authoritarian forms of control over students' thinking, or refrain from treating girls unequally from boys. Values guide the discrimination of action patterns even when they are objectively described. Nevertheless such low inferential accounts of people's actions and interactions enable them to offer an alternative view of the intentions and motives they manifest to those the observer may have in mind. This is more difficult if the observer portrays their actions and interactions entirely in terms of high inference statements dissociated from observable evidence.

For example, an observer may interpret a teacher asking students whether they agree with a point of view expressed in discussion as "pressurising them into a consensus position". The interpretation imputes blame to the teacher. But when presented with the observable evidence the teacher may defend his or her action as simply an attempt to discover what students think about the point expressed. In the absence of such evidence and faced with the bald assertion that (s)he was "pressurising for consensus" it is difficult for the teacher to resist the imputation of blame. If (s)he simply denies rather than accepts the interpretation (s)he can be charged with "defensiveness". It is a "no win situation" for the teacher because in the absence of concrete observable evidence (s)he is not in a position to use it as a basis for constructing an alternative interpretation of his or her intentions.

Pattern analysis constitutes a valuable triangulation technique because it processes observational data in a form which dissociates evidence from interpretation and thereby can be used to elicit a multiplicity of interpretations.

Issues and dilemma analysis

Data collected and processed by means of the techniques outlined above can be used to identify issues and dilemmas which face a practitioner in a social situation. "Issues" are constituted by different views or understandings of a situation and the sorts of actions which are appropriate and desirable in it. A triangulation strategy using the kinds of observational and interview techniques described above generates evidence about such differences of view, e.g. between a teacher and his or her students about what constitute appropriate teacher interventions to foster learning.

"Dilemmas" are constituted by ambiguous views held by individuals. A teacher, for example, may experience a conflict between ensuring that his or her students possess certain knowledge they are required to teach and giving them a measure of freedom to determine what they need to know for themselves. To take another example, a teacher may experience a dilemma between stretching a minority of very able students in her class and catering for the learning needs of the majority.

"Issues" may mask "dilemmas". For example, observation disclosed that a Biology teacher I was working with engaged in a pattern of frequently interrupting discussion to ask "does everyone agree with that?" (referring to a previous student contribution). Students in interview unanimously interpreted this pattern as an attempt by the teacher to secure their agreement to the views expressed. At first the teacher, when I interviewed him, emphatically rejected this interpretation, and argued that he was merely attempting to assess the degree of consensus/divergence which obtained in the class with respect to the views expressed. Later in the interview, the teacher began to reflect about the possibility that the way he couched the question was ambiguous, manifesting a dilemma he was experiencing between wanting to protect the expression of divergent views while at the same time securing agreement to what he considered to be the "correct" view by the end of the lesson. What at first appeared to be an "issue" between the teacher and his students later emerged as a "dilemma" for the teacher. An "issue" often constitutes an "externalisation" or "projection" of one aspect of a subjectively experienced dilemma.

Action-research facilitators should be careful to avoid forms of data analysis which rest on the assumption that the analysis is completed once "the controversial issues" have been identified. Such an analysis proffers a very different account of the problem to dilemma analysis. It suggests that the problem solely requires a resolution of conflicting interpretations between people while an understanding of a problem as a dilemma suggests that what needs to be resolved is an internal conflict within the individual. Many apparent issues are not so much directly resolved as "dissolved" by practitioners resolving their internal dilemmas.

Dilemma analysis involves a great deal of reflexive self-awareness on the part of practitioner-researchers. This can be developed through forms of discourse about triangulation data which enables practitioners to risk self-disclosure, to themselves as well as to others. Such discourse must overcome the defensiveness which underpins the transformation of subjectively experienced ambiguities (dilemmas) into interpersonal conflicts (issues). Issues between people in a situation often remain unresolved because the discourse between them fails to facilitate the withdrawal of "projections" and the consequent disclosure of dilemmas.

In educational action-research by teachers discussion with students may initially be too threatening for teachers to risk the self disclosure of their dilemmas. Discussing data with an outsider or professional peers may provide a less threatening setting for issues and dilemmas analysis than discussion with role-partners such as students. Once dilemmas have been articulated in a form which a teacher acknowledges and accepts then (s)he can begin to discuss how they might be resolved with students.

What follows is a suggestion about how to foster a process of analytic discourse between teacher researchers which has the potential to identify and clarify subjectively experienced dilemmas. The method outlined is a variant on one devised by Peter Posch (1988) at the University of Klagenfurt in Austria and used by the teachers' research groups he has worked with.

Analytic discourse method

Here the practitioner presents to peers some observational or interview data (or both) about his or her practice, in the form of an excerpt from a recording or transcript. The presentation places the material in context but avoids interpretation. It should be brief and last no longer than 10-15 minutes.

Peers are invited to ask the presenter questions in the light of the data provided. They are not allowed to offer or suggest their own interpretations. The presenter's role is to respond to such questions.

After a pre-specified period the presenter is given an opportunity to make a summary analysis of the data in the light of his or her responses to the questions.

The main purpose of this method is to maximise questions from others which promote self reflection and minimise conditions, such as the expression of judgmental attitudes, which prove threatening and promote defensiveness.

Although Posch calls the above procedure "analytic discourse method" it is, strictly speaking, only one method among many which can be used to structure group discourse about case study data generated through action- research. Below I will describe a method known as "nominal group technique".

Nominal group technique

This is essentially a procedure for allowing individuals in a group to freely express their ideas while at the same time enabling them to identify areas of consensus and divergence between them. In my view it can be fruitfully applied to support a form of analytic discourse between action researchers where they are attempting to draw comparisons between each other's case data. In describing the procedure I will attempt to illustrate how it might be applied in such a comparative analysis context. Let us assume that a group of 8 teacher researchers have come together to look at and discuss each other's case data, perhaps recordings of each other's teaching, with a group facilitator. Having spent time in advance studying the case material the procedure is as follows:

i)   Task Setting and Clarification (10 mins).

The facilitator writes down the task on a flip-chart or board, e.g.: Identify a) similarities, and b) differences in patterns of teacher intervention manifested in the case data. (S)he then requests questions from the group about the nature of the task and responds to each in turn. If necessary the task is reformulated to make it clearer.

ii)   Silent Listing (15 mins)

Each member of the group produces in silence a list of statements in response to the task, e.g. of similarities and differences in patterns of teacher intervention.

The facilitator clarifies in advance what is required; namely, statements of a sentence in length that (s)he can copy word for word onto the flip-chart, without having to contribute in any way to its formulation.

iii)   Round-Robin Listing (25 mins)

In turn each member is asked to select one item from their list and asked to read it aloud, e.g. one item from each of the similarities and differences listed. These are recorded on a flip-chart master list. With respect to the comparative exercise the master list will list "similarities" and "differences" in separate columns. Rounds of statement calling in turn are repeated until the items on the individual lists have been exhausted. Individuals are invited to call "pass" once all the items on their list have appeared on the master list. No discussion of items as they appear on the master list is permitted.

iv)   Clarification of Items (10 mins)

Members are given an opportunity to ask only clarificatory questions to the authors of statements on the list. As a result an item may be reformulated to clarify its meaning but only if this is acceptable to its author.

v)   Elimination of Equivalent Items (5 mins)

Items can be deleted from the master list at this point if the author agrees that a statement is strictly equivalent in meaning to another on the list. Items which simply overlap in meaning are left as they stand. Subsuming them under a more general or abstract statement should be avoided, since this may diminish perceptions of their practical significance.

vi)   Rank Ordering Items against a stated criterion (5 mins)

The facilitator gives a criterion, e.g. "which items on the master list have the greatest significance for how teachers handle value issues in environmental education?" Group members are asked to silently select 5 items they judge to be of most significance in terms of the criterion and to rank order them on a 5-1 scale; 5 being the upper and 1 the lower end of the scale. In the case of the comparative exercise five items will be selected from the 'similarities' and five from the 'differences' columns.

vii)   Tallying Items (10 mins)

The facilitator moves through the master list one item at a time and records the individual ratings and overall score for each. This is intended to give a fairly crude picture of agreements in judgement within the group.

viii)   Discussion of Results

It is only at this point that the facilitator gives the group an opportunity for discussion. Here individuals can discuss the results and their implications for practice and indeed further action-research. They are also given an opportunity to assess the value and validity of the procedure they have followed, either in part or as a whole.

ix)   Merging Master Lists

The views of several groups can be collated by compiling an overall master list from several group lists, selecting from each the six or so most highly scored items. With respect to our comparative example, six 'similarities' and six 'differences' will be selected from each list, and presented in two columns. This overall list can then be circulated to members of all the groups with the request that they select five items against the criterion and rank order them on a 5-1 scale. Again, with respect to our comparative example, five items will be selected from each of two columns. Those with the highest overall scores can then be selected out for inclusion in a "super-list" which provides a crude picture of shared understandings and insights across a number of groups.

The time frames stipulated for each element are adjustable and are intuitively based on my own experience of what might be reasonably accomplished in a 2-hour meeting/session. It is important that the whole procedure and the time-frames for each element in it is spelled out to participants in advance, and that in the process the facilitator is fairly strict on time-keeping.

This procedure minimises opportunities for facilitators to manipulate opinion personally but it has been accused of being a device for manufacturing a spurious consensus. In my experience most participants find it useful as a mechanism for expressing, sharing, and evaluating ideas, so long as the facilitator does not make too many claims for it and is aware of its limitations.

In addition to its application to the comparative analysis of case data, nominal group technique can be used as a group interview method to elicit and process people's perceptions and views of situations, events and issues.

Case study reports of action-research

Since a focus on particular practical situations is a key feature of action-research, reporting it naturally takes the form of the case study. However, case studies vary according to the type of research they represent, and their intended audiences and uses. In the context of action-research to bring about change the primary audience for case studies are fellow practitioners who use them as a means of comparing and contrasting experience across a range and variety of situations. This suggests that case study reports of attempts to bring about pedagogical change should be constructed in the light of something like the following criteria:

    i)   provide a narrative account of the change process as it unfolds from a variety of perspectives: teacher(s), students, and observers. The account should be highly readable, using non-technical language to tell a story and give the reader a sense of what it was like to be involved;

    ii)   portray the change process in context, highlighting those aspects which illuminate the experience of those involved;

    iii)   focus on problematic aspects of the change process;

    iv)   reflect about the problematic aspects from different angles or points of view;

    v)   reveal how understanding of the situation and the problems and issues involved develop in the light of new evidence;

    vi)   describe the curriculum and pedagogical strategies generated during the course of a developing understanding of the situation;

    vii)   assess the consequences of curriculum and pedagogical strategies, both intended and unintended, for the quality of the change process;

    viii)   describe, justify, and critique the methods and procedures used to gather and analyze evidence.

In the context of action-research case studies do not simply report "findings" detached from accounts of the research process. "Understanding" is being continuously modified through the insider researcher's practical interventions in it, and this in turn generates new possibilities for further action. It is this interactive process of action influencing reflection and vice versa that has to be described in case reports of action-research.

The construction of case studies which satisfy the criteria listed is not an easy task. In advising teachers on how to do this I have often found Stenhouse's distinction (1978) between case studies, case records, and case data a useful one. The case data simply consists of all the evidence collected during the course of the research. The case study consists of an interpretative account of the situation which is grounded in the case data. This involves a great deal of selectivity. A lot of the case data will be disregarded in constructing the account because it is judged not to be significant enough for understanding the relevant aspects of the situation. The case record consists of a selection from the case data, organised around the central interpretative themes explored in the case study, in a manner which would enable others to critique the validity of the interpretations represented in the latter.

Where an action-research programme involves practitioner researchers in comparing and contrasting cases across a variety of situations, as the ENSI Project does (e.g. across classrooms, schools, communities, and countries), then comparative discourse may be considerably enhanced if participants have access to the case records as a basis for their critiques of each other's case studies.

Summary reports

The similarities and differences identified through the comparative analysis of case studies and case records, together with explanations for them, can be reported in summary form. Items in such reports can be cross-referenced to relevant sections of the case studies and case records. Summary reports are a way of representing the insights distilled from the comparison of cases.

In the context of the ENSI project the pedagogical support persons may be in a more feasible position than teachers to produce Summary Reports of the action-research carried out within their respective countries, and the OECD consultants may be in the best position to produce the Summary Report based on cross-national comparisons. But it is important that such reports should be well grounded in the teachers' action-research, represented in the case studies, and that they should have opportunities to critique drafts of the reports.

Concluding remarks

The primary purpose of this monograph is to support the pedagogical support persons within the ENSI project in their role as facilitators of teachers' based action-research. It is offered as a resource rather than a prescription. The ideas, principles, research strategies and methods outlined above will hopefully be tested in the experience of pedagogical support personnel through their own action-research into their role. They have an important contribution to make to the continuing development of a methodology of Insider Research which supports the professional development of teachers and curriculum development in schools. The author would welcome reflective critiques of this monograph from pedagogical support personnel and the teachers they are working with as a contribution to the publications of the project.

References

ELLIOTT, J. (1991), *Action Research for Educational Change* Open University Press: Milton Keynes & Philadelphia, UK.

HOLLY, M.L. (1989), 'Reflective Writing' *Cambridge Journal of Education* Vol 19, No 1, UK.

KLEMP, G.O. (1977), *Three Factors of Success in the World of Work: Implications for Curriculum in Higher Education,* McBer & Co: Boston.

McCLELLEND, D.C. (1973), 'Testing for Competence rather than for Intelligence' *American Psychologist,* 28, 1-14, Boston.

McCLELLAND, D.C. (1976), *A Guide to Job Competency Assessment,* McBer & Co: Boston.

POSCH, P. (1988), 'Analytic Discourse Method', Mimeo, University of Klagenfurt, Austria.

SPENCERS, L.M. (1979), *Identifying, Measuring and Training Soft Skill Competencies which Predict Performance in Professional, Managerial and Human Service Jobs,* McBer & Co: Boston.

STENHOUSE, L. (1978), 'Case Study and Case Records: towards a contemporary history of education', *British Educational Research Journal,* Vol 4, No 2, UK.

WALKER, R. and Adelman, C. (1975), *Guide to Classroom Observation,* Methuen: London.

WINTER, R. (1989), *Learning from Experience,* The Falmer Press: London, New York, Philadelphia.

Chapter 3

NETWORKING IN ENVIRONMENTAL EDUCATION

by

Peter Posch
University of Klagenfurt
Austria

This chapter examines needs and prerequisites for networking in environmental education. The first section refers to two new educational tasks which confront schools when they involve themselves in environmental education, and which pose the problem of communication in education in a new way. Sections two and three examine two contrasting types of networks and their philosophical background: hierarchical networks and dynamic networks. Section four gives a few examples of dynamic networks in environmental education and section five analyses some of their implications for educational support.

New tasks in environmental education

Environmental education can be regarded as the most successful innovation in education in our time -- at least, if the investment of energy at school level is taken into consideration. The number of teachers and students who have become involved in environmental initiatives has increased sharply during the past ten years. The most remarkable aspect of this development is that, in general, these activities have not been mandated by authorities but are self-initiated by teachers and students. This is an indication that environmental education is a creative and autonomous response of teachers and students to the growing pressures exerted both by external societal changes (cf. Posch 1990a) and by growing discontent inside school. This response is expressed primarily by two interrelated tasks which -- it seems -- are increasingly complementing the traditional task of schools to transmit subject matter knowledge and predefined competencies. The two new tasks are:

-- the generation of "local knowledge" by teachers and students, and;
-- the active participation of teachers and students in improving environmental situations.

The generation of local knowledge

The following examples to illustrate this task are taken from the Environment and School Initiatives Project (OECD/CERI 1991). In a secondary school in the Tyrol, Austria, 13 to 14 year old students studied the use of energy in four small villages. They prepared a questionnaire, went from house to house in pairs, asked for collaboration and offered assistance in data collection. Nearly 70% of the households had filled in the questionnaire. The students processed the data at school and produced a comparative analysis of the use of energy for each house and for each village.

The results were presented by the students at a public meeting. People who had requested it were provided with proposals for saving energy on the basis of their individual data. The teachers involved and their students kept "research diaries" to facilitate reflection on the progress of work. A follow-up activity which -- though originally not intended -- emerged from this initiative was the establishment of several local initiatives to manufacture sun collectors (Mair, personal communication and BRG Imst 1990). In 1990 the project was followed by another project, in which the energy situation of a more sizeable community was analyzed (1991a).

In Mantova, Italy, five vocational upper secondary schools are co-operating to study the quality and the degree of pollution of ground and surface waters in the communities of Mantova. The activities are co-ordinated by a group of students and teachers and are financed by the communities on the basis of contracts. The responsibilities of the pupils range from the selection and drawing of water samples and on the spot analysis, via a detailed chemical, bacteriological and micro-plankton analysis in their school laboratories, to reporting and discussing the results with the authorities. Recently, they involved 12 lower secondary schools in this project (Sutti 1991 and personal communication).

In these examples students produce local knowledge, i.e. knowledge of specific conditions of their environment. This process has several features:

-- The knowledge produced is not a reconstruction of existing knowledge but is potentially "new" knowledge. It may provide information on issues which was not available before.

-- The knowledge is specific knowledge generated in specific contexts. It is potentially valid in this context but not necessarily in other contexts.

-- The knowledge is potentially useful for a specific audience. It may increase this audience's ability to understand situations and cope with demands.

-- For the students the generation of local knowledge implies an integration of experience-based judgement with available knowledge.

Responsible action to improve environmental conditions

A few examples may also illustrate this task: In an Austrian elementary school, students investigated the use of plastic bags and asked shop-keepers also to offer cloth or burlap bags, at a moderate price. A second enquiry was held a few weeks later and the pupils sent thank-you-letters to those shop-keepers who had taken positive action (Haas 1990).

Students of a secondary school in Norway conducted a market analysis on the buying habits of the local population regarding detergents, and at the same time provided information on the consequences of phosphates on the environment. They succeeded in modifying buying (and in consequence also selling) behaviour in favour of detergents without phosphates (F. Folkedahl, personal communication).

An Australian school analyzed the water quality of a surfing and swimming beach and found that coliform bacteria counts were far in excess of the guidelines for safe body contact. The students tried to engage in dialogue with the local Water Board who controlled the nearby sewage treatment plant. They were rebuffed and went public. As a result, a general and sustained community interest was mobilised and the Water Board was requested to undertake substantial improvements to their sewage treatment facility (Gough/Robottom 1990).

In a lower secondary school in Austria, a teacher in cooperation with a nature conservation association organised a regional campaign in schools to finance the acquisition of "meadows for butterflies and hedges for birds" to counteract negative consequences of land consolidation. Prior to 1990 36 hectares had been acquired. Since that time it has become part of a project to establish a nature part "Bohemian Forest" comprising 20,000 hectares (Zimmerhackl 1990; Österreichisches Zentrum für Umwelterziehung (ÖZU) 1990, 4f).

In a number of schools students made an attempt to change their immediate school environment: the classrooms and the school yard. The idea was to make the school a "place where one would like to live" (e.g. Schindler, pers. comm).

These examples show direct involvement of students and teachers in the improvement of their environment.

Such influence can have several forms of expressions:

-- Activities to inform other people. In many cases research activities to gather and analyze evidence (i.e. local knowledge generation) are a necessary prerequisite for this purpose.

-- Activities to convince others of the usefulness and feasibility of certain changes or to exert pressure (e.g. by personal example, by petitions, public hearing, letters, by involving the local press etc.).

-- Hands-on construction of alternative environments (by buying land for biotopes, developing the ambience at school, reducing waste at school etc.).

Activities to influence environmental situations confront students with open-ended situations and with controversial perceptions of reality and values. Such situations challenge them to use their intellectual, emotional, creative, and organisational capacities; they provide experiential knowledge that environmental situations are determined by human intervention and that students can actively participate in the construction of reality. A correlation is established between school learning and activities to cope with real-life problems. As a 15 year old student put it: "To prepare for life means to achieve something now" (Mair 1990b). The justification of these activities is not derived from their assumed learning potential but from the determination to realise values in the students' environment.

Both tasks, generation of local knowledge and exerting an influence on the environment, refer to educational situations which provide the chance to do something that "matters". They have arisen from the understanding that there are problems in our society which cannot be coped with successfully if the processes of learning, of knowledge generation, and of interventive action are separated from each other.

The emergence of these tasks, and the fact that more and more teachers and students have started to integrate them in their conception of teaching and learning, indicate that traditional barriers between school and environment, between learning and living, between theory and practice, are being reduced and that, on a more fundamental level, are changing from "hierarchical" to "dynamic" networks. This hypothesis will be elaborated and examined in the following sections.

Hierarchical networks and technical rationality

The term 'network' is used to indicate a structure in which elements are identified and related to (connected with) each other to allow exchange processes between them (influencing, learning, moving, transporting messages etc). The relationship can be one of time (e.g. sequences of activities) or one of space (e.g. places of activity); it can be a relationship between concepts or theories, or one between persons or objects.

There are networks in our natural environment (e.g. food chains), in our cultural, technical, economic, and social environment (e.g. systems of knowledge, road intersections, enterprises, friendships etc., e.g Fischer 1991).

A hierarchical network is a network with a pyramidal relationship of super -- and -- subordination with ranked (sets of) elements and lines of communication between them.

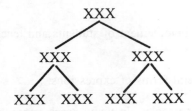

Fischer-Kowalski (1991) in her "liberal version" of hierarchical networks gives five characteristics:

a) The direct connection between two ranks is asymmetric. Depending on the end from which an exchange starts qualitatively different but complementary messages are transported. There is, for example, top-down task definition and bottom-up feedback. the total advantage of the exchange is greater for the higher points than for the lower points. The higher the rank the more information is available to it. As a result it can make better use of each single piece of information than any lower rank. This feature strengthens the centre at the cost of the periphery.

In education it is illustrated in the relative position of head and teacher, but also in the relationship between teacher and pupil (the teacher is expected to transmit information, the pupil has to take it in; the teacher is supposed to set the questions, the pupil has to answer them).

b) On each rank there are (sets of) elements that communicate with each other. This feature allows for considerable dynamics and differentiation and for the development of competition and solidarity. However, the contact between ranks is regulated. An example is the "official channels of communication" in the educational bureaucracy. The teacher is supposed to communicate with a higher level only via his or her immediate superior.

c) The connections between ranks are safe-guarded by rules defining the elements which belong to the network (or a subsystem within the network) and thus excluding elements ("outsiders") not belonging to it. Structure is developed by inclusion and exclusion. The clear distinction between inside and outside stabilizes the internal communication process and reduces complexity.

d) The decision to include classes of elements into or exclude them from the network is based on dichotomous judgements: relevant/irrelevant, good/bad, right/wrong, legitimate/illegitimate. Potential contradictions are thereby named and at the same time eliminated. In education, for example, the legitimate educational content is defined by the curriculum (or syllabus). Curriculum-bound transmission of systematic knowledge is thereby defined as relevant. Subject matter or problems or types of learning which are not referred to in this document (in general situational learning, open-ended learning activities, and controversial issues) are excluded.

64

e) The ranks and (sets of) elements within a rank are functionally differentiated (division of work). This reduces the number of possible connections. Only those aspects of each element become relevant which are needed for the defined function. In a hierarchical educational system, the "value" of a teacher (or student) is dependent on those characteristics which correspond to his/her function. Other characteristics are considered irrelevant.

The philosophical background of hierarchical networks is technical rationality. According to Schön (1983) this approach is based on three assumptions:

-- there are general solutions to practical problems.
-- these solutions can be developed outside practical situations (e.g. in academic or administrative centres).
-- the solutions can be transferred into practitioners' actions and solve the practical problems.

Consequences of these assumptions are the separation of theory and practice, of knowledge and action, of means and ends, and the emergence of two hierarchies: the hierarchy of knowledge and the hierarchy of credibility.

Basic science, applied science, and the technical skills of day to day practice constitute the hierarchy of knowledge. General, theoretical, propositional knowledge (e.g. in education it might be learning theory) enjoys a privileged position. Its application to practical problems constitutes the intermediate level of applied science (e.g. educational technology). The practical knowledge necessary to cope with every-day problems (e.g. in a school) offers the lowest level of prestige, partly because it is considered as a merely instrumental application of technical means suited to particular purposes. Partly, its low prestige stems from the experience that in reality practice is often a swampy lowland in which "messy and confusing problems defy technical solutions" (Schön 1987, 3). So much the worse for practical knowledge.

This hierarchy is operationalised in the classical Research-Development-Dissemination (RDD) model of innovation. Researchers produce the theoretical background for an educational innovation. In the development phase the theoretical framework is applied to solve a generalised practical problem. The result is a product for a specific group of consumers (a curriculum, teaching and learning materials, etc.). It is tested and directions for use are elaborated. The logic of application favours the tendency to make it as "user proof" as possible (e.g. by materialising it into an instrument with "inbuilt efficiency"). The product is then disseminated to practitioners. Strategies are applied to reach, train, and stimulate them to accept the innovation and to use it in a prescribed way (e.g. by information leaflets, training courses, administrative incentives and pressures, etc.).

A similar hierarchy can be found in legal and administrative regulations. Laws (general regulations) are higher in status than, for example, regional decrees which again carry more weight than local regulations. The result is a hierarchy of credibility. It implies that a person is the more credible, the higher (s)he is in the institutional power structure, i.e. the closer (s)he is to general regulations. The teachers is considered more credible than the pupils, the head of department more credible than the teacher, the principal more credible than the head of department etc. The hierarchy of credibility expresses a genuine mistrust of the practitioner. Within the conceptual framework of technical rationality she or he is working on a low level of generality and is merely applying what has been predefined in the academic and administrative power-structure above him or her. Improvements of school practice are in this view primarily a result of improved general and applied theories and norms transmitted to the practitioner (and of incentives and control mechanisms to ensure their correct application).

According to these assumptions, networking serves to effect the smooth and efficient top-down communicational knowledge and regulations, and to facilitate and control their use by the teachers. The most appropriate structure of communication, according to technical rationality, is therefore the hierarchical network.

Both technical rationality and hierarchical networks have promoted a specific culture of teaching and learning in school:

Its main characteristics are:

-- Predominance of systematic knowledge. It gives priority to well-established facts and enables schools to maintain a close relationship with the results of academic knowledge and to the process of knowledge generation.

-- Rigid specialisation. The knowledge is compartmentalised in subject matter fields which more or less correspond to the academic disciplines. This again facilitates the orientation on academic knowledge structures. On the other hand, complex, real-life situations tend to be disregarded because they cross the disciplinary borders.

-- Transmission-mode of teaching. This mode facilitates the retainment of the systematic character of knowledge and its reconstruction by the student. It tends to discourage the generation and reflective handling of knowledge.

-- Prevalence of top-down communication. it facilitates the control process for predefined knowledge structures and discourages self-control and co-operation between students (or teachers).

These characteristics indicate a relatively "static" and "standardised" (Mayer 1990, 11) culture of learning in which it is assumed that the processes of teaching learning can be predetermined and in which the teaches' and students' ability to define and cope with the problems autonomously, and to monitor themselves, appear to be counter-productive.

Hierarchic networks and technical rationality have been extremely efficient. Technical rationality has led to a stupendous growth of knowledge and to an unprecedented extension of human capabilities to access, store, process, use, and communicate information. It has surrounded human beings with an ever-increasing array of artificial "cognitive limbs" (Arranz 1987) extending the limited human anatomical outfit.

The hierarchical network, as the social organisation of technical rationality, has made possible an enormous functional differentiation of work and mass production. Both have contributed to the high standard of living and life expectancy in industrialised societies and to a stale mass education system, providing systematic knowledge by specialised personnel in special sites, distanced from accidental influences of every day communication.

Until recently, technical rationality and hierarchical networks have maintained a relatively unchallenged dominance. Three developments can be made responsible for the emergence of an alternative paradigm:

One is the dramatic growth of complexity. This can be seen as a consequence of the profusion of "cognitive limbs". Arranz (1987) also uses the even stronger metaphor of the ever growing "artificial tentacles of the human cephalopod". Their parallel development, their interaction with each other and with natural systems, produces an enormous multiplicity of influences. Another development is closely related to it: the decreasing predictability of intended and unintended effects. This is a direct consequence of increasing complexity and is related to the well-known paradoxical phenomenon that the more knowledge accumulates the more new questions arise. Finally, the risks or "death potentials" of possible futures have risen sharply in recent years. They indicate that the "carrying capacity" of some ecosystems may have been reached. These developments appear to be "natural" outcomes of the predominance of technical rationality.

Technical rationality has, in a sense, produced its own contradiction. its strength depended on the "stable state" (Schön), where privileged knowledge could be applied to problems of practice because its effects could be foreseen and controlled. For nearly two hundred years this assumption seemed to have been defensible. However, by acting on its basis, man devaluated it and produced many of the complexities, uncertainties and controversies of our time. At the same time, hierarchical networks became less and less able to fulfil their task. The main reason is probably that they were "constructed" for top-down operationalisation/co-ordination of know-how and for positive feedback. Their limits becomes obvious if a multiplicity of effects and side effects of human intervention call for the production of local knowledge and for the rapid utilisation of negative feedback.

Arranz draws a gloomy scenario of the future of mankind by extrapolating the present development. For him chaos is pre-programmed. He believes that the inextricable maze of human beings' cognitive limbs will eventually reach proportions which would produce their own dynamics and would defy human control. As a result, the cephalopod would collapse under its own weight and complexity.

I do not believe that this is the only answer, but it highlights the importance of a search for an alternative rationality, and a corresponding network of communication which would counteract the 'death potential' of technical rationality and still retain its 'life potential'. The attempt to identify an alternative will be made in the following section.

Dynamic networks and reflective rationality

In a comfortably equipped former classroom i a suburban school in Vienna (Austria) teachers of several neighbouring schools meet for a two to three hour afternoon session every other week. They come with their children who are taken care of by a student. They exchange experiences, discuss themes and problems of mutual interest, discuss and develop materials; sometimes they invite an external speaker etc. To prepare these sessions a small group of teachers meets one afternoon in the intervening week to plan the agenda for the next meeting.

The costs of this self-organised exchange of experience are very low and could be borne by the teachers themselves (as actually happened in the initial phase). Nonetheless some "soft money" is provided by the regional teachers' centre: the teachers who organise the afternoon (generally three to four teachers) and the student taking care of the children are paid a small fee ($ 8.00 per hour). the teachers' centre also covers the maintenance of the room and provides some small additional services (e.g. they hired the van needed to transport some second-hand furniture which the teachers acquired cheaply).

This is a simple example of a non-hierarchical network set up by the teachers themselves. It is unbureaucratically supported (but not taken over) by the regional teachers' centre. It represents a small step beyond informal communication and, not being confined to the context of an individual school, provides a new quality of opportunities for mutual professional assistance (Schneck 1989).

Another example:

Bratteberg School is situated on the island Öckerö (Sweden). In this school, an attempt was made to reorganise school-life in order to counteract the negative effects of the economical difficult situation on the island. Teachers, parents, local businessmen and others founded the "Alliance for Better Learning" to over come the isolation between the school and the population. Its main task was to support the initiation of projects and to give the pupils the opportunity to take an active and creative part in the cultural and economic life of the community. Numerous projects were implemented, which were partly of a long term nature. Among other things they established a fish farm, a greenhouse, a studio for radio and TV productions, and a wind power plant. One third of the total time available for lessons is used to carry out the projects. The projects are partly financed by the alliance, partly they finance themselves by commercial activity. (Rapp 1991)

Characteristics of dynamic networks

Dynamic networks differ in several respects from hierarchical networks (cp. Fischer-Kowalski 1991):

i)   The direct connection (interchange) between two elements (and classes of elements) is symmetric. From each element a variety of messages is transported. The total advantage of the exchange is distributed evenly among the elements. Because of the symmetric relationship an exchange on the exchange process is possible. Each element is able to change places in the sense that it can take another element's perspective. It facilitates meta-reflection and the development of shared policies.

ii)   The connections between elements are paved by exchange processes (e.g. by comparing, influencing, learning). They are not defined by pre-specified routes. Their duration can vary. The examples given above show networks of a relatively stable, long-term character. The other extreme is illustrated by the organising of an afternoon at a commercial secondary school in Austria, in which students of another school were invited to present their experiences with an environmental project and to assist their hosts in starting a similar initiative (Karl Schweitzer, pers. comm.)

iii)   The connections are not safe-guarded by predefined rules but are defined and charged by shared interests. Nothing is by definition included in or excluded from the network. A connection that does not exist is one that presently does not exist but might exist at another time. The decision to participate or not is a matter of negotiation between the elements concerned. Relationships can develop quite spontaneously. A Finnish teacher whose students were concerned with waste problems found out about an Austrian primary school which had already taken initiatives in the field. The Finnish students presented themselves and their concerns in written form, on tape and with slides and the exchange started with a high level of involvement on both sides (E. Amann, 1991).

iv)   There is no externally established functional differentiation. This means that the connections can be multidimensional. As a result each element of the network can be involved in a potentially unlimited learning process. Learning in this context means constructing new connections (or new dimensions within a connection) without having to give up the existing ones (although they may be less used). This contrasts with a pyramidal structure in which new connections have to be defined by another rank (e.g. by a new boss) and in general substitute the old ones. An example of the multidimensional character is the "Alliance for Better Learning" (see the example at the beginning of the chapter) providing a supportive structure for a great variety of student initiatives.

The essential feature of dynamic networks is the autonomous and flexible establishment of relationships to assist responsible action in the face of complexity and uncertainty. They are answers to specific situational characteristics (see also Ochsenbauer, 1989):

-- Complex, low-structured specific situations -- in which often even the problems are in need of being defined -- call for specific knowledge to cope with them. "General knowledge" is not sufficient.

-- This specific knowledge can only be generated within the situation and by those who through their action (or non-action) are elements of it. It cannot be produced in another context but is derived from a "situational understanding" (Elliott/Rice, 1990).

-- The knowledge thus generated is not applied instrumentally to solve the problems but expresses itself holistically in actions comprising cognitions, value orientations, and feelings.

Dynamic networks contradict one of the traditional assumptions of schooling the assumption of a separation of school and society. If dynamic networks develop it is difficult to say where the educational organisation ends and where society and its abundance of personal and institutional relationships begins.

It is interesting that quite similar developments have been identified in the economic system (cf. Ochsenbauer, 1989, pp. 264ff.).

Dynamic networks are in a sense an extension of the idea of specialisation by providing access to a variety of external resources (and know-how) to teachers as well as students.

These characteristics call for another form of rationality, one that is able to complement technical rationality and to substitute it wherever it fails to cope with local complexity. In the following sections the attempt will be made to elaborate this alternative form of rationality and a corresponding concept of institutional learning. Both should help in understanding how the emergence of autonomy and self-organisation are a precondition for the substitution of hierarchical structures of communication by dynamic networks.

Reflective rationality

Donald Schön (1983) in his seminal book on the reflective practitioner has elaborated a theory of reflective action which provides a conceptual background for an alternative to technical rationality and a theoretical basis for dynamic networks.

Donald Schön distinguishes three types of professional action (see also Altrichter/Posch/Somekh, 1993):

Action of Type I: Knowledge in action

The normal state of knowledge is tacit knowing-in-action. It is characteristic for this type of knowledge:

-- That there is no division between thinking and acting: "Although we sometimes think before acting, it is also true that in much of the spontaneous behaviour of skilful practice we reveal a kind of knowing which does not stem from a prior intellectual operation" (Schön, 1983, p. 51);

-- That the actor often is not conscious of having acquired the knowledge;

-- And that the actor normally is not able to express his knowledge verbally: "He knows more than he can say".

Action of Type I is a result of socialisation in certain traditions which because of their relatively consistent structure require frequent and similar types of activity.

Action of Type II: Reflection in action

Tacit knowing in action is efficient as long as there is a perfect fit between the demand of the situation and intentions embedded in one's action. If problems arise this is no longer sufficient and a need arises for reflection in action.

"Reflection in Action"...is central to the art through which practitioners sometimes cope with troublesome "divergent" situations of practice (Schön, 1983, p. 62).

When someone reflects in action, he becomes a researcher in the practice context. He is not dependent on the categories of established theory and technique, but constructs a new theory of the unique case. His inquiry is not limited to a deliberation about means which depends on a prior agreement about ends. He does not keep means and ends separate, but defines them interactively as he frames a problematic situation. He does not separate thinking from doing, rationalising his way to a decision which he must later convert to action. Because his experimenting is a kind of action, implementation is built into his inquiry. Thus reflection in action can proceed, even in situations of uncertainty or uniqueness, because it is not bound by the dichotomies of technical rationality (Schön, 1983, p. 68f.).

Donald Schön (1983, p. 56) conceptualised this "research in the practice context" as "reflective conversation" with a situation. The following activities mark typical steps of this "conversation":

-- The process begins if a situation occurs which cannot be coped with by routines. The result is surprise, dissatisfaction or failure;

-- The practitioner tries to make sense of a situation he encounters. His experience offers a repertoire of examples, images, interpretations and actions to define the problematic situation. He uses them to view the new situation as an already-known one in analogy to one he is already familiar with. He names it and tries to reflect on the consequences which follow his framing of the problem.

When a practitioner makes sense of a situation, he perceives to be unique, he sees it as something already present in his repertoire... (He sees) the unfamiliar, unique situation as both similar to and different from the familiar one without at first being able to say similar or different with respect to what. The familiar situation functions as a precedent, or a metaphor, or -- in Thomas Kuhn's phrase -- an example for the unfamiliar one" (Schön, 1983, p. 138).

-- The practical consequence of this first problem definition is tested in a frame experiment. The resulting experiences are used to re-conceptualise the situation and to re-establish the fit between the situation and action.

-- This process requires a double "vision":

At the same time that the inquirer tries to shape the situation to his frame, he must hold himself open to the situation's back-talk" (Schön, 1983, p. 164).

Coping with a problematic situation involves a combination of "advocacy and inquiry" (Argyris *et al.*, 1985, p. 258). "Advocacy" refers to the attempt to impose one's interpretation of a situation on that situation. Inquiry refers to sensitivity to the situation's back-talk through the unintended effects of action.

-- The evaluation of such frame experiments requires a holistic evaluation of a new situation. Instead of asking, "Did I achieve the ends I set?", he asks, "Do I like what I get?". In a situation in which he acts responsibly the practitioner cannot judge the situation only in view of the intended consequences but he has to take into consideration also all of its effects and side effects. According to Schön such an experiment is considered a failure (and the process of reflection in action has to be resumed) if the totality of effects and side effects are judged as a change to the negative. On the other hand the experiment is successful if the total situation improves even if the intended consequences have not occurred.

-- The practitioner's main interest lies in understanding a situation in order to improve action in it.

The process spirals through stages of appreciation, action, and re-appreciation. The unique and uncertain situation comes to be understood through the attempt to change it, and is changed through the attempt to understand it" (Schön, 1983, p. 132).

Action of Type III: Reflection on action

Actions of Type III are those where the actor steps out of the flow of action, distances himself from action and objectifies it. Reflection is a kind of secondary action which is directed on (or "laid over") this objectified form of primary action. Primary action is "brought to a stand" and viewed as an object of reflection. Cognitive objectivation is also a feature of action Type II. The distancing from the stream of action, however, enables the actor also to achieve a "real" objectivation by collecting data representative of a situation and by storing them in material form. Thereby new possibilities of analysis, presentation, reorganisation, and optimisation of action are accessible. In addition, knowledge can be communicated, discussed and criticised. This is an important prerequisite for the further development of a common base of practical knowledge.

Reflection on action is a type of action which usually is regarded as a domain of academic research. Schön (1983), and Altrichter (1990) have argued that research is characterised by all three of these types of action. It is based on "natural interpretations" and routines of action. It is oriented by reflection in action, and specific phases of the research process are reflection on action. The same seems to be the case with the professional action. The centre of professional competence is reflection in action with which complex professional situations are coped with. It is embedded in the unquestioned self-evidences of non-reflected routines (knowledge in action), and is complemented by reflection on action if a serious problem is to be solved or if one's own knowledge is communicated to others (Altrichter, 1990).

Donald Schön developed his epistemology of practice for the (academic) professions. I believe that this limitation to a specific clientele is unnecessary and unjustified, because complexity, insecurity, and uniqueness are pervading more and more situations in the public vocational and private domains. As a result, autonomous local initiatives in varying degrees are required from more and more people. This cultivation of the ability to reflect in and on action is becoming a necessity for practically everybody.

In the following section the concept of reflective rationality is used to elaborate a model of institutional change that is consistent with the emergence of dynamic networks. It views institutional learning as an assimilation process.

Institutional learning: the assimilation process

A simple example gives some clues on how the "assimilation process" might be understood: the concept of roundness can be derived from the form a hand must develop in order to hold a round object, for example a tennis ball. Here, an existing structure (the hand) creates a form (a substructure) in order to hold the new object. The hand is "accommodated" to the object. The new structure is then integrated into the memory of the individual. It has been learned. The whole process is called an assimilation process. Its result is a differentiation of the available structures of the organism to increase its capacity to understand and cope with the environment.

The concept of assimilation has been introduced by Piaget (1975) in the context of fundamental epistemological issues. Piaget describes the development of the individual as a process of differentiation of (originally genetic and later on learned) structures while interacting with the environment. He uses the complementary terms "assimilation" and "accommodation" to refer to two aspects of the integration of "reality" into the living organism. This integration is accomplished by the structures available to the organism (assimilation). At the same time, the structures are adapted to reality (accommodation) -- for example, by new combinations of existing structures -- if the reality resists being integrated.

The term "structure" is used as a hypothetical construct to explain individual behaviour. The concept of roundness is such a structure. Once learned, it is available for a great variety of individual actions. Such structures are expressed in our actions. Generally, we do not consciously apply structures to our actions, but the structures are embedded in them and are expressed without our determination to apply them. They are "tacit knowing" (Polanyi, 1967) or "knowledge in action". However, if difficulties arise -- if the available structures do not sufficiently reproduce the information they encounter -- the structures enter consciousness. They become an object of reflection. Reflection, in this sense, is a strategy to accommodate a structure to regain the capacity for smooth assimilation. Difficulties arise if the incoming information and the structures available for assimilation do not correspond: if there are incongruencies (or differences) between the structures and the events which they try to understand and cope with (i.e. to assimilate).

Incongruencies are a result of the "back talk" of the "real" world. Schön (1983) has used this vivid term to describe how again and again our structures are confronted with a reality "unwilling" to be incorporated by them. The result is a "conversation" between structures and situation, which results in a new combination of structures in order to regain the capacity of tacit assimilation. In this sense, assimilation can be viewed as an ongoing (mostly unnoted) process by which an organism becomes what it is at any given time.

Can the concepts of assimilation and accommodation be applied to the process of institutional learning? By analogy to the human organism, it seems possible also to regard an institution, for example a school, as an organism. It has a "memory", it "acts", using the available "structures". It "understands" and copes with "changing environments". In a human organism, it is assumed that the structures are organised in sets of structures, subsystems, systems (e.g. the physical system, or the view of life of a person) that are more or less integrated into a coherent whole.

In a similar vein an institution can also be split into a number of more or less complex and more or less integrated (sub)systems. Therefore, incongruencies between reality and available structures can develop, not only between an institution and the outside world but also within the institution. Subsystems can be in conflict with each other -- for example, two departments of a school. By analogy to the tacit state of most structures of the human organism, it is also assumed that most structures of an institution which are expressed in its "actions" and which manage the day-to-day assimilation (understanding and coping) process, are tacit knowledge. They are a "hidden agenda", because they govern behaviour without being consciously applied.

The word "hidden agenda" implies that there is also an overt agenda. The overt agenda refers to what is intentionally communicated by actions. "Hidden" refers to all the rest of meanings which are also communicated -- unintentionally and unconsciously. A hidden agenda can, for example, say much about the relative importance of subjects in the curriculum. This message may be quite different from what is intentionally communicated about it. It is assumed here that it is the hidden agenda, the "knowledge in action" that "really" matters in the assimilation process of an institution.

Institutional learning is in this sense the development of the tacit knowledge of an institution. This can happen in a rather diverse manner. Some changes may go unnoticed. Small incongruencies between the implicit structures and the situations encountered may lead to spontaneous adaptations; other more conspicuous "bad fits" enforce a reflection in action by which knowledge in action becomes conscious and is modified in the process. If the incongruence increases, the need to conceptualise knowledge in action and its implications becomes stronger, providing a basis for more substantial reflection on action. At the same time, the security provided by tacit knowledge is reduced, which can be interpreted as loss or even as threat to the institution (Menlo, 1985).

It is assumed that, in general, no more tacit knowledge than is necessary to understand and cope with a problematic situation, becomes conscious and subject to analysis and modification. The economies inherent in this principle could explain why fundamental institutional changes are very rare. The bulk of knowledge in action retains its implicit character and defines the general approach to assimilation. This is probably an essential condition for the functioning of institutions in complex and unstable environments.

The assimilation perspective on institutional learning can be summarised by three features:

-- It refers to the perspective of the institution confronted with changes in its environment. It does not refer to the perspective of the supporters of specific responses to such changes (e.g. of an innovation to be institutionalised).

-- Institutional learning is first and foremost regarded as an "intuitive" process of understanding and coping based on the "feel" for a situation. The extent to which it becomes a rational and reflective process depends on the perceived discrepancies between environmental pressures and institutional practice and on the extent to which prevailing institutional structures are able to enter a process of reflection and to accommodate to a new situation.

-- The assimilation perspective is a primarily dynamic view of institutional learning. Institutions are momentary stages in an ongoing process of change. The knowledge to cope successfully with a complex and changing environment is local knowledge generated by the practitioners within the institution in a process of a "reflective" conversation with a situation" (Schön).

The assimilation perspective expresses a relatively high regard for the potential of organisations to develop themselves. It assumes that institutions such as schools "want" to exert control over their own fate and "know" best what actions will ultimately work. The first assumption implies that a school's ability to "understand" the environment and to cope with pressures is necessary for its survival and is therefore highly valued. The second assumption implies that substantial changes demand changes in the tacit knowledge of an institution, and that these cannot be accomplished *for* the institution but have to be generated *by* the institution (for example, by the individual school or groups within the school) through systematic reflection on activities and on their contextual conditions and consequences.

Dynamic networks presuppose institutions that are able to organise themselves and control their interaction with the environment. The assimilation perspective provides a model of institutional development that is in line with this requirement.

Dynamic networks in environmental education

Teachers and students who get involved in the generation of local knowledge and in responsible action to improve environmental conditions generally develop interests in three respects: in external support, in legitimation, and in political impact.

External support: Environmental school initiatives create a strong demand for direct contact with external experts, and with public and private institutions to obtain information and resources and to offers services.

An example is the school involved in the energy project described in Section 1 (BRG Imst, 1990). The core group were students of two forms and two teachers (with a third teacher co-operating for specific purposes). They initiated contact with an energy expert who became more or less integrated into the core group for periodic advice. Communication also developed with offices of the regional government to gain legitimation and to obtain financial coverage for the expert. Contact was also established with the mayor, with several councillors and officers of the community investigated, in order to get the official backing by the community (i.e. a decision of the community council in support of the project), including a financial contribution and necessary materials (e.g. maps of the appropriate scale). Finally, communication with the population was established for the presentation of data and proposals.

Legitimation: Legitimation is a critical asset in any activity which is marginal and not yet established in the formal structure of educational tasks. Legitimation can be derived through regulations and materials defined by the hierarchical power structure. Examples are syllabi, curricula, approved textbooks or assessment schemes referring to environmental initiatives, or governmental decrees in support of environmental education. This, however, is not the only source. Legitimation can also be derived through association with other persons or groups potentially sharing similar values. Any activity which deviates from common practice is in need of this kind of "lateral" legitimation. As a result, in most environmental initiatives a close relationship is sought with parents of the students in order to win them as partners (e.g. Haas, 1990). Similarly, the support of the press and of influential groups is in strong demand. In one project, the contact to the press proved vital. Pupils of a vocational secondary school mapped illegal waste dumps in different municipalities of their region and informed the responsible mayors and the public. Considerable conflict arose with public authorities: they considered the students' activities completely outside of any school responsibility. However, the students were increasingly supported by the local and regional press and won the case. Numerous illegal dumps had to be closed and removed (Schweitzer, 1991).

Another important form of "lateral" legitimation is provided by links to other public or private institutions -- for example, local governments, or by being part of a regional, national or international project. In this sense, the international Environment and School Initiatives Network has important legitimating functions. However, legitimation is not only a matter of finding other people of similar value structure. It is also a matter of convincing others of the legitimacy and necessity of environmental involvement. In this context, documentation and reports on action research play a significant role. They enable the teachers and students to argue their case and to provide evidence that their activities are in line with value orientations of other people, even if they do not correspond with traditional expectations of schools.

Political impact: It is a specific characteristic of environmental school initiatives that they have a political dimension "here and now" and that they provide opportunities for teachers and students to take part in the shaping of conditions influencing their lives.

Teachers and students involved in successful environmental school initiatives are sooner or later intrigued by the experience that they are gaining influence not only inside school but outside. They experience a shift in the distribution of power in society which can be felt in diverse ways: an increased willingness to listen and to co-operate on the side of public institutions, easier access to resources, invitations for consultation, etc.

In many cases this shift of power is accompanied by conflicts. Examples are provided by the waste project mentioned above, in which both teacher and students were faced with severe attacks from political representatives, or by the Australian water analysis project described in Section 1. In most cases the conflicts are coped with by establishing liaisons with other groups or institutions. This often involves taking advantage of typical features of hierarchical networks. If, for example, a regional authority co-operates, it can become difficult for a local authority not to co-operate.

In most cases the interest in increasing political impact implies contacts with non-educational institutions. There are, however, also tendencies to broaden the operational base by creating links with other schools. The four schools originally involved in the Water Analysis Project (Mantova) opened their network to twelve lower secondary schools in the region (Sutti, pers. comm.). The school dealing with the energy project (mentioned in Section 1) established a link to the elementary school of the community investigated in order to make it familiar with the issues and to stimulate activities for which the school could claim ownership but which would be in line with the overall aims of the project . (These aims were to create consciousness in energy matters and to improve conditions in the community.)

Links emerging from joint ventures of groups of schools are still limited to the local level. They could have a considerable impact if they also developed on a regional, national or even international level. For this development, however, neither the consciousness of most teachers nor the present communication facilities are developed enough. But the idea is well expressed by the intervention of a 16 year-old student, a participant in the energy project (Mair, 1990):

> The polluters are linked on a world-wide scope. One should also link all people involved in environmental education. The efficiency of activities against unacceptable states of affairs and abuses would increase. We should build a network of students who investigate the energetic and environmental situation of their immediate localities, develop improvements and exchange data via computer networks. Then we could react more quickly to positive and negative environmental changes, could go public more effectively and could exert more influence on the regional and supraregional energy politics.

This sounds utopian but points in a direction in which interesting developments can be expected.

The three demands for external support, for legitimation, and for political impact, are the basic motives to initiate dynamic networks. Especially the last one, the demand to increase the political impact of environmental school initiatives (and of schools in general) has important side-effects.

At present, the self-definition of the educational system suggests a passive other-directedness. It is assumed that the system is a mere recipient of demands from the power structures in society. A shift in the power balance means that schools participate in the public discussion on educational tasks with more self-confidence. Not only representatives of established lobbies would present their demands on schools. Also, schools (teachers and students) would present their views of social problems and their demands on social power structures.

Types of dynamic networks in environmental education

The characteristics of dynamic networks allow for a considerable variety of structures. However, on a very provisional basis, one can distinguish two types of networks which have specific strengths and weaknesses -- the school-mediated network and the broker-mediated network:

75

The school-mediated network

This type of dynamic network is initiated and sustained by the teachers and students of one or more schools. The network that emerged during the energy project described in Section 1 was quite large (Mair, 1991):

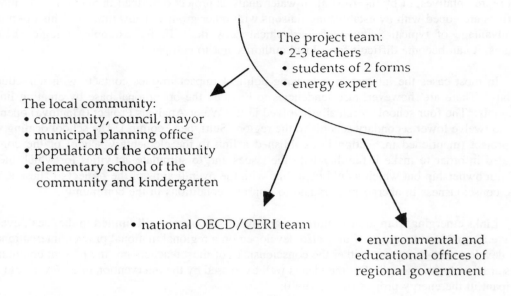

The project team:
• 2-3 teachers
• students of 2 forms
• energy expert

The local community:
• community, council, mayor
• municipal planning office
• population of the community
• elementary school of the
  community and kindergarten

• national OECD/CERI team

• environmental and
  educational offices of
  regional government

Another example is the Water Analysis Project (Mantova) comprising, in each year, teachers and students of five vocational secondary schools, twelve middle schools, and a number of local and regional institutions (the most important of these is the government of the community in the area where the samples are drawn (Sutti, pers. comm.).

A third example is the development of a link between an Austrian primary school and a Finnish comprehensive school to exchange experiences on their handling of waste projects (Ammann, 1991).

In all of these cases the networks are limited to those persons, groups or institutions which are expected to contribute to the schools' project activities, and the networks are the result of initiatives taken by teachers and students of the schools concerned.

The main strength of this type of network is its functional integration into the activities of an environmental project. The usefulness of investments into the network can relatively easily be discerned by all participants. The weakness of this type of network is its relatively low institutional stability because it is anchored in a specific school initiative. The conclusion of the project, therefore in general is also the end of the network.

There are, however, interesting attempts to stabilise this type of network. one strategy to stabilize the network is by stabilizing the environmental project and by including it into the mainstream curriculum. This was accomplished by the Water Analysis Project (Sutti 1991). Another strategy is to stabilize it by institutionalising the network. This was accomplished by the establishment of an "Alliance for Better Learning" in Bratteburg school (Öckerö) described in section 3.

A third strategy to stabilize the network is by expanding it. This strategy is presently being used by the school (BRG Imst) which initiated the energy project. In this school a "municipal energy-saving model" was originally developed fore four small villages (See section 1). The impact of this project resulted in a second tryout in a larger community which became phase 1 in the plan to establish a network. The plan to extend the network has several phases (Mair 1991b):

Phase 1:

-- Tryout of the "Municipal energy-saving model" and of the accompanying computer software in a larger community and with assistance of an energy expert.

Phase 2:

-- Tryout of the model by nine other Austrian schools of different types. The teachers and students of these schools are introduced in a workshop by teachers and students of the school in which the project was initiated (BRG Imst).

Phase 3:

-- Modification of the model on the basis of a systematic reflection on experiences (action research) by the teachers and students involved.
-- Production and translation of a user handbook and translation of the software.
-- Contacts to interested school in other countries.
-- Publication of a network-newspaper among the participating Austrian schools.

Phase 4:

-- Set-up of electronic mail communication among the Austrian schools and publication of pilot-studies on its operation.
-- Identification of interested schools in foreign countries and introduction into the model by teachers and students of BRG Imst.
-- Operation of the projects, action research, and communication on experiences
-- Development of cooperative initiatives among participating schools
-- Edition of an international network-newspaper and establishment of links to other institutions.

Phase 5:

-- International electronic mail communication
-- Development of neighbourhood links (local networks) by the schools involved.
-- Dissemination of experiences through INSET activities

Phase 6:

-- Presentation of results at an international conference

The whole networking enterprise is expected to be established by 1994. Phase 1 has begun in 1990 and in 193 the project has moved into Phase 4.

This last example highlights a serious limiting factor of school mediated networks -- if they grow larger: the demands in time and management capacity. A technical means that may facilitate the development of school-mediated networks is provided by electronic mail systems. As yet there are only few examples of this kind of communication available that are relevant to schools, although electronic mail is increasingly being used by researchers. One of these examples is the Global Rivers Environmental Education Network. This network links schools in Australia and the USA, that are involved in chemical analyses of water quality. They share a data bank at the University of Michigan and are also connected with each other. They use the data bank for comparative analyses and the network to exchange experience, to ask each other fro advice, and for informal communication (Robottom 1988).

There are a number of arguments that favour electronic mail communication:

-- Quick communication between school involved in similar projects could stimulate work and could improve its quality. Very successful teachers and students could be relatively easily "accessible" by other interested schools. Critical feedback on their research finding and methods could be facilitated.

-- Electronic mail would provide the opportunity to create and use data bases. For some types of projects data-sharing could considerably extend the sources of information available to the individual school.

-- The network could make it easier for groups of (not necessarily neighbouring) schools to develop cooperative projects (this is probably the most attractive long term argument).

There are, however, also some caveats:

-- For some of the uses mentioned above also surface mail would suffice. From past experience we know however that it is hardly used. This could happen to electronic mail, at least when the novelty effect is over.

-- Most projects do not depend on communication between schools. As a result communication via electronic mail would not answer existing needs but rather open additional dimensions. In view of most of the present environmental projects its value therefore could be rather low.

-- The establishment of computer communication may not be in line with an environmental philosophy to save scarce resources.

Nonetheless, electronic mail provides a number of attractive and still untapped opportunities and can (among other things) facilitate the emergence of school-mediated dynamic networks.

Broker-mediated dynamic networks

Brokers are managers of interfaces between schools and from schools to other institutions (cp. Atkin/Atkin 1989). This type of network is set up and managed by institutions which are outside or on the margin of the educational hierarchy (although they may be part of the educational system). They can be more or less related to specific environmental projects.

An example of a project-related of this kind is the Norwegian network involving schools in environmental surveyance activities (Ministry of Education and Research 1990). In Telemark county pupils of fifty primary and lower secondary schools are involved in water analysis. Each school is responsible for three experimental areas localised near the school. The ecological quality of the water samples is tested in each school with the help of macro-fauna. The tests are forwarded to the Norwegian Hydro Research

78

Institute where advanced analysing methods (such as ion-chromatography) are used. The results are fed back to the schools where work with the data continues and where comparative analyses are made and published. The schools are also linked to local fishing associations, to the environmental department at eh office of the country governor in Telemark, and to the Telemark college of education.

Several different surveillance projects are presently in operation in Norway. Their basic ides as that "through active participation and in contact with adults, pupils experience themselves as responsible participants in work which preserves and protects the environment. Their investigations are considered to be a link in the public environmental surveillance warning services." (p. 12)

The schools are elements of a complex model of communication:

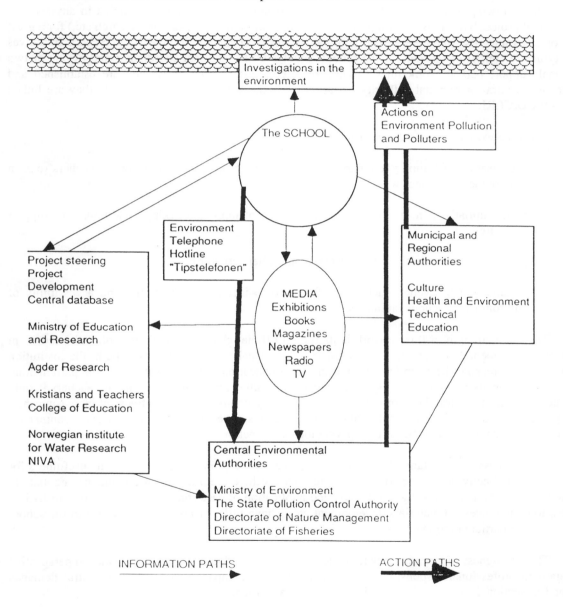

This illustration shows the lines of interaction between school projects and local and central institutions and authorities. The purpose of the network is to establish routines for cooperation across organisational boundaries in favour of environmental education as well as collection of data and data-based action.

The strength of networks of this kind is their being anchored both in a specific structure independent from the schools' initiatives and in the operational process of the school initiative. A weakness is the specificity of the network limiting its usefulness only to one type of environmental project (in the case of our example to water analysis). Another weakness is the sensitive power balance between the individual school and the broker.

The following example of a broker-mediated dynamic network is not specialist in any specific environmental project but serves general purposes (dissemination, training, advice, research etc.) for a great variety of environmental initiatives. The national networks of the Environment and School Initiatives Project typically consist of teachers of the schools involved, of a national coordinator and of one or two educational support persons sometimes assisted by a committee. Generally they are established and financed by a central or regional authority but are outside the hierarchy. Internationally they are linked through OECD/CERI.

These networks fulfil a variety of tasks:

-- organisation of training seminars provided by the project teachers to other teachers (e.g. in environmental project work);

-- policy initiatives in environmental education (to improve working conditions and support structures);

-- publication of research (action research and other research);

-- organisation of events (such as conferences) to increase the visibility and accessibility of environmental school initiatives.

The main strength of this network is its formal official character involving political interests in support of environmental education. A strength is also its dual function. It serves both, the institution financing it by increasing the visibility of environmental education policy and it serves the participating teachers. However, its facilitative influence on the school initiatives of the participating teachers is only an indirect one: it offers training, for example in potentially controversial initiatives by increasing their visibility and legitimation, international contacts, access to resources and last but not least a context for mutual encouragement and friendship (the "psychological" function).

Its weakness is its distance from the actual project work going on in schools. Its usefulness for specific operational activities of the participating teachers is therefore a matter of continuous negotiation. Many activities of the network -- the production and publication of case studies, its contribution to INSET activities, to conferences, to materials development etc -- have little, or no direct relevance to the school initiatives of the participating teachers.

The willingness of teachers to participate in such a network depends on their widened perspective with regard to professional responsibility and on the network's capacity to fulfil their central demands mentioned in section 1: support, legitimation and political influence.

Dynamic networks and support structures

Dynamic networks depend on the stimulative potentials of those innovations that are already existent in the teaching profession. Ernest House (1974) begins his seminal book on *The Politics of Educational Innovation* with what appeared to him as an "enormous conundrum: How can so much effort directed toward changing the schools produce so little change?" (p. 2). In the final chapter of his book (p. 305) he writes (referring to Galtung, 1973):

> *Part of the answer may be in the metamorphoses of the vertical division of labour, as prescribed in the research, development diffusion paradigm of change. A horizontal division of labour would bring the invention, production, and distribution of innovations closer to the people who must use them so that they will be more useful in conception, better implemented, and will produce fewer inequities. The features of such a horizontal division of labour might mean shorter, less alienating development cycles where participants can see and understand what is going on and have immediate control. This would mean more self-reliance and the utilization of the local, indigenous expertise and resources at hand.*

The emergence of dynamic networks in environmental education is such a horizontal division of labour. However, dynamic networks do not develop by chance. They develop if the tasks of the educational system are reconceptualised to include the generation of local knowledge and the responsible action on environmental conditions. These two tasks lead "naturally" to an overcoming of the barriers between school and environment, and to the establishment of dynamic networks. They induce a shift in balance from a static view of learning (transmission of predefined knowledge for future application) to a more dynamic view (tackling low-structured situations of present-day significance).

The growth of this movement -- and at the same time a smooth transition to a more dynamic learning culture -- is highly dependent on a redefinition of the role of educational support:

The most difficult reorientation will be to complement technical rationality or the doctrine of "transferability" (House) by a reflective rationality and a logic of "supporting growth". The doctrine of transferability implies that innovations can be developed and tested outside schools and be transferred to them. The logic of supporting growth is based on the understanding that local initiatives exist already and that their growth process can be supported symbolically and instrumentally. House (p. 243) provides another metaphor to indicate the direction of this shift:

> *Government activity should be stimulating and regulating like withdrawing or inserting a lead rod in an atomic stock pile... Directions and energies must be mobilized within the system itself.*

The metaphor should not be overstrained but it acknowledges that innovative potential is already there. It need not be imported and imposed. Moreover, if specific innovations are forced upon schools, this tends to reduce their coping power and problem-solving capacity, and increases their dependence. This understanding implies a fundamental change in perspective on the side of educational support. In this respect the responsible bureaucracies could learn from the findings of Peters and Waterman (1982) who studied the conditions for success of the most successful American enterprises. They found the following characteristics:

-- Problems are actively defined and co-operatively tackled. Contributions to problem definition are valued even more highly than contributions to problem solution.

-- Control comes after the event. The expectation is: "Try it and we'll see", and not: "Ask for permission before you do anything".

-- Closeness to the customer is aspired. His satisfaction with the services is valued highly. To get to know him and to listen to him in order to find out what he needs and wants is among the central activities of successful enterprises. They trust that the customer knows best what is good for him or her.

-- To try is the essential thing. To accept risk is expected. Failure is not penalised if it stimulates learning.

-- Informal communication in small teams is highly valued and an important stimulus for the spreading of ideas.

-- They assume that people have an interest in doing a good job and trust them.

-- Achievements are honoured in various non-spectacular ways. They assume that everybody should be able to feel successful in his place.

According to Peters and Waterman, such characteristics contribute to environments in which initiatives and innovations develop and in which self-confidence and involvement grow. On the other hand, the much larger group of unsuccessful enterprises contradict nearly all of these characteristics: punishment prevails over acknowledgement, rules replace a common philosophy, restrictions and controls substitute the active search for meaning, and political leadership takes the place of a moral one. Although there are many differences between schools and enterprises, this list of criteria could provide some food for thought.

In view of emerging dynamic networks, educational support and administrative intervention would have to concentrate on three tasks:

i) The first task is to confront schools with developments and pressures in society but *not* to impose the solutions (Ekholm, 1988, p. 20). Traditionally, administration tends to establish barriers between school and society in order to sustain a hierarchical power structure. The emergence of dynamic networks moves schools closer to other institutions in society and to their diverse and often conflicting demands. Therefore, schools have to develop their own educational philosophy informed by exchange processes with other institutions. It is important that schools are not passive recipients of these demands but that they actively use information on developments in their environment to define their role in society. The shift from a recipient of prescriptions by syllabi, tests, regulations, etc. to an institution with a self-defined and shared policy is a delicate and probably long-term process. To stimulate this process will be an important and difficult task of administrative systems and support structures.

ii) The second area in which support will be necessary is to assist schools in the process of finding idiosyncratic solutions to problems, to encourage school-generated innovations, and to facilitate their spreading. Resources should be made available where the innovations occur, i.e. in schools. They should allow teachers and students to initiate innovations and to create the networks they think appropriate. The support structures (teacher centres, development centres) should be school-dependent rather than administration-dependent. Communication within the system and across system boundaries is a prerequisite for the development of dynamic networks. To stimulate face-to-face communication among teachers and with people "from outside" is therefore an important new support task:

Ideas move along the social network of personal acquaintance... Indirect contact suffices to spread simple, well-structured routine information. Direct contact is much more effective where there is an element of uncertainty or when results are unpredictable.

These are likely to be encountered in problem-solving situations, planning or negotiation, any of which might involve innovation (House, 1974, p. 10).

Personal, informal contacts are the breeding ground for dynamic networks. They can be stimulated in various ways:

-- If teachers have the opportunity to visit other teachers whose work appears to be interesting or to invite them into their own school, e.g. as proposed in the model of collegial INSET (Posch, 1990c). Observing how other teachers and students develop their initiatives and to discuss with them how they cope with difficulties and how they utilise strengths and compensate weaknesses can be a powerful stimulus for innovations (cf. Ekholm, 1988). Even if experiences gained in one complex situation cannot be technically applied to other situations, a kind of "naturalistic generalisation" can occur (Stake, 1985). This is the kind of generalisation that occurs through vicarious experience. A direct or mediated understanding of an innovation in another school generates a set of illuminating hypotheses which allow a fresh perspective of one's own situation. One can grasp an idea that materialised in one context and can use its power to construct one's own concretisation, adapted to one's own situational context and personal strengths and weaknesses. The result is not a copy nor an application of a general principle but is a new solution for which ownership can be claimed. In this sense, dynamic networks provide cross-situational links which allow a spread of innovative activities without "disseminating" anything.

-- If local and regional programmes are organised to stimulate communication, such as the programme "Teachers report on their practice" where teachers involved in innovations discuss what they do with an interested public (similarly structured are the "Fora on innovations in schools" -- cf. ARGIS, 1991), and conferences where teachers and students reflect on experiences and illustrate their practical activities, e.g. the annual conferences of the Collaborative Action-Research Network in the United Kingdom.

iii) The third task is to stimulate self-evaluation to maintain and increase quality. Teachers who leave the "stable state" of systematic knowledge transmission have to cope with open-ended, uncertain, unpredictable, sometimes contradictory situations, entailing risks (of course, static-learning cultures also imply risks but these are considered normal system elements and are not identified as such). It is imperative for them (and for the students) to reflect on what they do and by doing so to become clearer about their own values. This implies a shift from external control to self-evaluation and to professional peer-evaluation (Elliott, 1989). Evaluation should be in close relationship to professional practice and primarily inform teachers and students rather than the authorities. In this context, action research has proven to be a methodological approach of high potential. However, it creates new demands on educational support: training, organisational support, and frameworks for local, regional, national and international communication on findings and experiences.

The long-term aim of support should be to strengthen those values within the school which are fundamental in any process of innovation: high regard for problem-finding, for customer orientation, for reflection on aims and policy development, for an experimental attitude to actions, for the acceptance of controlled risks, and for the potential of the human resources of the organisation. Schools differ enormously with respect to these values. Elsewhere (Posch, 1987), three types of schools with specific attitudes to innovation were distinguished: policy-active, policy-conscious and policy-unconscious schools.

-- *Policy-active* schools take initiatives in systematic reflection on their situation, and base their activities on their own policy -- the policy being a concern of the whole staff or of sub-groups within the staff. They organise the internal flow of information and the communication with the school's environment. They feel responsible for the philosophy of the school and for its translation into policy. If external support is needed to execute the policy it is actively invited. These are the kinds of schools in which dynamic networks prosper.

-- *Policy-conscious* schools are conscious of a need for a reflective stance, but they somehow do not have the abilities, experiences or other preconditions to actively develop a policy. Rather, they take what is offered to them. They may be quite active but concentrate on means instead of aims, on deficits instead of strengths.

-- *Policy-unconscious* schools are unaware of the relationship between reflection and action. Often, such schools have a low institutional identity and are heavily dependent on, and quick to react to, outside pressures. They open doors to information but do not use it actively. Responsibility is avoided, and general discussions substitute individual and collective reflection in and on action. Personalistic answers to problems are preferred to structural ones, and this keeps initiatives on a low level. These are the kinds of schools that invite and rely on hierarchical networks.

It should be a challenging task for educational support systems to stimulate the development of a policy-active value structure in schools and to enable them to find their own answers to developments in society. This is not primarily a technical problem but a "process" of institutional and professional growth. The growth metaphor is based on the notion that the readiness to innovate is not only a matter of competence and of external resources but also a matter of self-confidence and of the experience to be able to have an impact on the conditions of work. To actively build on one's own strengths and on those of other people are important elements in this growth process. It seems evident that such elements cannot be prescribed, but rather evolve in a professional culture. Environmental school initiatives, and especially the two new tasks mentioned in Chapter 1, can provide forceful stimuli to develop this culture.

A cynical but probably accurate description of the state of political intervention in the area of policy in a controversial field where powerful economic and technological interests are at stake, is reflected in a remark made by a high-level federal German politician at an unofficial meeting (reported by ecologist H. Rieseberg): "I can do everything provided that something happens."

The "something happens", however, can be interpreted in two ways: as a catastrophe such as Czernobyl or Seveso, which would enable political intervention to reduce environmental hazards and pollution; or, more profoundly, as a change in the state of consciousness of a wider population. "Consciousness" would include not only knowledge, problem-solving capacities, and values, but also the practical experience that individual and joint initiatives can achieve improvements and can create contexts also for political consequences. Such a concept of active citizenship can be a powerful motor of change in a democracy. Therefore, the consequence is not to wait (some would even say "hope") for the next generation of catastrophes but to provide the necessary experiences "here and now".

The school has the chance to become the first public opportunity for young citizens to construct reality.

References

ALTRICHTER, H. (1990), *Ist das noch Wissenschaft? Dartstellung und Diskussion einer von Leheren betriebenen Aktionsforschung,* Profil, München.

ALTRICHTER, H., POSCH, P. and SOMEKH, B. (1993), *Teachers investigate their Work. An Introduction to the Methods of Action Research*, Routledge, London.

ALTRICHTER, H. (1991), *Quality Features in an Action Research Strategy,* ARGE Umwelterziehung, Vienna, ESI-Series No. 12.

AMMANN, E. (1990), *Projekte - Eine Chance gerande für verhaltens - und lerngestörte Kinger?* ARGE Umwelterziehung, Vienna, USI-Reihe No. 17.

ARGIS (Arbeitsgemienschaft für Innovationen an der Schule) (1990), *Forum für Innovationen an steirischen Schulen - Eine Dokumentation*, Graz (Pädagogisches Institut).

ARGYIS, C., SCHÖN, D.A. (1974) *Theory in Practice: Increasing Professional Effectiveness* Jossey Bass, San Francisco.

AGRYIS, C., PUTNAM, R.and MCLAIN SMITH, D. (1985), *Action Science - Concepts, Methods, and Skills for Research and Intervention* Jossey Bass, San Francisco.

ARRANZ, R.M. (1987), *Abgrund Mensch - Der Mensch im Gefüge der Natur unter dem Gesichtspunkt der Informatik,* Univ. Salamanca, Salamanca, MS.

ATKIN, M., ATKIN, A. (1989), *Improving Science Education through Local Alliances - A Report to Carnegie Foundation of New York,* Network Publication.

BRG (Bundesrealgymnasium) IMST, (1990), *Schulprojekt Energiekonzepte,* BRG Imst, Imst.

EKHOLM, M. (1988), *Inservice Education of Teachers and School Development,* Swedish National Board of Education, Stockholm.

ELLIOT, J. (1985), "Teachers as Researchers", HUSEN, T., POSTLETHWAITE, T. (Eds.): *International Encyclopedia of Education*, Vol.9, Pergamon, Oxford pp. 5042-5045.

ELLIOT, J. (1991), "Environmental Education in Europe -- Innovation, Marginalisation, or Assimilation", in: *OECD/CERI (Ed.): Environment, Schools and Active Learning* OECD, Paris

ELLIOT, J. (1989), "Educational Theory and the Professional Learning of Teachers: an Overview", in: *Cambridge Journal of Education*, Vol. 19, No. 1, B1-101.

ELLIOT, J. RICE, J. (1990), The relationship between disciplinary knowledge and situational understanding in the development of environmental awareness", in: Pieters 1990, pp. 66-72.

FISCHER. R. (1991), "Hierarchie und Alternative - Charakeristika von Vernetzungen", in: Pellert 1991, pp. 121-164.

FISCHER-KOWALSKI, M. (1991), "Das pyramidale und das unbegrenzie Netz", in: Pellert 1991, pp. 165-194.

GALTUNG, J. (1973), The European Community - A Superpower in the Making", in: *Journal of Peace Research* pp. 81-117.

GOUGH, A., ROBOTTOM, J. (1990), "Environmental Education and the Socially Critical School", in: *Journal of Curriculum Studies* April.

HAAS, K. (1990), *A Primary School's Initiatives*, ARGE Umwelterziehung, Vienna, ESI-Series No. 5.

HOUSE, E. (1974), *The Politics of Educational Innovation*, McCutchan, Berkeley.

MAIR, G. (1990), "Lernen durch Handeln in Projekten - Schülerinnen beeinflussen die kommunale Umweltpolitik" in: Bundesarbeitsgemeinschaft Bildung/Die Grünen: *Forum zur ökologischen Bildung*, vom 14-15.9, in: Mimberg (1990), BAG Bilgung/Die Grünen, Berlin, 8-10.

MAIR, G. (1991a), Das Projekt *"Kommunales Energiesparkonzept einer Gemeinde"*, BRG Imst, Imst, MS.

MAIR, G. (1991b), *Kommunales Energiesparkonzept - Umweltschultz - Netzwerk*, BRG Imst, Imst, MS.

MAYER, M. (1990), *Evaluating the Outcomes of Environment and School Initiatives*, Centro Europeo dell'Educazione, Frascati, MS.

MENLO, L. (1985), "A reconceptualisation of resistance to change and its application to the institutionalization process", paper presented at a meeting of the International School Improvement Project in Luzern, MS.

MINISTRY OF EDUCATION AND RESEARCH (1990), "Environment and School Initiatives - A review of Policy Developments", in: *Environmental Education. Country Statement Norway*, Ministry of Education and Research, Oslo.

OCHSENBAUER, C. (1989), *Organisatorische Alternativen zur Hierachie*, GBI-Verlag, München.

OECD/CERI (Ed.) (1991), *Environment, Schools and Active Learning*, OECD, Paris.

Österreichisches Zentrum für Umwelterziehung (ÖZU) der österreichischen Naturschutzjugend (2a/1990) Club information.

PELLERT, A. (Hrsg) (1991), *Vernetzung und Widersprunch - Zur Neuorganisation von Wissenschaft*, Profil-Verlag, München.

PETERS, T.J., WATERMAN, R. (1982), *In Search of Excellence. Lessons from America's Best-Run Companies*, Harper & Row, New York.

PIAGET, J. (1975), *Das Erwachen der Intelligenz biem Kinde*, Klett, Stuttgart.

PIETERS, M. (Ed.) (1990), *Teaching for sustainable development*, Report on a workshop at Veldhoven, Netherlands, 23-25 April 1990, Institute for Curriculum Development, Enschede.

POLANYI, M. (1967), *The Tacit Dimension*, Doubleday, New York.

POSCH, P. (1987), "The Assimilation Perspective", in: MILES, M.B., EKHOLM, M., VANDENBERGHE, R. (Eds.) (1987), *Lasting School Improvement - Exploring the Process of Institutionalization*, Acco, Leuven, pp. 173-189.

POSCH, P. (1990*a*), *Dynamic Qualities and Environmental Sensitivity in Education*, ARGE Umwelterziehung, Vienna, ESIP Series No. 9.

POSCH, P. (1990*b*), *The Project "Environment and Statistics"*, in: ARGE Umwelterziehung, Vienna, ESIP Series No. 10.

POSCH, P. (1990*c*), *Kollegialer Erfahrungsaustausch*, IFF, Klagenfurt, MS.

RAPP, N.J. (1991), "Environmental School Initiatives as Part of School Life", in: OECD/CERI (Ed.), *Environment, Schools and Active Learning*, OECD, Paris, pp. 80-83.

ROBOTTOM, I., MUHLEBACH, R. (1988), "Expanding the Scientific Community in Schools - A Computer Conference in Science Education", *Australian Science Teachers Journal* pp. 3-12.

SCHNECK, P. (1989), "Dezentralisierung der Lehrerfortbildung im Regionalen PI-Zentrum Wien", in: *Erziehung und Unterricht*, H.5 (1989), pp. 317-319.

SCHÖN, D.A. (1983), *The Reflective Practitioner*, Temple Smith, London.

SCHWARZ, G. (1985), *Die heilige Ordnung der Männer - Patriachalische Hierarchie und Gruppendynamik*, Westdeutcher Verlag, Opladen.

SCHWIETZER, K. (1991), "Emancipation through Environmental Projects?", in: OECD/CERI (1991), (Ed.) *Environment, Schools and Active Learning,* OECD, Paris, pp. 39-45.

STAKE, R., (1985), "Case Study", in NISBET, J. (Ed.) (1985), *World Yearbook of Education 1985 - Research, Policy and Practice*, Kegan Page, London, pp. 277-285.

SUTTI, A. (1991), "The Water Analysis Project - An Alternative Model for Environmental Study", in: OECD/CERI (Ed.) (1991), *Environment, Schools and Active Learning*, OECD, Paris, pp. 59-65.

ZIMMERHACKL, K. (1990), *Wiesen für Schmetterlinge und Hecken für Vögel - Grundzusammenlegung als ökologischer Konflikt*, ARGE Umwelterziehung, Wien, USI Reihe No. 9.

Chapter 4

EVALUATING THE OUTCOMES OF ENVIRONMENT AND SCHOOL INITIATIVES

by

Michela Mayer
Centro Europeo dell'Educazione -- CEDE
Frascati
Italy

Introduction

The aim of this paper is to discuss the role of evaluation in Environmental Education projects. Firstly I will discuss the epistemological status of evaluation in conventional educational research with respect to demands on environmental education action-research. Then I will propose to identify some common elements, theoretically derived and empirically identified in the previous Environment and School Initiatives Project, as "indicators of the quality" of the schools initiatives, proposing as an example the research carried out in Italy.

This quality indicator system can be used for comparison between environmental education projects within a country and between countries. For such comparison, there is a need for instruments which can be applied directly by the teachers to the school initiatives they are involved in and which can also be used to describe and possibly "measure" the qualitative and quantitative dimension of each chosen criterion. A discussion of some of the possible instruments is presented in the final part of this paper.

The status of evaluation in educational research

Environmental education is currently one of the most important sources of innovation in education along with education for development and education for multiculturality and peace (Visalberghi 1989). In all these cases the innovations cross all disciplines and place primary importance upon the growth of values and the fostering of "positive" modes towards the society. It is precisely because of the complexity of these themes and objectives that their evaluation is not an easy task.

Evaluation in education cannot be a neutral process which guarantees *per se* the objectivity of the results, but it is -- like any technique or scientific theory -- a theory-laden operation, full of values and consequently "ideological".

The values we are sharing in this OECD project, values related not only to environmental problems but also to educational procedures, do not allow us to believe in something as "objective evaluation" or as "a strict control of variables". The implicit paradigm in this project opposed to the "agricultural- botany" model that informed many "experimental designs" or "quasi-experimental designs" in curriculum innovation (Robottom, 1989).

The agricultural metaphor is based upon an image of science, and upon an unlimited faith in "technical rationality", that no longer has support in science itself and in its epistemology. As Popper and Lakatos have pointed out, each observation is intrinsically subjective and depends upon the theory which guides it. Even if knowledge can become intersubjective through dialogue and confrontation, this does not guarantee correspondence with an external reality, given that even the scientific community constitutes a social entity and is thus permeated by values (Kuhn, 1970). Nor could one speak of scientific method as a guiding path to know reality, given the variety of methods used by the sciences (Feyerabend, 1975) and the different levels upon which reality manifests itself. These levels depend upon the questions we ask rather than upon the answers we manage to find.

The conventional methods in educational programme evaluation refer to a conventional image of science, and identify the need to comprehend with the need to simplify and to quantify.

According to Morin (1985):

"It has often been said that scientific explanation lies in explaining what is complex and visible by recurring to what is simple and invisible. But in this way, it would completely dissolve all that is complex and visible, while it is also the complex and visible with which we must deal".

It is exactly this "complex" and "visible" with which environmental education must deal and thus, by adopting rigid and quantitative methods of evaluation, we run the risk of neglecting those elements which characterize it best.

Of course the consciousness of the inadequacy of this conventional image of science and of the "agricultural model" for educational research varies from country to country: in the U.S.A. and in the U.K., where more emphasis has been given to "educational empirical research" and to the evaluation of centrally developed programmes, the criticism emerging in the '70s proposed an "alternative paradigm" to this positivistic approach; in other countries, such as Italy or Spain, where the traditional approach to education is an idealistic one, more concerned with philosophy than with science, the need for empirical studies and for quantitative data received, till a few years ago, the attention of the more innovative among teachers, administrators and researchers, looking for theories based on the reality of educational phenomena.

The alternative paradigm proposed in the anglo-saxon countries contrasted the emphasis on objective data, and the possibility to consider a "programme" as a "treatment" that can produce similar results in different contexts, and stressed the importance of studying the particular contexts of programme implementation. In his fundamental revision of the appropriateness of experimental research in education, Cronbach (1975) argued that the primary aim should become "interpretation in context" not "generalisation".

"The positivistic strategy of fixing conditions in order to reach strong generalizations fits with the concept that processes are steady and can be fragmented into nearly independent systems. Psychologists toward the physiological end of our investigative range probably can live with that as their principal strategy. Those of us toward the social end of the range cannot."

Then, it is the belief in the uniformity of phenomena, not only natural but also social and educational phenomena, that allow for generalisation in space and time. But in education and in social science, phenomena are time-bounded and space-bounded. What we need in order to describe and interpret a phenomenon, as Cronbach argues, is more history than science:

"The two scientific disciplines -- experimental control and systematic correlation -- answer formal questions stated in advance. Intensive local observation goes beyond discipline to an open-eyed, open-minded appreciation of the surprises Nature deposits in the investigative net. This kind of interpretation is historical more than scientific. I suspect that if the psychologist were to read more widely in history, ethnology, and the centuries of humanistic writings on man and society, he would be better prepared for this part of his work."

Cronbach, History, with all sciences related with time -- where it is impossible to identically reproduce a given phenomenon -- is a rational and logical products of the human mind, but it does not share the stereotypical scientific methods proposed for natural sciences.

An Italian historian, Carlo Ginzburg (1986), proposed for human sciences a "circumstantial paradigm" versus the "galilean paradigm", typical of natural sciences. In a "circumstantial paradigm", what matters is the difference not the similarity: small differences, small signs, enable Frate Guglielmo in Umberto Eco's "The Name of the Rose" to describe the Abbot's horse without having seen it, or the wise farmer to forecast weather, or the art critic to recognize a masterpiece. The circumstantial paradigm has ancient and noble origins: all novels concerned with "serendipity" are dealing with the rational ability to recognize traces, signs, clues, that when correctly interpreted allow one to reconstruct the whole story, to link together all the apparent oddities, to show the hidden links.

The same type of rational reconstruction and understanding is also used in natural sciences -- astronomy, geology, palaeontology, as well as in ethnology and environmental sciences -- where it is very difficult to design an experiment in a strict sense.

In Environmental Education, there is the need to define intents, methodologies and instruments of meaningful evaluation in order to be consistent with this image of rational understanding. It would be an evaluation aiming to gather together and not to discard, to comprise and not to select, a formative evaluation for all those involved; students, teachers and researchers alike.

At the same time, evaluation must take into account the specific aspects of Environmental Education, and look after the congruency between environmental values and teaching-learning behaviour, between environmental attitudes and cognitive attitudes, between the image of the natural and social world and the image of the inner world where knowledge is constructed. Some issues can be "recognised" both in environmental sciences and in education, and this "isomorphism" has to be stressed. Here are some of these issues:

-- environmental sciences and education are strongly concerned with "the future", they are working for something made to last, and not to be consumed in a few years;

-- "ecology is a science based more on experience than experiment" (Conti, 1991), and the same can be said for education;

-- both environment and education have a need for a global approach, where "descriptions are complex, holistic, and involving a myriad of not highly isolated variables" (Stake, 1980);

-- the complexity of the problem -- environmental or educational -- is not one of the amount of knowledge, but of the character of unforeseeability of the interactions involved;

-- in both cases -- environment and education -- there is a need for awareness of values and ideologies which yield not only the answers given to the problems, but also the questions posed;

-- environmental and educational issues are always controversial, as a result of conflicts between different scales of values and images of the world;

-- both present an interaction between knowledge, ways of thinking, beliefs, attitudes, and behaviours;

91

-- in both cases, it is difficult to distinguish the observer from the object of observation, and consequently the evaluation of a process from the impact of the evaluation itself on the process evaluated.

The evaluation we need for the ENSI project must be oriented at the same time to the complex and dynamic nature of education and to the complex and dynamic nature of environmental issues, in the search for consistency and for the one generalisation we are seeking: a "naturalistic generalisation" (Stake, 1980), that can enable us to recognize one particular feature in new and foreign contexts.

Criteria for comparing projects: the "quality indicators"

The first phase of the Environment and School Initiatives research showed that it was possible to reach common agreement on the "quality of an environmental education project", so that it was possible in each country to choose school-initiatives that were representative of this quality.

A second step is to identify and to compare the projects characteristics that were, implicitly or explicitly, considered as important in each country. A comparison on this point will allow not only to identify evaluation "criteria" but possibly also to construct a common model of environmental education.

I shall call the elements of this model "*quality indicators*". In this way, at the microlevel of school initiatives, we use a concept which is widely used in comparative research at the meso and macrolevel. "Indicator" is a word often used as a synonym of "statistical index" or group of indexes, and it is thus reduced to a pure quantitative measure. The most commonly used indicators in educational systems are performance indicators:

"time series data that reflect and record change across a number of significant dimensions relevant for judging the effectiveness and efficiency of a system in achieving its goals" (Norris, 1991).

For these performance indicators, the major assumptions are: first, these kinds of indicators are meant to reflect both quality and output, second, educational quality can be readily defined and measured, and the performance indicators can stay the same over space and time.

This is not the conception of quality in education implicit in the ENSI Project, nor is it my proposal for an identification of quality indicators. First the reduction of a quality indicator to a pure quantitative measure is not logically founded: we have "biological indicators" in environmental science that are qualitative and quantitative at the same time. Second, in medical diagnosis, in police investigations, among art "connoisseurs", knowledge is based on symptoms, tracks, signs that something has happened. As proposed in the first paragraph, we have to apply a "circumstantial paradigm", and not a Galilean experimental perspective, in order to reach an understanding of the processes we are carrying on with schools in the ENSI project. So we can look for "*signs*" that, as far as environmental education is concerned, our work is going in the right direction.

When speaking about quality indicators, reference is often made to a "check-up" process, and in fact the evaluation of a system by a group of indicators is a process that is similar more to the intuition of a medical diagnosis than to the reduction and simplification typical of natural sciences.

In the OECD Washington Conference on educational indicators this was one of the proposed definitions:

"In my vocabulary, indicators are just information assumed to be relevant to some individuals, as a basis for decisions, or simply for increased understanding" (Eide, 1987).

92

Criteria, and indicators, cannot be defined as isolated signs: it is the whole of the symptoms that allow us to recognize the health or the illness in a body. In OECD educational policy, quality indicators are based on an explicit or implicit *model or theory*, in order to be meaningful.

Indicators may be composed of indexes and must be connected in a system:

"Ideally, a system of indicators measures distinct components of the system of interest, but also provides information about how the individual components work together to produce the overall effect. In other words, the whole of the information to be gained from a system of indicators is greater than the sum of its parts" (Oakes, 1987).

The problem is how we can agree on some quality criteria and, at the same time, what kind of "information we consider as relevant", what are the concrete elements that supply evidence that a given situation conforms, or not, to the defined criteria.

Therefore, as an example of what could be done, I want to present the work carried out by a group of Italian teachers in 1989-90.

Proposals for a quality indicators system

As the evaluation criteria in the first phase of ENSI were only intuitively defined, at CEDE we needed to assess their effectiveness. This need to research "quality" criteria for Environmental Projects was in harmony with the need of the environmental association *Lega per l'ambiente*, which was facing the same problem of quality inside its educational sector, and with the interest of *ISFOL* (Institute for worker training) for the evaluation of quality of vocational courses oriented to new environmental professions.

Starting from this common interest, a research group was set up in 1989-90 with the aim of identifying a set of "quality indicators" based on a common conception of environmental education. The research was conducted by researchers of the three institutions (Ammassari and Palleschi from ISFOL, Cogliati Dezza from Lega per l'Ambiente and Mayer from CEDE), in close collaboration with ten teachers involved in environmental education projects from different Italian regions and different school levels, from primary to vocational and technical schools.

Because there is no agreement on a single definition of "quality" and of Environmental Education, our group started comparing different points of view in order to build a shared value system. In fact, establishing a system of quality indicators implies "a series of value assumptions about the importance of a wide range of objectives" (Eide, 1987).

A quality indicator system can be interpreted only "in the context of educational values and experience with schooling" (Oakes, 1987). Our set of values was inspired by the results of the International Conferences of Stockholm, Tbilissi, and Moscow, and can be summarized as follows:

-- the awareness that man is part of nature;

-- the awareness that man needs nature for his physical and spiritual survival;

-- the awareness of our responsibility toward the whole human species for the present and for the future.

Almost everybody could accept these statements as general aims for environmental education. However, different points of view arise when we try to go on from these statements to consequent actions and behaviours. This is especially true in the field of education: what do the general statements mean in concrete teaching and learning situations? In our group we stressed two main consequences:

-- the need to go beyond "far-west" culture towards a "spaceship" culture; which means the need to replace, in all subjects and in all disciplines, the concept of "growth" and that of "development", having a positive value, with the concepts of "respect of limits", and "self-regulation";

-- the need to give value to differences, not only to biological differences among species or among ecosystems, but also to individual differences, for example among pupils.

At present, the school system seems organized in order to avoid differences instead of making the most of them. As Heinz Von Foerster pointed out (1971):

"Consider, for instance, the way our system of education is set up. The student enters school as an unpredictable "*non-trivial machine*". We don't know what answer he will give to a question. However, should he succeed in the system, the answers he gives to our questions must be known. They are the "right" answers. Tests are devices to establish a measure of trivialization. A perfect score in a test is indicative of perfect trivialization: the student is completely predictable and thus can be admitted in the society."

This is but an example of how general environmental values could be full of consequences for teaching-learning behaviour. The ecology of our planet is related to the "ecology of mind" (Bateson, 1972), and the latter to an ecology of teaching-learning processes.

In the group, we identify other consequences directly related to school practice:

-- The development of an attitude of tolerance towards conflictual, ambiguous or unforeseeable circumstances. In the same scientific disciplines, it is important to be aware of the provisional and hypothetic character of knowledge, i.e. the limits of "laws", "theories", and "models".

-- The transition from a school where knowledge is "transmitted", to a school where knowledge is "constructed" together with attitudes and behaviours, as an active creation of "personal meaning".

-- The equally needed transition from a school based on "individual competition" to a school, and classwork, based on cooperation and solidarity.

-- The changing roles of teachers and students within schools, on the one hand, and of schools towards the community and the local environmental problems, on the other.

These general educational values are very close to the aims established by the ENSI project:

-- Broadening environmental awareness, extending the scope of environmental education, integrating various disciplines in moving towards a culture of complexity and overcoming the obstacles of a reductionistic and mechanistic approach to reality (OECD-CERI, 1986).

-- Influencing the learning-teaching process: "pupils or students had a substantial role in defining their projects, they took responsibility for carrying them out, and the objective of their work was to change the local environment" (Kelley-Laine K., 1990). In other words, the educational process is fostering "dynamic qualities" in students (Posch, 1986).

94

To these aims we added the ones that Laura Conti, a famous Italian ecologist, proposed in Linz at the final conference of ENSI's first phase (Conti, 1991):

-- to teach children to be aware of the future, to identify themselves with their own future and to recover their past, in a society that only values the present,

-- to teach children to "predict the unpredictable", to recognise fortuitous and not obvious links in natural and social processes.

All these elements, values and educational aims, based on values, allow us to start defining some elements of evidence that can be collected in school projects. This work was done during a one year process of reflecting together on the different experiences the teachers are living in their school life, seeking criteria and elements that could describe the consistency between teaching-learning strategies and the agreed aims -- and values -- of environmental education, trying to apply this criteria and to identify these elements in their own practice.

In this quest we used, first implicitly and then explicitly, one model of Environmental Education based on the agreement reached on the "quality" we want to assure and to realise in educational processes. We defined a system of "quality indicators" accepting the OECD general definition. However, for us quality indicators are rarely statistics, more often they present observable features or behaviours, which can be interpreted as signs of the consistency between the environmental education project and the model and the value system mentioned above.

We have grouped our indicators into three sets connected to the observation fields: where and when signs and traces, can be noticed. We have called these "*field indicators*", each one of them being composed of indicators, and we have listed the "indexes" that enable us to recognize the presence or absence of these indicators in the project examined.

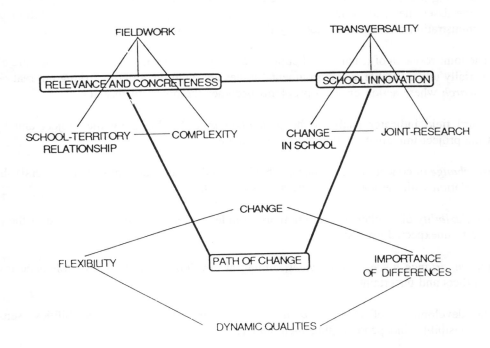

The first field indicator is the *relevance and concreteness* of the project in the local situation. An environmental education project has to face problems considered relevant by pupils and by the local community, in which the school could intervene by producing information or promoting actions in an effective way. The indicators which describe the conditions for an effective intervention are:

-- *Fieldwork*, considered not only as an active way to gather data, but also as an important educational tool to broaden perception abilities, to develop an overall vision, and to establish a feeling of belonging.

-- *School-territory relationship*, where not only is the school brought into the environment, but also the environment into the school. An environmental education project presents the school as an active partner in the local social system.

-- *Complexity* of the approaches and processes, which must reflect the complexity of environmental equilibrium, going from a systemic perspective to the recognition of intrinsic uncertainty, stressing the role of the observer and the importance of different points of view.

The second field indicator relates to *school innovation*: the relationships among the "actors" of the project, mainly students and teachers, who have to change in order to be consistent with the explicit values. Teaching methods and strategies have to change as well, together with assessment and evaluation techniques. The indicators describing this innovation are the following:

-- The *transversality* in environmental education of contents, methods and actions, that are no longer related to one or few disciplines. This creates, as a result, connections not only among different disciplines, but also among different teachers, their methods, their value systems and their behaviours.

-- The change in school, that is, all the structural and organizational changes that are consistent with the value system, implicit or explicit, in the project (for instance, the possibility of modifying the time schedule according to the needs of the project; or the importance given, in the assessment, to collective work done during the project; or the recognition by the administration of extra work done by the teachers involved in the project, ...).

-- The joint-research of teachers and pupils, facing open situations and problems, that are always partially unpredictable, as environmental issues are, with the aim of carrying out real *action-research* where action on local problems becomes the object of research.

The third field indicator analyzes the *path of change* developed by the project and by the processes that the project implements. Points to examine are:

-- the *change* of conceptions, attitudes, behaviours and values that pupils (and teachers!) showed in relation with the approaches and strategies used;

-- the *flexibility* of teacher programming as an index of receptiveness to the need of the pupils and to unexpected events;

-- the *importance given to differences*, aiming at developing an attitude of tolerance towards conflicts and uncertainty;

-- the development of *dynamic qualities*; that is, decision making abilities, sense of responsibility, independent judgement and action.

The first two set of indicators offer a synchronic image of a project, one from a point of view outside the school, the other from a school perspective. The third set of indicators follows the diachronic processes the project implements. These three sets correspond to the significant dimensions of the ENSI project:

"*intervention* in the local environment and *collaboration* with the local community, *organisational change* in the school, and *pedagogical change*" (Elliott, 1991).

Every indicator was articulated by indexes, and for every index we prepared many questions, corresponding to an identified set of variables. The outcome has been a check-list, partially organized as a questionnaire, directed to teachers, where the answers and the elements to be recognised are generally qualitative and not statistical. The effectiveness of the questionnaire was confirmed by a comparison with the case study prepared on the same projects. Even if "ethnographic information" did not come out in the questionnaire as in the case study, the "quality" of the project seemed to be well represented, together with the consistency between the project and the values proposed for environmental education.

Moreover, the information given by the indicator system is greater than that given by the sum of the individual indicators. The indicators are connected in a network, where some connections change as the project develops and where it is possible to investigate different features. Consistency is one of them: consistency between school innovation and action in the community; consistency between the latter and the curriculum; consistency through the different steps of the project; consistency among the problems, the experiences proposed and the values expressed.

The indicator system seemed to be a valid and reliable tool for project evaluation in Italy. It not only enabled researchers to identify "good projects", but it offered teachers a comparison, an "identikit" of a "good quality" project, even if, as with every identikit, it did not represent any real project.

The whole research -- the indicator system, the questionnaire, together with case studies and the application of the system on vocational education -- has been published by ISFOL, who funded the research (Ammassari and Palleschi, 91).

The system has been validated with and for Italian schools. However, if applied to ENSI school initiatives in other countries, probably the general values and the environmental education model could remain the same, while the indicators system has to be adapted to the local situation and to the national educational system. Some of the proposed indicators, however, were present almost in all the projects presented in the general conference in Linz, although in different national contexts and school systems. So one way to use this work is to discuss internationally if all the indicators we proposed are "necessary" and if they are "sufficient".

Obviously, indexes and the check list have to be constructed in the cultural context on which the project is based. The evaluation of the importance of an innovation, or of what could be considered an innovation in environmental education, depends on the general local attitude toward the environment and toward the school system. In strongly centralised systems, for instance, modifying the curriculum of only one discipline in order to introduce environmental issues can require a great effort and may be considered a meaningful innovation. In other systems, a specific length of time is already allocated for classroom practical activities and projects, and the only use of this time is no longer an innovation. In the same way, some "environmental problems" are more easily faced in one country than in another, because of the different sensitivity of the population or of the political system.

Let me give an example. In the Italian situation, "fieldwork" is a good indicator both of a meaningful environmental initiative and of educational innovation. Very few schools allow teachers to do fieldwork -- and the teachers are not prepared for it --. When fieldwork is provided in the curriculum, it is often restricted to the gathering of technical data. No space is given, except in a few primary schools, to perception abilities, to a holistic view of the territory, to the feelings of adventure, that can support and motivate cognitive abilities and value growth. So our questionnaire included the elements we wanted to develop in our schools:

-- the space given to development of perception abilities;
-- the freedom left for free exploration of the field;
-- the space given for a global approach to the field and to the problem;
-- the quantity of knowledge the students need to perform their fieldwork;
-- the type of data they are requested to gather (whether quantitative or also qualitative);
-- the amount of time dedicated to fieldwork in the whole environmental project.

For other countries and other school systems these kinds of questions could receive absolutely predictable answers and, perhaps, they will need to qualify their fieldwork in other directions related to their specific contexts.

The path of change: instruments for formative evaluation

The third set of indicators describe the pedagogical change as one of the major dimensions in environmental education and this set represented a challenge for our research group and our teachers. Looking for expected and unexpected changes, being open to "surprises" and prepared for "unprogrammed" teaching actions, seemed more difficult to realize than to promote concrete action for the environment or innovations in school structure.

In this case we also found reference to the indicator system useful. The need to go deeper into the chosen indicators and indexes in order to find common elements to look for, obliged the teachers to shift from common assessment methods to more sophisticated observational methods and to formative evaluation.

Among the educational objectives we derived directly from the characteristics of environmental education, one in particular seemed very important: to make the most of differences. This means, on the one hand, to avoid "trivialization" of students, and on the other, to use as many differences as we can in the educational process: differences in abilities, in points of view, in values. It is not to perpetuate social diversity and disadvantageous situations, but rather to allow each student to carry out his or her own choices and to use his or her abilities to the utmost. It is therefore necessary for an environmental project to readily have common aims, shared by all students, and specific aims which characterize the personality of the individual. The presence of both, will allow the students to increase their own possibilities for choice. This means that objectives and aims, including the cognitive ones, are not proposed and evaluated only by the teacher but are presented to and discussed with the students, in such a way that each student can independently evaluate the point s/he has arrived at and be able to establish personal goals to be examined within a group discussion.

The diversity of the students' knowledge and attitude is not a variable that teachers are prepared to handle. Students, in fact, are often considered by their teachers as "tabulae rasae", empty tablets ready to be written upon. But also children in primary schools carry within themselves a richness of conceptions, sometimes implicit, and ways of viewing the world.

This "*common-sense knowledge*" often opposes scholastic knowledge not with simple "errors" or misunderstandings, but with "tacit" theories (Polanyi, 1966). Sometimes they are explicated only by action, but have a remarkable internal coherence and thus are difficult to modify. These "epistemological obstacles" as they are called by Bachelard (1938) can be overcome, but not eradicated, and will wind up becoming part of that epistemological profile which is totally personal and individual and which corresponds to the personal construction of a concept. In order to collaborate on this construction, the teacher must be aware of these "obstacles" and perhaps also of the "experiences" and "rules" which have produced them.

As Ausubel says:

"If I had to reduce all educational psychology to just one principle, I would say this: the most important single factor influencing learning is what the learner already knows. Ascertain this and teach him accordingly" (Ausubel, 1968).

The primary instrument for recognizing the presence of these "alternative" conceptions is the interview, or the written questionnaire with open answers to "legitimate" questions. If, in fact, we agree with Von Foerster and consider as legitimate only those questions for which we do not know the answer, or for which the school has not yet furnished one, we thus stimulate the student not to recall the right answer, but to present their own beliefs.

Numerous results have been obtained using this method in the field of science teaching. One example taken from my own research in physics education: to the question;

"What does gravity mean to you?"

asked at the beginning of a physics course, a girl replied

"Gravity is the force that keeps objects suspended (!) in air"

and continued

"I heard it on T.V. ... They said that once the Shuttle is launched, it remains in orbit due to gravity."

In this case, the girl coherently connected the implicit theories taken from the perceptive-motorial field -- heavy objects fall if not opposed by force -- with information presented by the mass-media, otherwise scientifically correct.

The common sense knowledge is not always coherent; but it almost always opposes a more global point of view and is in its way more "systemic" in respect to the reduction of simple elements proposed by scientific disciplines.

In the field of scientific education, studies in this direction have developed a quantity of techniques from the interview in an experimental situation to group interviews, from open questionnaires to multiple choice questionnaires, to the continuous observation in class, and have placed a wealth of data and proposals at the attention of teachers. These methods assist in eliciting conceptualizations and facilitate reflection, both for teachers and students. The latter often manage to criticize their own concepts only after having expressed them.

The diversity thus constitutes a point of departure which does not necessarily need to be rapidly converted into "accepted knowledge", but instead must be respected, even if disputed, and most of all understood and used.

Alternative conceptions are often strongly connected with *initial beliefs*; and these are generally related to commonplace notions and to the overabundance of information, so characteristic of our society, and characterized by the lack of critical reflection. Examples of these notions, which connect information or misinformation to an image of the world, are examined in the study which accompanied the Dutch project of the introduction of environmental education into the curricula (NME-VO Project).

"There is no need to use oil and coal sparingly, for when these are finished we can switch to electricity" (reported by De Jager, 1987).

"Acid rain? Yes, I've heard of that; in that place called Tsjernobyl something has exploded. That's called radioactive or something like that. And that's rather dangerous and it causes all kinds of fruit in warm countries going to pieces" (reported by Kortland, 1988).

"Environmental pollution? yes I think that the worst form of environmental pollution is due to plastic bags. Yes, plastic bags are the things that pollute the most" (Italian T.V., children 10-12 years old)

These replies not only testify to the scarce knowledge of the situation, but also to the difficulty of recognizing and accepting complex connections consequent to one's way of living: it may be easier to give up using plastic bags than electricity or automobiles. One cannot operate on a knowledge level alone, but also on the level of relationships between knowledge and the image of their future utility. It is only through the ability to imagine a future which is acceptable on an individual level and sustainable on a planetary level that certain ideas can be accepted and thus understood.

A strategy which can be utilized to record and analyze not only the concepts, but also how their relationships to each other are established, is that of "*concept mapping*" proposed by Novak.

"Concept maps are intended to represent meaningful relationships between concepts in the form of proposition. Propositions are two or more concept labels linked by words in a semantic unit ... A concept map is a schematic device for representing a set of concept meanings embedded in a framework of propositions ... concept maps should be hierarchical ... the same set of concepts can be represented in two or more hierarchies. Concept mapping is a technique for externalizing concepts and propositions" (Novak and Gowin, 1984).

The map helps to render connections explicit which often remain implicit, and to bring them into discussion. This is also one instrument to assist reflection upon one's own knowledge. The teacher can construct a concept map of the initial knowledge which his/her students have and compare it with the maps which were constructed during the project. Alternatively, the student can construct his/her own map with respect to the proposed concepts, and use it as a means of comparison with his/her classmates, teachers and with him/herself in successive points during the course of learning.

To become aware of change and its causes is an equally important part of change itself. I would like to point out that among the strategies and instruments proposed so far, certain elements have remained constant:

-- first, the *growth of awareness*, by individual reflection upon one's own objectives, concepts, and conceptual networks;

-- secondly, collective discussion and comparison making the most of one's own diversity and *accepting the diversity* of others;

-- finally, *self-evaluation* in respect to the processes involved, and not only to the achieved "outcomes".

This kind of evaluation is in itself an educational and formative action, and a prototype of the ideal process of evaluation of knowledge. This, in fact, requires assuming *responsibility* with respect to one's own opinions and points of view, exercising *critical abilities* during discussions and in comparison with others, while at the same time encouraging *non-competitive behaviour*, inspired by the respect and the utility of diversity.

The same conceptual itinerary could then be applied to those aspects in environmental education which are harder to recognize and describe: *values and attitudes.*

Also in this case, the first step is to elicit the system of values and the image of the world that lies beneath these values. This is not an easy task and it is necessary to find direct and indirect methods in order to explore the students' points of view. One method we tried in our research (Ammassari and Palleschi, 1991) was that of "free word association". We asked different groups of students in secondary schools to write their free associations in relation to the words: town, nature, energy, environment, car, limit.

The words they associate are "clues" not only to their knowledge but also to values and beliefs. So, for instance, if "town" received prevalent negative associations (noise, pollution, chaos, dirt), and "nature" positive associations (beauty, freedom, colour, peace), "energy" received positive associations before having carried out environmental projects and more critical associations after. "Environment" is almost always considered not as a synonym of nature but as "environmental problems", meaning pollution, waste, illness, and so on. The concept of limit -- that is so important in a new environmental culture -- is always associated with prohibition, restriction, wall, end or even "death" (!).

Another question we posed was to find the possible relationship between word pairs: for instance "air-town", "house- landslide", "highway-polluted sea", "mechanized agriculture-eutrophication". In this way we want to look for the capacity of students to imagine non-trivial relationships and interactions, to predict the unpredictable, as suggested in Laura Conti's paper (1991). But in these answers, too, it was possible to recognize values and attitudes mixed with "conceptions" and "misconceptions". These kinds of elements allow teachers to grasp some of the images of the world that students already have, and allow students to elicit them and to reflect on them.

Another point is whether students are able to recognize values and attitudes in other people's positions, in newspapers, in mass media. There could be exercises of summarizing and making charts and questionnaires on the comprehension of a text in order to see whether the students are capable of grasping the fundamental points of a discussion. There is need of analysis of conflictual positions, in order to learn to distinguish between data and theory, questions and answers, emotional images from logical propositions, diversity due to different life experiences, and sometimes, due to differing cultural contexts, and finally to distinguish explicit positions from implicit ones relative to a scale of values.

The recognition and evaluation of attitudes is strictly related to this kind of problem. Questionnaires on interests and attitudes are widespread in various field, environmental education included.

Usually, questionnaires are proposed on a Likert-type response format, in order to allow easy scoring and easy comparison among different samples. The assumption is that both the student and the researcher attribute the *same meaning* to the items. But different studies showed that students' points of view are not captured by a Likert-type questionnaire (Aikenhead *et al.* 1987), and that, for example in scientific education, to measure attitudes and to interpret the results is particularly problematic. We might legitimately expect the same kind of problem in environmental education, since the almost ideal unidimensionality of Likert-items is in sharp contrast with the multidimensional aspects of environmental education.

An alternative methodology has been proposed by Aikenhead (1988). He proposed to derive a multiple choice questionnaire from the categorisation of students' previously written paragraphs on the proposed statements. The empirically derived "students' position choices" seem to reduce ambiguity and, at the same time, improve the understanding of different attitudes and opinions. This methodology might be used in environmental education too, if we want to construct usable questionnaires, comparable in different countries. But, as far as a classroom project is concerned, written comments to a set of statements could become a basis for a very good class discussion, for an exercise of consciousness and reflection on students' own opinions, and a follow-up exercise of group confrontation.

Value and attitude descriptions should not be separated by *behaviour* observations. It is possible to use observation grids, but one useful strategy to record behavioural observations is that of taking "anecdotal records" regarding the behaviour of this or that student. This method is useful, above all, if we want to keep only a few subjects under observation; for example, during the first phase of ENSI many teachers said that environmental education helped students with cognitive or social disadvantages to become part of the class group. To confirm this hypothesis, "anecdotal records" seem a fair strategy. Of course, students diaries, their self-evaluation, and teachers diaries can confirm and/or add new points of view to the observations made.

These methods allow us to record changes that happen mainly in the field of social behaviour within the class. Parents and relatives could be involved in order to give their point of view. But because this is not always possible and not easy, another possibility is to use questionnaires along the lines of "What am I willing to do for ..." as proposed in the NME-VO Project.

Another useful tool for eliciting values and for starting to deal with different points of view and conflicts is the "role play". There are many "role playing" games proposed on environmental issues, by UNESCO and other National and International Organisations, that could be used as a way to elicit values and attitudes. The problem is that "values" and attitudes" are those proposed by the "role play" and not necessarily the ones of the students. What seems more interesting in order to know the student's own opinion, is a discussion following the game, where the student is asked to evaluate not only his/her behaviour or the behaviour of the classmates, but the game itself, its rules, its play cards, its descriptions of the roles. We found particularly useful to transform the actual conflictual situations presented by a concrete school project in a "role play": interviewing people in the street, collecting data, reading newspapers, could become the activities the group needs in order to play its role as realistically as possible. Knowledge is in this way closely connected with decision making, with behaviours, with attitudes and values.

Conclusions

The characteristics of environmental education demonstrate the need for a different role and status of evaluation in educational research.

Quality indicators may be used to identify evaluation criteria. A comparative study seems possible on different systems of quality indicators and on the indexes and concrete elements that characterize the same indicator in different countries. The challenge of ENSI is whether it is possible to share common criteria, i. e. common quality indicators, for environmental education and, at the same time, whether it is possible to find different national or regional ways to put these criteria into the school practice. In other words whether it is possible to built a common project toward common aims without reducing the richness in diversity of the countries and schools involved.

In the indicator system presented, a central point is given to the change of values, behaviour, attitudes and knowledge demanded by environmental education projects. To guarantee flexibility and appropriateness of a school project, a continuous formative evaluation is needed. This formative evaluation is not aimed at a standardization of students, but towards respect for individual differences. Observation grids, questionnaires, interviews, words association, written essays and group discussions, may all be used in order to describe knowledge and beliefs, values, attitudes and behaviour. Some conventional tools can be adapted to environmental education needs; others, such as the Likert-type questionnaire, need substantial modifications; some new tools, such as "role play" and "conceptual mapping", have to be experimented.

This kind of evaluation will allow us to describe changes and compare them with local and national contexts, i.e. with values and beliefs regarding environment and education, shared in the school and in the community.

These instruments will not substitute more holistic instruments such as "case studies" or "ethnographic descriptions", but they will only add elements for reflection and meta-analysis both within projects and between projects.

Acknowledgements

This is a revised version of the paper presented at the initial meeting of the second phase of the ENSI project at OECD. This new version, therefore, presents research results and quotations that were not available at the time. I would like to thank John Elliott and Peter Posch for their kind advice and strong support in helping me with my work.

References

AIKENHEAD, G.S., FLEMING, R.W., RIAN, A.G. (1987), High school graduates' belief about science-technology-society, I, Methods and issues in monitoring student views, *Science Education*, 71(2), pp. 145-161.

AIKENHEAD, G.S. (1988), "An analysis of four ways of assessing student beliefs about STS topics", *Journal of Research in Science Teaching*, 25 (8), pp. 607-629.

AMMASSARI, R., PALLESCHI, M.T., (Eds.) (1991), *Educazione Ambientale: gli indicatori di qualità, Un percorso coerente dalla scuola elementare alla formazione professionale*, (Environmental Education quality indicators, A consistent path from primary school to vocational training), Franco Angeli, Milano.

AUSUBEL, D.P. (1968), *Educational psychology: A cognitive view*, Holt, Rinehart and Winston, New York.

BACHELARD, G. (1938), *La formation de l'esprit scientifique*, Librairie Philosophique, J. Vrin, Paris.

BATESON, G. (1972), *Steps to an Ecology of Mind*, Intertext Books, London.

CONTI, L. (1991), "The environmental perspective", in *Environment, schools and Active Learning,* OECD CERI, Paris.

CRONBACH, L.J. (1975), "Beyond the two disciplines of scientific psychology," *American Psychologist*, Vol. 30, No. 2, United States of America.

EIDE, K. (1987), *The need for statistical indicators in education*, paper presented to the OECD Washington Conference on Educational Indicators, United States of America.

ELLIOTT, J. (1991), *Are 'Performance Indicators' Educational Quality Indicators?* Paper presented at the annual conference of British Educational Research Association, Nottingham Polytechnic, United Kingdom.

DE JAGER, H. (1987), *Students' beliefs concerning environmental issues*, Paper presented in the 4th Symposium on World Trends in Science and Technology Education, Kiel.

FEYERABEND, P. (1975), *Against Method: Outlines of an Anarchist Theory of Knowledge*, New Left Books, London.

GINZBURG, C. (1986), *Miti, emblemi, spie*, Einaudi, Torino.

KELLEY LAINE, K. (1990), "The Environment at School", *The OECD Observer*, pp. 13-16, Paris.

KORTLANT, K. (1988), *Environmental education within the science subjects in secondary education: why, what and what for?*, Paper presented at the Joint Seminar AIF-ICASE, Caserta, Italy.

KUHN, T. (1970), *The Structure of Scientific Revolutions*, 2nd ed., University of Chicago Press, Chicago, Illinois.

MORIN E. (1985), "La via della complessità", in *La sfida della complessità*, BOCCHI, G. and CERUTI, E. Eds., Feltrinelli, Milano.

NME-VO Project (1987), "Energy-household" Questionnaire, *Centre for Science and Mathematics Education*, University of Utrecht, Netherlands.

NORRIS, N. (1991), *Evaluation, Economics and Performance Indicators*, Paper presented at the Annual Conference of the British Educational Research Association at Nottingham Polytechnic, United Kingdom.

NOVAK, J. D., GOWIN, D. B. (1984), *Learning how to learn*, Cambridge University Press, Cambridge, United Kingdom.

OAKES, J. (1987), *Educational Indicators, A guide for Policymakers*, Centre for Policy Research in Education, Rutgers University, The Rand Corporation, University of Wisconsin-Madison, paper presented to the OECD Washington Conference on Educational Indicators.

OECD (1986), *Proposal for a co-operative project on Environment and School Initiatives*, Meeting of Country Representatives, Paris.

POLANYI, M. (1966), *The Tacit Dimension*, (Italian version, Armando Armando, 1979), Roma.

POSCH, P. (1986), *The Project Environment and School Initiatives*, Introductory statement at the meeting of Country Representatives, OECD-CERI, Paris.

ROBOTTOM, J. (1989), "Social Critique or Social Control: some problems for evaluation in Environmental Education", *Journal of Research in Science Teaching*, vol. 26, no. 5, pp. 435-443

STAKES, R. E. (1980), "The case study method in social inquiry," in *Toward a science of the singular*, Helen Simons Ed., CARE Occasional Publications no.10, University of East Anglia, Norwich.

VISALBERGHI, A. (1989), "Educazione all'ambiente, educazione allo sviluppo, educazione alla pace," in *Una scuola per l'ambiente, Risultati di una ricerca promossa dall'OCSE*, M. Mayer Ed., I Quaderni di Villa Falconieri, no. 18, Frascati, Italy.

VON FOERSTER, H. (1971), "Perception of the future and future of perception", *Instructional Science*, pp. 31-43.

PART TWO

EVALUATION PERSPECTIVES FROM THE CROMER CONFERENCE

EDITORIAL

by

Bridget Somekh and May Pettigrew
Centre for Applied Research in Education
University of East Anglia
Norwich, United Kingdom

The Cromer conference on evaluation was a forum for exploring the values and assumptions built up by all the participants over many years experience. In the morning sessions, members of the Centre for Applied Research in Education made a series of presentations on their practice as educational evaluators; and in the discussion periods, over lunch, walking on the beach -- during a boat trip on the network of rivers known as the Norfolk Broads -- the ideas about evaluation arising from these sessions were interrogated, elaborated and challenged. In a multi-national group, whose members were experienced in either environmental education, or evaluation, or both, there was a high degree of awareness of the politics of evaluation. This was a project which had implications for many different interest groups: as one participant said, "Identifying aims (for the evaluation) is difficult for some countries, for example where there are six distinct government ministries involved there are (six) distinct sets of aims." In addition, the conference took place at a time of political upheaval and euphoria when the map of Europe was being re-drawn following the 1989 revolutions in the old Eastern Block countries: hence, even as we welcomed project participants from a newly liberated Hungary, we shared in the tension and uncertainty of the participants from the former Yugoslavia as they received news of the outbreak of civil war in their home town of Ljubljana.

Any one of the participants at the conference could probably have suggested an approach to evaluating ENSI from his or her experience. But there was a need for a coherent statement of methodology which might form the basis for an approach which could be adopted -- and adapted -- across all the participating countries. Many countries in the ENSI programme were using action research as a means of supporting curriculum development, and the roots of CARE's tradition of evaluation were closely linked with the origins of the action research 'movement' among teachers in Britain (see Introduction). So, it was appropriate that the statement of methodology came from CARE. But, the impact and importance of the conference lay in the generation of new ideas about evaluation, applicable to ENSI. The cultural differences between the countries ensured that all the approaches would never be the same, but the common experience of the Cromer conference went a long way to ensuring that each approach would have the ENSI stamp.

The papers which follow have been constructed from the experience of the conference. Some originated as documents handed out in the morning sessions. Others have been written at a later date on the basis of tape-recordings of presentations and discussions. The one on interviewing was written for another purpose, but is included because we believe it to be particularly apt. The predominant thrust of the papers is a presentation of the CARE evaluation tradition, although they incorporate a number of contributions from ENSI participants. Ideally, they should be read in the spirit in which they were originally intended: they are not to be treated as expert statements setting out a prescription for action, but as starting points for discussion, re-definition and extension. The following questions are adapted from some the conference participants posed at the beginning of the second day. They may be of use as a starting point for interrogating the papers as you read.

-- Should an evaluation represent diversity or rest on clear aims and concepts. Is the aim to cultivate or limit contradictions?

-- Is the audience for the evaluation the teachers and students involved or representatives of the power structure and funding agencies? Other possible audiences are other schools and research communities.

-- Is the aim of evaluation to improve environmental education or to legitimate environmental education? In at least one country it is necessary to evaluate in order to show environmental education can build up science education and mathematics, and can reduce student dropout rates. In this case it will achieve legitimacy by helping achieve other aims.

-- Should communication of the evaluation be through informal or formal means? Should there be multimedia reporting using video or computer conferences, or written studies?

-- Should the evaluation be carried out by insiders or outsiders?

-- On what level should the evaluation concentrate -- school practice, or policy development, or the support structure between them?

-- If there are differences between the cultures of different countries, are there also differences in the attitudes to change and the way change is introduced and supported?

-- Is there something distinctive about change problems in environmental education? Is there a danger of supposing that all perceive problems in the same way?

-- How important are concrete descriptions in showing how teachers actually develop interdisciplinary work and assess dynamic qualities?

-- Should the evaluation include a section entitled "Tales of the Unexpected"?

-- Is there a danger that we can get too consensual? You could get more of a framework than is useful. It can inhibit the pursuit of idiosyncrasies and sacrifice depth for coverage. So hang back a bit from that consensus view.

Chapter 5

**VALUES, POWER AND STRATEGY IN EVALUATION DESIGN
SOME PRELIMINARY CONSIDERATIONS**

by

Barry MacDonald
Centre for Applied Research in Education
University of East Anglia
Norwich, United Kingdom

The way we think about evaluation now is not the way we thought about it thirty years ago. That was when, at least in some Western countries, State sponsored curriculum development began to feature as a significant element of post-war socio-economic reform. The major influence on the way we think now about evaluation has been that experience of successive attempts, by various means, to devise and secure improvements in what our school systems provide for children to learn. At the height of the curriculum development movement, in the United Kingdom for example, there were some two hundred sponsored curriculum innovations in action across the country. Today there may be a handful, but to all intents and purposes the curriculum development strategy is dead, abandoned by its political backers as a failure -- it is not effective enough, it is not cheap enough, it is not quick enough. In short, it does not work. What is more, it's all the fault of the professionals, you and me, who had most of the responsibility and therefore must take the blame.

This conclusion is not confined to the United Kingdom. It is shared by the United States, by Canada, by Australia, by New Zealand, and others with a long investment record in the transformational power of voluntary, professionally led initiatives.

And what do we have in place of curriculum development as a strategy for improving schools? We have standardisation of curriculum, we have specification of what has to be done at all levels, we have accountability for delivery of the specification through performance indicators of a quantitative kind. In other words, we have a non-developmental prescription for schooling controlled by output testing. That model is already in place in some countries and appears to be spreading to many others. Within such a model there is little room for the kind of curriculum initiative with which you are currently engaged.

How did we get here, and what are the implications of this massive reverse for the Environment Programme which in some ways, in some of the countries involved, appears to belong to a vanished past? We got here through approaching curriculum development in ways that were based on wrong assumptions about the nature of the problem of curriculum and about the problem of change. As these assumptions were shown by experience to be inadequate or misguided, approaches were modified to take account of experience.

Looking back, we can distinguish a learning curve, or a sequence of phases, each of which constitutes a modification of strategy to take account of previous failures. Now let me say at once that not every country that has been involved in curriculum development has gone through this sequence in the order which I will describe. Different countries have started at different points in time, and some late starters have taken account of experience elsewhere, as well as of their particular circumstances and traditions. Nevertheless, I would contend that, allowing for variations, approaches to the problem of changing the curriculum have shown an evolutionary pattern; from the simple-minded and mechanistic to the sophisticated and organic. But not enough to save the curriculum development movement.

In the initial phase it was assumed that the problem was simple and the solution could be achieved by simple means. So we commissioned people to write new textbooks and we made them available to the schools. That would do the trick. It did not work. On to phase 2. In this phase, the textbook was replaced by a more imaginative collection of learning materials, and accompanied by extensive guidance for the teacher in the use of materials. This was the packaged curriculum. It did not work either, and by the end of this phase, as the "no significant difference" results began to accumulate, the idea of smuggling into the schools any kind of iron clad, teacher proof innovation had its day. On to phase 3, which involved a switch from teacher proof strategies to teacher led strategies. Here the teacher was seen as the major resource, the motto was "no curriculum development without teacher development", and investment was concentrated on in-service professional development. The idea was that you change the teachers, who will then change the curriculum. This phase was particularly strong and influential in the United Kingdom during the seventies, but it could be said that its very success exposed its limitations. Individual teachers cannot change the institutions in which they work, and the curriculum is institutionally held in place. And so we came to phase 4, where the school is seen to be the unit of change and therefore the target of development strategies.

So we have moved from a textbook phase through a package phase into a teacher development phase and finally school development phase. In that process the people who have led the initiatives have changed their role, from subject expert to teacher developer to organisational theorist.

The main point to note is that throughout all these phases the schools were still failing to deliver the transformations promised by successive cohorts of educational developers. Neither stick nor carrot, nor the various combinations of coercion and incentive that characterised the late period of curriculum intervention, could overcome the apparent intransigence of established practice. For the politicians, who had worked hard on public opinion to land the schools with more than their fair share of responsibility for the economic and social ills of the nation, this posed a dilemma. Ultimately the voters would hold them responsible for doing something about the schools. Their response was to abandon the curriculum development ambition and replace it with a fixed rather than an evolving curriculum brief, and a punitive system of accountability for performance. That is where we are now and that is roughly how we got here.

Presently, I shall focus on the ENSI Initiative, to see what kind of phenomenon it is in this context, but I want first to offer a parallel sketch of how evaluation has changed in response to, and in interaction with, these changes in the approach to the problem of curriculum change.

In the beginning, when curriculum development projects could be defined in very basic treatment/outcome terms, evaluators were attached to projects as measurement specialists, offering scientific proof as to whether or not the student learning objectives of the new curriculum had indeed been attained. Pre- and post-testing of learning gains was the mission of the evaluator. Now that might have been O.K. if the projects had been as successful as they hoped, but they were not and so, whatever difference the projects were making, it didn't show up on the instruments. It appeared that, far from the transformational scenarios confidently predicted by project leaders, nothing much seemed to have happened. Of course, the agencies with major responsibility for master-minding the modernisation of schooling began increasingly to ask "Why?" and they turned to evaluators for answers. But evaluators could not tell them why because they had not been asked to look at why anything happened, just whether it happened.

Within a short time the role of the evaluator changed from that of psychometric technician to that of ethnographer. With the realisation that changing the curriculum was a more complex task than it had first seemed, the task of the evaluator expanded to encompass the interpretation of educational settings, so that the developers and strategists of change might better understand the processes in which they were intervening. And, instead of a narrow focus on student learning, evaluators began to think in terms of assessing the impact of the project, a much broader concept of outcomes. It was during this period that psychometrics gave way to the more naturalistic methodology of case study, portrayal and descriptive and narrative accounts of projects in action. And the notion of authoritative proof of accomplishment gave way to the notion of informed judgement, with evaluators supplying the information.

But still, at this time, evaluators were operating on the assumption that change comes from the top, so that the important audience for their reports were the most powerful actors in the system, those who made policy. It was their understanding, their judgements that mattered. And that meant seeing them as decision-makers. That may sound obvious, but it entailed a big change from the classical position of the detached scientist. Now evaluators had to study the anatomy of decision-making, so that their data matrices might better match the knowledge components of executive choices. Not the rhetoric of decision-making, but the reality. In this way, and not at this time fully consciously, evaluators began to nibble at the exercise of power, and to expand their field of interest to encompass more than the implementation efforts of schools.

As this aspect of evaluation expanded, and as it became increasingly clear that the difficulties of changing the curriculum could not be attributed, at least solely, to the perverse obstinacy of schools threatened by enlightenment, another fundamental assumption bit the dust. That was the assumption that our societies are under rational command, or that at least they would be if only they had the information on which rational command could be exercised. That is not how, in general our societies operate. That finding, in turn made a nonsense of our notion of serving a hierarchically structured decision-making model, and of our simple-minded assumption that what we did as evaluators was, in political terms, non-problematic.

Suddenly, it seems now in retrospect, evaluation became politicised in its consciousness, and highly problematic as an occupation. New questions, hitherto not posed, came to the fore. "Who am I helping with what I am doing?" became a central issue, an issue not unrelated to the problem of change as we identified blockages to change far removed from the discretion of schools, teachers and learners. We became aware that we were part of a process of strengthening the knowledge base of the more powerful actors in the system at the expense of the less powerful, and moreover without securing a noticeable benefit to educational development in return.

For some of us, that meant another shift of role, from the managerial feedback role to what we might call a mediation model of knowledge creation and transfer, a negotiation model, or if you like, a broker model of evaluation, in which the interests, rights and obligations of a whole range of constituencies have to be taken into account in deciding what knowledge is to be generated, for whom and about what. For years, we had been happily extracting information and knowledge from the school system, without putting much of its back, on the assumption that such data would be used to benefit schooling, and for no other purposes. That will not do any more. Nothing in evaluation is straightforward. Everything we do has to be justified, not just technically, but ethically and politically. It is not just curriculum developers, but evaluators too, who operate, implicitly or explicitly, with a theory of change.

You can see in this account some parallels between the thinking of developers and the thinking of evaluators. The experience of developers led them to reject the notion of securing change in schools through packages devised outside schools and sent back in for teachers to implement. In place of that they sought more investment in the grassroots, in the human resources of the schools, in the notion of schools as sites of continuous auto-regeneration, whose diverse creativity would shape and guide national policy of a responsive and supportive kind. Action research evolved as a major expression of that strategy of change, and of the politics of teacher professionalism. In like fashion evaluators, looking to make a more influential contribution to development, are less inclined to prioritise management needs, more inclined to prioritise direct feedback to the workforce, and keen to explore collaborative processes of evaluation that can help to internalise learning.

Now I think that through all these cumulative changes we can see a clear line of development with regard to the definition of the evaluation task and the concept of the role. Beginning with the conventional research paradigms from which evaluators were recruited, there was the tendency to see programmes as quasi-experiments from which, concentrating on their amenable aspects, some scientific generalisations could be usefully extracted. This phase was followed by a more holistic view of the innovation as an intrusion into a settled culture, which had to be interpreted and understood if it was to be effectively influenced. That was the ethnographic or anthropological phase, utilising an expanded database and increasingly concerned with detailed study of the contexts and processes of new implants in the school system. This was still largely focused upon the experience of implementation at the grassroots level. Case study at this point meant case study of innovating schools. Then came, as a result of continually expanding the framework of explanation of school-based phenomena, a redefinition of innovation as an intrusion into established systems of power, and as attempts to redistribute power in support of new values.

At this point the concept of the case was redefined as the whole programme, including participants at all levels of responsibility for its origination, management and implementation. It is not hard to see the political implications of such a redefinition, or to understand how that changed the role of the evaluator to that of someone who is mediating power relationships by virtue of choices she/he makes about who gets to know what about whom. And if you see, as we do in the Centre for Applied Research in Education, the public function of evaluation as holding the exercise of delegated power to civic account, with respect to all levels of action, then this puts a premium on the independence of the evaluation.

I imagine that most of the participants at the Cromer Conference, as Pedagogical or Administrative Support persons within the Initiative, see their role in some sense as a mediating role within hierarchical power systems, both protecting and stimulating activity in the schools and districts and at the same time trying to satisfy those "up there" who are financing the initiative. All I am saying at this point is that evaluators also have a mediating role.

So the programme is the case, and case study evaluation is a study of what particular people in the case do and think in their specific circumstances at particular points in time. Now let us ask, with respect to the Environmental Education Initiative, what is it a case of? I will tell you what I think it is a case of. I can do that because I come from outside it, I have no involvement with it, and I am not going to evaluate it. So here are some thoughts, based on the little information I have gleaned from conference papers. Clearly, it is an interesting case. At one level, it is a wholesome and harmless initiative, which has little children going out and planting perhaps a beetroot? What could be more wholesome than that! At the other level, it is an international conspiracy. Is it a specific curriculum innovation, or is it an attempt to take one single issue and restructure educational systems through it? It is fairly clear that some people had that in mind. Is it, in fact, an attempt to get an international response to a problem which can only be solved internationally? Here we have a planet in serious danger. We live increasingly in a habitat that nobody wanted and, in a sense, nobody made, but which we do not seem able to do anything about. So, at one level, this initiative can be seen as the first stage in a grand plan to put a brake on that process and, if possible, to reverse it.

Now, this is highly relevant to how we plan evaluation. Some may say, 'the answer has to be international in order to get any leverage in our own country'. In this case the international aspect becomes important. So that, in conducting an evaluation those with that view, have to take seriously what use can be made of the data in Paris if in fact that level of action or influence is important to the overall plan. But there are other things to take on board. Many of the ENSI participants were involved in this initiative before evaluation came along. Some may have been commanded to engage with the initiative, some may have had nothing better to do, but most have probably a strong commitment to it. If this is true it raises the question, 'what are you going to do about evaluation?' If I come in, I have no such commitment. I can come in and look at this initiative from whatever perspective seems to illuminate it and make it understandable to people outside. But I would say to participants, 'if it is a conspiracy to which you are party, then you might want to look at it quite differently. You might want to say, "what can we afford to do strategically at this point in time?' "Now one of the things that is interesting about the papers I have looked at is the delicate issue of this being seen as a political initiative, as a dangerous form of subversion. And I notice that reassurance is being given to those who might harbour such a deeply wounding suspicion. Children have to be introduced to the realities of the world, to the costs and the benefits, to the fact that nations are all having to compete economically to survive, that industry is essential, various forms of pollution have a certain justification. But nevertheless underneath that there is a view that if this kind of initiative gets looked at critically in that kind of light, too soon, it will not yet have gained enough purchase to have a future. Now, obviously, strategically one gets an initiative like this by going in the "soft way". It is another harmless OECD project for volunteers; those naive people in the schools, who happily do a little bit on the environment and keep everybody happy by saying, 'yes, we are doing something about environmental education, yes' -- and so forth. But, we know enough about the history of innovations, we know that so long as it is at the margin it will get assimilated, ignored or shut out of the school. Either way, it is no good. It has got to be moved into the centre of the curriculum, into the mainstream.

My question to ENSI therefore is, 'what is your strategy and timescale for doing that? Does your investment still at this stage need to be on improving the quality of the work in the schools, or is the emphasis to be shifted to another level? Do you need to do anything about the networks you have got, to strengthen those? Is that where the action is in the next phase?' It is very interesting because here is an initiative, a curriculum development initiative, which has already been going for seven years and there is no reason why it cannot go on and on. Now that is unusual because nearly all curriculum developers have been asked to transform the world in less than five years, sometimes three. Now here an interesting issue arises. Is this a case of an educational initiative, or is this a case of a movement, which is a different thing? Is it a movement, or is it a finite curriculum development? What is the case? What is the strategy of change? There are two tasks: one is to realise the values in a viable operational form in schools -- that is to specify the curriculum in action; and the other one is to secure it -- to root it in the system so that it can grow. Both these aims have to be part of this strategic thinking.

Now, those who are outside evaluators, like me, would just go in and would report everything that is happening, all aspects of it. But participants are mostly inside, probably with some kind of commitment to the enterprise. So for those people, what does evaluation mean? What kind of evaluation? What is it for? Is it an insider evaluation to strengthen the inside, in other words to supplement the product of the action research, which already generates a large amount of formative data? Is that what it is? Or is it insider evaluation for outsiders, to influence them, and, if so, have participants got to be selective in how they represent the work, or not selective? Or are some of them outsiders looking in? You can have an outsider evaluation for insiders, or you can have an outsider evaluation for outsiders. I would say to participants, 'What you do is a question of where you stand in relation to the future of the Initiative and the contribution your evaluation can make to that future.

There is danger in evaluation and there is promise. And there are always unanticipated consequences, although sometimes these are confused by unacknowledged intentions. In designing evaluations, try to be clear about your values and priorities in relation to the values and priorities of the Programme. And about your evaluation strategy. There is high risk and low risk evaluation. A high risk evaluation, which is honest, which reports everything as objectively as possible, may gain credibility for the initiative, or may expose it, perhaps prematurely, to unfair criticism. A low risk evaluation, cosmetic or compromising, may do little harm, but may fail to stimulate the kind of constructive critique that can help the Programme to improve and help others to understand the levels of support needed if the task is to be accomplished.'

The question of priorities is an important one for a group like this to consider. At this stage, for instance, how important is the international nature of this initiative? If it is important, then participants need to pay attention to the extent of their individual contribution to the construction of an overview. Comparable data, common foci and themes will feature prominently in such designs. On the other hand for some, the priority may be influencing own state national policy-making, or developments in a particular locality. It may be for others, that interest in this initiative is not so much an interest in environmental education *per se*, but in exploring the feasibility and fruitfulness of classroom action research, or in the possibilities more generally of ways of improving schools. In that case, it could just as well be a programme in drugs education, or information technology. When I read ENSI documents I see an emphasis on breathing new educational life into atrophied school systems, and I do not care which country we are talking about, that need will be there. This initiative has a very strong educational line, and one that is readily generalisable to the whole process of schooling. This is high ambition, and we know from thirty years of evaluating innovations in schooling that it is the truly educational component that is most resisted, the educational values that get lost as innovations are stripped down for assimilation into the mainstream curriculum culture.

Let me conclude by offering this advice to participants: it is important to be clear about what you are up to in this particular innovation. What is your view of your school system, its functions and its possibilities? Schooling can be seen as a conspiracy by the State against people, or as a conspiracy by educators like us against the State, or as any number of things in between. Where do you stand? All I am saying is that at the outset, when we are going to design evaluations, issues of this kind cannot safely be left off the agenda.

What are you going to do and why are you going to do it?

What is the Initiative a case of?

Do you want an evaluation to help the internal development of the Initiative, or one which is about informing outsiders, either because they are entitled to know and to judge for themselves, or because you feel that unless you begin to do that the Initiative will remain powerless?

Chapter 6

EVALUATING ACTION RESEARCH PROJECTS

by

Bridget Somekh
Centre for Applied Research in Education
University of East Anglia
Norwich, United Kingdom

Reading through the considerable body of papers and books which have emanated from the ENSI Programme, it seems clear that there was a significant shift in OECD policy for ENSI part way through the second phase of funding. ENSI was set up with an infrastructure designed to facilitate development of environmental education on a collaborative, international basis: each participating country was asked to appoint a pedagogical support person and an educational administrator with some influence at the policy level. Each pedagogical support person worked with teachers in a number of schools. In the majority of countries this work took the form of supporting teachers in carrying out action research into curriculum development in environmental education. Teachers tried out ideas with the students in their classrooms and researched their educational outcomes, making changes as and when necessary to improve the learning opportunities for the students. The educational administrators were there in the background to offer advice and maintain good communications with national policy-makers and with the OECD through Kathleen Kelley. However, during 1990, the OECD agenda shifted. A new requirement was introduced: the pedagogic support people were to be asked to carry out an evaluation of the work in schools. The Cromer conference was set up specifically to introduce participants to evaluation methodology. The action research work in schools was, meanwhile, continuing. In a letter to participants on 21/12/90, Kathleen Kelley clarified that at the conference there would be a double agenda:

    i)   "the preparation of reporting research of school initiatives";

    ii)   "to plan the evaluation of Environment and School Initiatives and to structure reporting".

This double agenda posed some problems for the ENSI pedagogical support people which I will try to address in this chapter. Evaluation should be a feature common to all educational programmes, since it provides the means of ensuring an incremental increase in the stock of public knowledge about their conduct and outcomes. The difficulty of the double agenda set out in Kathleen Kelley's letter was not that a single project should be asked to conduct both action research into development and an evaluation, but that *the same individuals* should be asked to lead both of these rather different activities. The effect was to ask those individuals to work with the same people in two different ways, governed by different principles of procedure. In the current political climate this is not an unusual problem, but that does not make it any the easier to handle. It seems to result from an increase in the pressures for accountability placed upon officials of governments and international organisations, coupled with a decrease in the money available to mount separate evaluations. In this chapter I want to draw on my own experience of dealing with a very similar problem in the Pupil Autonomy in Learning with Microcomputers project (PALM).

I will begin by analysing the different assumptions which guide the conduct of evaluation and action research, and then present a document developed in the PALM project as part of a strategy for coping with the problem.

The different assumptions which underpin evaluation and action research

To a certain extent, evaluation and action research can be conceptualised as being on a continuum: detached evaluation being at one end of the scale, participatory action research at the other. There are, of course, different approaches to evaluation, and in order to minimise the problems when one person is carrying out a dual role, it is essential to adopt an evaluation methodology which is well towards the middle of the continuum. In CARE, the traditions of action research and evaluation spring from a common root, in the development work of the Humanities Curriculum Project (HCP) directed by Lawrence Stenhouse, and the HCP evaluation directed by Barry MacDonald. Through the influence of Peter Posch and John Elliott, both of whom worked with Stenhouse, the ENSI Programme has direct links with HCP; and the evaluation methodology presented at the Cromer conference is rooted in the procedures of democratic evaluation which MacDonald developed for HCP (MacDonald, 1974). Hence, there is a consonance of values between the ENSI programme's action research approach to development and the evaluation methodology which the pedagogic support people were being asked to adopt. The problems arising from one person being asked to act as both a facilitator of action research and an evaluator are rooted not in value conflict but in a conflict of roles and relationships, and a conflict of starting points. Thus:

-- evaluators need to stand back from a project and retain their independence;

WHEREAS

-- action research facilitators need to work integrally with the participants in the situation;

-- evaluators observe, consult, empathise and reflect back their perceptions to the participants;

WHEREAS

-- facilitators of action research have a more active, promotional role in supporting and encouraging participants;

-- in an evaluation, the participants do not take the role of evaluators, at least initially;

WHEREAS

-- action research incorporates evaluation as an integral part of the process carried out by participants;

-- for evaluators the tension is: how much to allow themselves to collude with the participants;

WHEREAS

-- for facilitators of action research the tension is: how to prevent the participants from becoming dependent upon them;

-- the role of an evaluator is primarily analytical with a secondary developmental purpose;

WHEREAS

-- the role of an action research facilitator is to promote an integrated process of development and analysis;

-- the importance of evaluation for action research projects.

Although there are problems which arise from asking the same person to carry out the dual role of evaluator and action research facilitator, there are also reasons why this can be an advantage. Action research incorporates evaluation as part of a cyclical process of question raising, data collection, analysis, evaluation, planning and development: as a result, when outsiders conduct evaluations of action research projects there is an overlap of roles and some duplication of effort. This, too, can be stressful for all concerned. More often the alternative to an evaluation carried out by the action research facilitator is not another kind of evaluation, but no evaluation at all. To an extent, I assume largely for political reasons, this was the case in ENSI. It would have been difficult for the OECD to impose a team of independent evaluators on all the participating countries, so instead they were offered the *option* to participate in a formal policy review. However, only 6 countries decided to take up this option. The 'insider' evaluations carried out by the pedagogic support people were, therefore, the only evaluations to be carried out in the majority of countries.

Without an evaluation of any kind, action research projects face:

-- difficulties in carrying out a cross-case analysis of a number of linked action research projects, in order to establish trends and hypotheses by means of cross-case comparisons;

-- difficulties in effectively reporting the action research carried out by participants on a part time basis;

-- difficulties in accessing power and exercising influence on policy makers.

These difficulties, as well as the benefits to be gained from an additional 'insider' evaluation, can be illustrated through the work of the Pupil Autonomy in Learning with Microcomputers Project (PALM), 1988-90. In PALM, a team comprising myself as coordinator, three teacher-facilitators and a full time secretary supported over 100 teachers in 24 schools, carrying out action research to improve their use of computers as tools for teaching and learning. As an action research project, PALM was essentially local and domestic: without an evaluation, it was difficult for the teachers, as participant researchers, to go beyond their own frame of reference in interpreting their individual cases. There was also a problem for the project, as a whole, in moving from the analysis of individual case studies to analysis across cases: the teachers were much more interested in writing about their own work, than in collaborating with the central team to carry out cross-case analysis and reporting. Furthermore, it was difficult for the PALM teachers to take full responsibility for disseminating their work: fifty-six teachers wrote forty case studies for the PALM *Teachers' Voices* series (as sole authors or collaboratively), but their action research projects had been undertaken in addition to their full time teaching jobs; they had relatively little time for writing and most of them had little or no prior experience of communicating their ideas through written publication. They needed somebody else to share the burden of reporting the project's work, to ensure it was done effectively; for their research to make any impact, they also needed support from people with access to those in power and the ability to influence policy. The dilemma for myself and the PALM facilitators was that we had to take some responsibility for reporting while, at the same time, ensuring that the teachers maintained control over their research and over how it was reported. When we were asked by the local education authority inspectors to carry out an evaluation, this provided a rationale for a more equal sharing of the burden of reporting, although inevitably it also sharpened up this dilemma of ownership and control.

There is a further problem in the effective dissemination of the outcomes of action research projects and their impact on policy, which relates to the style of reporting. In a recent paper, Herbert Altrichter (in press) describes how the action research movement in German-speaking countries, which flourished after 1968, was very vulnerable to marginalisation by researchers in the established positivist tradition, because of its manner of reporting. Papers were written in a tentative and reflective style, raising questions and problematising issues, rather than being assertive and definite and instructional. An evaluator may be able to guard against this vulnerability by mediating between the reflexive voice of action research and the pragmatic needs of policy-makers. One of the participants at the Cromer conference articulated this need when he spoke of the importance of representing the work of the project effectively to the Minister of Education in his country. He needed to construe his role more widely than as a facilitator of teachers' action research if he was to operate effectively in this political context; paradoxically, the rather less teacher-centred concerns he was being forced to prioritise as an evaluator might help him to raise the minister's awareness of the teachers' work in ENSI.

An action research approach to evaluation

Is there a way of re-construing the dual role of action research facilitator and evaluator? I have said that there seems to be a conflict of roles and responsibilities, and of starting points, between the two endeavours; but I have also suggested that evaluation is important in overcoming some difficulties commonly experienced by action research projects. In a political context with a strong demand for accountability, but limited available funding, projects like PALM and ENSI are more and more likely to find that individuals are required to undertake such a dual role. One way forward may be to take an action research approach to evaluation: in other words, to re-construe evaluation as action research at the system and policy level.

I start from an assumption that evaluation takes place within a social and political context which it intends to influence. This is a value position which is broadly consonant with the CARE approach to evaluation put forward at the Cromer conference, but there is some difference of emphasis. In a previous paper (Somekh, 1990) I have built upon this assumption to develop a model of evaluation which aims, first and foremost:

-- to explain and illuminate the mixed motives of individuals;

-- to free the flow of communications;

-- to 'e-valuate' by analysing/constructing a coherent set of shared values.

Such an approach to evaluation is collaborative, and re-generative. Its rationale lies in Giddens' notion of the duality of structure, in which social activity can be understood in terms of *both* human agency and systemic structures (1984). The implication of Giddens' theory of structuration, is to allow not only for the causal explanations, which underpin the analysis of social events in terms of structures and organisations, but also for the multi-layered reflexivity which seeks to understand social events in terms of the conflicting demands of both routinised and conscious human actions. In terms of this kind of social theory, an evaluator needs *at the same time* to have sufficient detachment to understand the broader operation of power beyond the frame of reference of the individual, and to collaborate with individuals at all levels in the system to reconstruct the system itself. Giddens says that, "to formulate a coherent account of human agency and of structure demands ... a very considerable conceptual effort" -- but his formulation offers a resolution to the conflicts endemic in the dual role of action research facilitator and evaluator. The facilitator/evaluator participates in exploring and illuminating the mixed motives and differing values of individuals to each other, and in so doing collaborates in freeing the flow of communications. In partnership with the participants, the evaluator supports the process of reconstructing a coherent set of shared values. The reason why people so often complain of the unfairness and irrationality of systems, whether they be countries, or schools, or whatever..., is because each person in the system takes decisions according to his or her own values; when there are no shared values, the decisions taken by one individual must seem irrational to someone who would have taken completely different decisions based on a different set of values. Through an evaluation process which supports the development and continuing regeneration of a shared value system, the apparent irrationality of structures and organisations is reduced.

This approach to evaluation, like action research itself, suits the intrinsic concepts of environmental education as described by John Elliott in Chapter 2:

"Environmental problems are full of 'value-complexity'. Different sets of human values will tend to conflict and problem solutions will tend to reflect different preferences in prioritising values ... Environment problems raise controversial value issues. They are not simply technical problems."

It also fits with Michela Mayer's vision, set out in Chapter 4, of a kind of evaluation:

"intended to gather and not to discard, to comprise and not to select, a formative evaluation of all those involved, students, teachers and researchers alike."

Such an evaluation engages with individuals at many layers in the system, adopting collaborative strategies which set out to reconstruct the social order, in however small a way. Ministers, government officials, OECD officers, ENSI national coordinators, teachers, students, parents and other members of the local community are all potential collaborative partners and informants in the evaluation. This approach seems consonant with the concern in many of the ENSI projects to involve the whole community in environmental initiatives: in it there is no dividing line between an action research process, construed as local and "grass roots", in which facilitators support the development work of participants, -- and something different called evaluation in which an "independent" outsider collects observations and participants' perceptions, in order to interpret the Programme and its participants to policy-makers and the public. I think it would be a pity to approach a Programme such as ENSI in that way.

I think there is an alternative -- which is to say, 'We have been engaging in action research -- now, how can we take the concepts and methodologies of action research and operate, still bringing the teachers with us, collaboratively, at a much higher level in terms of the system of our country.'

Finding an evaluation strategy: an example drawn from practice

In the PALM project, we did not have the same opportunities as some of the ENSI teams to operate at the national policy level, but we worked closely with our main sponsors, the National Council for Educational Technology, and with the Information Technology inspectors in the three local education authorities which were our co-sponsors. During the second year of the project we were asked repeatedly by one of these inspectors, "How will I know if the £40,000 I have spent on the PALM project would have been better spent not doing action research but choosing another, alternative way of working?" This question could only be answered by carrying out an evaluation of our work. However, it would clearly be impossible to conduct the kind of comparative study which the inspector had in mind. The problem seemed insoluble until we reflected on the political imperative which lay behind his question. What he needed was reassurance that his money had been well spent. The kind of evaluation with which he was most familiar was an analysis of the performance of an experimental group against a control group, but if we could persuade him of the trustworthiness of an alternative methodology, we might equally well satisfy his need.

As a first step we produced a position paper designed as an educative document. It began by formulating a statement of the values which underpinned the project's development work, which we called *The PALM Operating Philosophy*, and went on to set out tools and criteria which could be used to evaluate its work on the basis of these values. The document embodied a strategy: it was designed to further the aims of an action research approach to evaluation. It was intended to be used to stimulate discussion with participants and policy-makers which would:

-- explain and illuminate their own values as well as those of the PALM project;

-- be a forum for communicating our intentions as to the conduct of the PALM evaluation;

-- provide the basis for analysing/constructing a coherent set of shared values, in the light of which we could write and they could subsequently read the report.

The document is set out in full below.

Working in a way which did not fracture our collaborative relationship with the PALM teachers, we tried to influence the thinking of the three inspectors, while at the same time answering the practical, value-for-money question we had been asked. We chose a smart design for the front of the report, incorporating the project's palm tree logo, and used a language which would communicate our ideas in a reasonably straight-forward way. We had to face up to the possibility that the project had been working according to a set of values which might be quite different from the values assumed by the inspectors. Evaluation is by definition a matter of value judgement. What we wanted to avoid was a situation where we reported on the project in the light of one set of values and the inspectors read the report in the light of a quite different set of values. The 'Operating Philosophy' of the PALM project was derived from an analysis of our methods of working with teachers. Talking through that document with the inspectors was a form of action research, in that it developed mutual understanding. What happened at a crucial meeting was that they readily endorsed the statement of values and this led to a full discussion of the implications of these values for the methods we could or could not adopt in carrying out an evaluation of the project's work. It was clear to the inspectors as much as to us that a comparative evaluation of an experimental group and a control group would not only be impossible at this late stage, but would be contrary to the principles upon which we were operating. We were proposing to gather extra data and produce an additional evaluation report, but the majority of the tools and criteria which we specified for the evaluation were an integral part of the action research process. The additions were some in-depth interviewing (to be carried out on our behalf by visiting consultants) and a questionnaire which we asked every teacher to complete. So, we did have to do a small amount of extra data collection specifically for the evaluation, but it was possible to do this without taking up too much extra time, or infringing the ethical code which guided our work with teachers. By means of this strategy we carried out an evaluation which was supportive, rather than destructive, of our role as facilitators of the teachers' action research.

In the PALM project we used this strategy with inspectors from local education authorities and officers of the principal funding organisation. I have also used the same strategy at a different level in another project, with civil servants responsible for administering national policy. In a project like ENSI, with access to policy-makers at different levels, such a strategy can be used to carry out action research, of a kind, at the national policy-making level. Such an approach may be crucial in order to ensure that the work of a project is adequately disseminated. In other words, cannot the way in which evaluators negotiate with policy-makers and choose what papers to feed them, and in which they set up meetings and present documents for discussions, actually be a kind of action research? And if evaluators do not do those things, are they not actually producing evaluation reports that nobody reads -- because they have not interacted sufficiently with policy-makers to make the report readable, by creating its functionality?

As the PALM project enters its final six months of funding we need to bring the question of how to judge its success sharply into focus. The action-research methodology employed by PALM ensures a continuing process of self-evaluation for all teachers and team members (and many pupils). In effect no separate evaluation is necessary. However, it is important that there is clarification of the issues to inform discussions between members of the PALM team, representatives of the four sponsors and the PALM

Director. It is important too for the PALM team members to clarify these issues as we move into the major writing up phase.

This document sets out evaluation tools and criteria for PALM, in the context of the project's operating philosophy and aims. This is important in order to ensure that the project's success is judged in the light of its aims and aspirations.

Operating philosophy of PALM

i) The curriculum is constructed within the teaching/learning process on the basis of a range of resources selected as appropriate by the teacher. Curriculum policies provide no more than the framework within which this process curriculum operates. Therefore curriculum change consists in change in individual classroom practice.

ii) I.T. is a tool which has the power to enrich the learning experience when it is integrated with the curriculum. The teacher plays a crucial role in setting the educational context for pupils' learning experiences with I.T.

iii) The success of any innovation depends upon practitioners' making it their own by relating the theory of the innovation to their own values and practices.

iv) Effective learning involves pupils in asking questions, investigating and experimenting, and drawing conclusions on the basis of reflection.

v) In order to support change, the management infrastructure needs to encourage a culture in which it is acceptable to experiment, take risks and learn from both successes and failures. This style of management is based on a concept of partnership in educational responsibility.

vi) Management of innovation is an innovation in itself. Managers need to engage in their own process of reflection leading to planned action. This is true at all the levels of the support infrastructure (including, of course, the PALM team).

vii) Teacher ownership of innovation presupposes a free exchange of ideas in a broad professional discourse. Therefore, PALM teacher-researchers have an important role in the dissemination process, both as writers of reports and leaders at meetings and workshops.

Aims of PALM

i) to work in partnership with teachers to research the role of information technology in developing pupil autonomy in learning;

ii) to investigate the effectiveness of action-research as a means of teacher professional development in the I.T. innovation.

Evaluation tools of PALM

It would not be possible to evaluate PALM's success on the basis of quantitative data such as the number of schools and teachers involved, frequency of computer use and range of software used, although data of this kind is being collected and will be useful as background information. The quality of PALM's performance can be more effectively measured by qualitative criteria such as those set out in the following section. The appropriate evaluation tools then grow naturally from the process of self-evaluation inherent in PALM's activities. For example:

i) PALM teachers' writing demonstrates the quality of their research and development work;

ii) PALM team members' writing represents the project's processes and achievements;

iii) in some cases PALM pupils' writing gives accounts of their work within PALM;

iv) transcripts of key meetings, including the two PALM conferences, reflect the quality of teachers' thinking;

v) interviews with a sample of Heads, senior staff, teachers and pupils elicit their perceptions;

vi) a questionnaire to all PALM teachers collects some quantitative data and a broad spread of perceptions on key issues;

vii) the project's outcomes will be clearly set out in the Shared Perspectives series, which will draw out common themes and knowledge from the whole range of the project's writing.

Evaluation Criteria of PALM

Effective educational change takes place over time. In this sense PALM is an ambitious project which introduces action-research as a strategy to support long-term educational change. In two years PALM can only be a beginning.

The evaluation criteria set out here are those which we consider appropriate for judging the project's success in pursuit of its ambitious aims. For convenience they are divided into "process criteria" and "dissemination criteria." These two kinds of criteria are closely related since the "dissemination" of PALM entails representing the research outcomes in terms of educational processes.

1. Process Criteria

a) *Relating to teachers*

-- achievement of a deeper understanding of the nature of pupils' learning using microcomputers -- particularly, but not only, autonomous learning;

-- an increase in confidence to experiment with a range of microcomputer applications to enrich learning for pupils;

-- achievement of a deeper understanding of their own role in curriculum development -- particularly, but not only, in relation to microcomputers;

-- development of the ability to reflect on their practice and relate it to their own educational theories -- particularly, but not only, in their use of microcomputers.

b)   *Relating to pupils (of all ages, abilities, gender and race):*

-- an increase in confidence in their use of microcomputers;

-- an increase in autonomous learning experiences in their use of microcomputers;

-- development of greater ability to discuss the value and limitations of using microcomputers for different purposes.

c)   *Relating to schools:*

-- an increase in the opportunities for professional dialogue between staff particularly, but not only, in relation to use of microcomputers;

-- creation of a context supportive of experimentation and change -- particularly, but not only, in relation to microcomputers;

-- those with responsibility for leading I.T. development within the school increasing their understanding of their role and improving their ability to support colleagues;

-- the setting up of structures to enable PALM activities to continue after the funded phase of the project comes to an end.

d)   *Relating to the three LEAs:*

-- use of PALM's accumulated knowledge and experience to inform and enrich other I.T. related support;

-- making PALM's accumulated knowledge and experience available to other practitioners;

-- establishment of structures to enable PALM teachers to play a role in the support of I.T. development in the future.

2. Dissemination Criteria

a)   *The PALM writing in the "first debate" relating to autonomy in learning with microcomputers":*

-- presents the project's accumulated knowledge and understanding of the relationship between microcomputer use and the development of pupil autonomy in learning;

-- reflects the variety and quality of the teachers' research;

-- provides a range of materials suitable for different audiences and purposes, with adequate guidance on "reading routes".

b)   *The PALM writing in the "second debate" relating to teacher professional development in I.T.:*

--   presents the project's accumulated knowledge and understanding of the way in which PALM's action-research methodology supports the professional development of teachers using microcomputers;

--   reflects the variety and quality of the project's research into its methods of support;

--   provides a range of materials suitable for different audiences and purposes, with adequate guidance on "reading routes".

c)   *The PALM writings and presentations, overall:*

--   make its processes and methodology accessible to -- policy-makers at the LEA and national level;

--   Advisory Teachers of I.T.;

--   I.T. coordinators and responsibility post-holders in schools;

--   the academic research community;

--   enable those PALM teachers who have registered to gain academic accreditation.

(PALM Team, February 1990)

References

ALTRICHTER, H. (1986), "Visiting two worlds: an excursion into the methodological jungle including an optional evening's entertainment at the Rigour Club", *Cambridge Journal of Education*, 16: 2, pp. 131-142, UK.

ALTRICHTER, H. (in press) paper on the action research tradition in German speaking countries, to be published in a book edited by Robin McTaggart at Deakin University, Australia.

ELLIOTT, J. (1989), *Environmental Education in Europe: Innovation, Marginalisation, or Assimilation?* Report on ENSI commissioned by OECD/CERI, Paris.

MACDONALD, B. (1974), "Evaluation and the control of education", In MACDONALD and WALKER, (eds), *Innovation Evaluation Research and the Problems of Control,* CARE, University of East Anglia, UK.

MAYER, M. "Evaluating the outcomes of environment and school initiatives", unpublished paper of the ENSI Project, OECD, Paris.

PALM, (1990), "How will we know if PALM is a success?" Working document of the *Pupil Autonomy in Learning with Microcomputers Project,* CARE, University of East Anglia, UK.

SOMEKH, B. (1990), "The evaluation of teaching with computers", *The CTISS File*, no 10. Computers in Teaching Initiative Support Service, University of Oxford, 13 Banbury Road, Oxford, OX2 6NN, UK.

Chapter 7

THE CONTENT OF PROGRAMME EVALUATION

by

Saville Kushner
Centre for Applied Research in Education
University of East Anglia
Norwich, United Kingdom

"...her old role had been that of an observer of roles, and now she wanted to attempt the opposite, not portraiture, which presupposed a subject, but reconstruction, raking together scattered leaves to build up the subject of her portrait, never being sure, all the while, whether the leaves she was heaping up actually belonged together, or whether, in fact, she wasn't ultimately making a self-portrait, in short a crazy enterprise..." Friedrich Durrenmatt, *The Assignment*, Picador, 1988.

There was nothing 'brief' about the briefing papers. These were a large bundle of documents I was handed to help prepare my presentation at the Cromer conference. The theory, I supposed, was that familiarity would breed relevance -- or, at least, acceptability. The reality was that the bundle of papers succeeded in breeding fear and confusion. What I was afraid of was having to get to grips with other people's complexity without having the chance to talk to them about it first. What I was confused about was that when I finally came to look at these documents ENSI looked familiar to me as a programme of research and development, when it ought really to have grown in mystery since it was clearly a complex business covering such a diverse range of cultures. My view was clearly being manipulated through these documents. How was I to make sense of the fact that I could make sense of ENSI before I even spoke with people involved in it?

This was an evaluative act, reviewing documents to improve my judgement about what I ought to be saying. Educationalists are compulsive meaning-makers and as soon as data is available, analysis and judgement commences. But it pays to stay sceptical about your ability to make judgements before you have at least spoken to people involved. In any case, I found the briefing papers untrustworthy as a source. Here was data -- reports of conferences, reports written by children, biographical data on programme 'leaders', scholarly papers, lists of programme members, etc. Were these the 'contents' of my small evaluation?

Here, then, was an opportunity to engage the conference on the question of what are the appropriate contents of an evaluation. My decision was to select examples from these documents and to present them to the conference participants as a kind of case study of ENSI -- a case made up of this collection of 'scattered leaves'. The result ought to be a combination of content and reconstruction, for the two can barely be separated. With their own knowledge of the programme participants would be protected from the worst effects of my ignorance and prejudice and might have an experiential and cognitive framework with which to judge the quality of my reconstruction.

What follows are some of the extracts I used along with a flavour of the commentary I gave as I presented them on an overhead projector. I have added my own personal reflections about the case I study -- what I was thinking then as I talked to participants in the conference session and something of what I think about my attempt now some months after I gave the presentation. These reflections appear in italics.

Slide 1: A list of programme participants

Australia, Victoria	a	Ian Robottom	Deakin University
Austria	A	Günthar Pfaffenwimmer	Ministry of Education
	a	Peter Posch	University of Klagenfurt
	a	Franz Rauch	
Belgium	I	Claude Bustin	Mission Form Cont
	I	Dirk Coolsaet	Coordinator
	I	Luc Henau	Inspector Geography/Ecology
Canada	c	Lyn Burton	Environment Canada
	a	Catherine Beattie	McMaster University
Denmark	a	Christian Christensen	Coordinator
Eire	I	Sean Morrow	Pedagogical Advisor
Finland	A	Reijo Laukkanen	National Board of Education
	a	Kyosti Kurtakko	Pedagogical Support
France	a	Maryse Clary	
Germany	A?	Dietmar Bolscho	Coordinator
Hungary	I	Judith Szunyogh	Senior Advisor
Italy	aA	Michela Mayer	CEDE
	aA	Bruno Losito	CEDE
Japan	a	Noviyuki Nasu	University of the Air
	a	Kazuo Watanabe	Ministry of Education
Netherlands	a	Maarten Pieters	National Institute for Curriculum Development
	aA	Bert van Beek	Innovation Institute
	aA	Harrie Eijkelhof	Utrecht University
Norway	aA	Astrid Sandas	Ministry of Education and Research
	aA	Per Bjorn Foros	Pedagogical Support
Portugal		a woman to be announced	
Scotland	?	Colin McAndrew	OECD Project Officer
Spain	ac	Ramon Lara Tebar	University of Madrid
Sweden	c	Harriet Axelsson	Expert
	cAa	Olle Nordgren	National Board of Education
Switzerland	?	Regula Kyburz-Graber	Coordinator
United States	c	John R Paulk	TVA
	c	Lynn Michael Hodges	TVA
Yugoslavia	a	Barica Pozarnik	Ljubljana University
	a	Majda Skerbinek	Ljubljana University

I policy evaluation participation; **a** academic; **A** administration; **c** ?

Before the conference we held planning meetings in CARE and those of us who were unfamiliar with the programme tried to speculate about ENSI. We had a list of people who would attend the conference and, lacking more incisive data, we resorted to stereotyping them. There are letters alongside the names on the list. A small 'a' stands for 'academic'; a large 'A' stands for 'Administrator'; an 'I' stands for ... well, I forget. There are question marks and against some people there are large and small 'a's. We were trying to work out the balance of professional 'types' -- about the character of the programme as represented by this group. Was this a group more concerned about management and control or more concerned with theorising about educational aspects -- do those divisions make any sense? And who was the "woman to be announced?"

We had additional data to bring to bear -- our personal record made up of previous experience. We had worked in a European programme before and we knew a little about France -- there is a British stereotype about French administration. Denmark has a stereotype for the British, too -- Denmark was hostile to European-wide programming or whatever. We had a view that given the interlacing of research institutions and the state it was difficult to engage in politically independent research in Germany. So here we had tiny morsels of data which interacted with prior experience, prejudices, half-remembered images. These were strangers coming to the conference, but we worked the little data we had on them to try to reduce their strangeness.

Is it, then, important to see ENSI as an international project -- or rather, what is the significance of its internationality? I am already complicit in eroding cultural differences by colluding in this crude stereotyping -- by imagining, for example, that an 'academic' in one country means the same thing in all others. But this programme does appear to be coordinated -- in fact, I have met the people doing some of the coordination -- and they must face this tension all the time. So this must be an issue for the programme.

As I show this slide it causes a lot of humour -- the 'woman to be announced' arrived and is here. She is a well-known person in this international peer group. But I also sense that treating such a list as data -- as a 'content' of an evaluation -- may be unfamiliar and, itself, a reason for bemusement. But it does generate some ribaldry -- the stereotypes are already giving way to a more human sense of these people. The list of names was undoubtedly useful and stimulated some analytical thinking for my evaluation -- but it also served to obscure. Documentation is a poor vehicle for personality -- more so for laughter.

Things could get a little tricky from here, I recall thinking. This next slide is a fragment from someone's work -- I think the 'someone' is in this conference and this could be embarrassing for him. Using his diagram can too easily look like choosing a 'sitting target' -- setting him up. To cross over the line from evaluative description to voyeurism is as compelling and role-changing as crossing into a city's red-light district. But I have made my slides and if I don't use them I have no other presentation.

The school in this diagram, I explain, lies at the centre of a network of advice, information and political action -- with links to the media, to political institutions and to research institutions. Here is a model of the politicised school. The uppermost text in the diagram says "Investigations in the environment" and political action appears to flow from that via the efforts of pupils.

This does not reflect what we routinely think about curriculum development projects -- certainly in Britain those dotted lines suggesting 'action paths' would frighten many politicians and even parents. The scale of the ambition represented here (and mirrored elsewhere in ENSI documentation) goes well beyond the elaboration of a new school discipline. This diagram has implications for the reform of schooling and for a reconceptualisation of the role of schools in their communities.

But, as data, this diagram starts the mind on the process of analysis and one of the ways that happens is by creating metaphors in the mind. Data collection and analysis do not happen one after the other as many writers and evaluation designs suggest -- they come together. Some analysis is an act of will, a striving against intellectual inertia, trying to get the mind to take this data somewhere it has not been before. But a lot of analysis is involuntary -- like when those metaphors 'come to mind' seemingly of their own accord. The pupil-as-police officer was one metaphor that arrived in this way.

At the bottom of that slide is a paragraph taken from another paper that lay among my documents. "Responsible action ...", it says, and describes a process through which pupils held shopkeepers to account for acting properly towards the environment. There is a morality, here, and, somewhere, the appeal to an authority which so far I had not found properly cited. And, too, there was the clear image of some very controversial activities going on. It is not hard to imagine some shopkeepers raising an eyebrow when being told what to do by schoolteachers through the agency of children.

But then, I talk from a knowledge of Britain (England, in fact) and things may be different in other countries which may be more tolerant of such interference in the community's business. Is this anecdote reported here -- and the model represented by the diagram -- expected to hold their meanings across national boundaries? And what of boundaries within a country? I was beginning to sense, in ENSI documents, a model of intimate and benign communication drawn from a vision of the small village being forcibly translated in the more complex and controversial territory of modern urban communities. But that just serves to raise the question -- what are the visions which drive this programme?

Slide 2: A diagram from a scholarly paper (by Peter Posch)

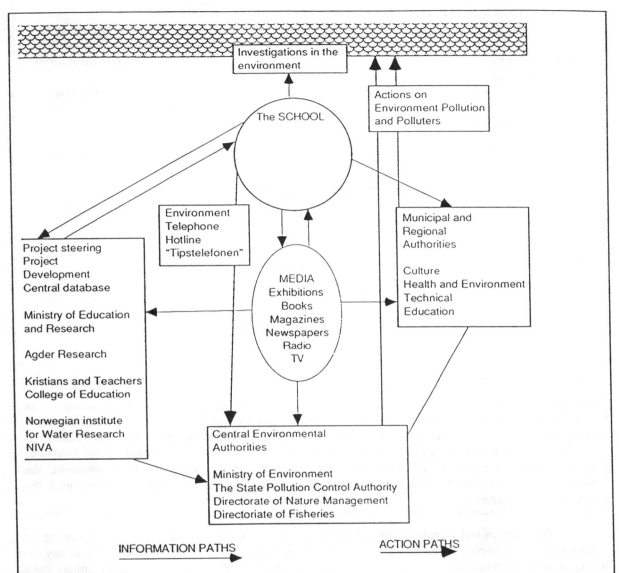

This illustration shows the lines of interaction between school projects and local and central institutions and authorities. The purpose of the network is to establish routines for cooperation across organizational boundaries in favour of environmental education as well as collection of data and data-based action.   (....)

Responsible action to improve environmental conditions

A few examples my illustrate also this task: In an Austrian elementary school, students investigated the use of plastic bags and asked shop-keepers to offer also cloth or burlap bags at a moderate price. A second enquiry was held a few weeks later and the pupils sent thank-you-letters to those shop-keepers who had taken positive action (Haas 1990).

Slide 3: Open and closed information

```
        ORGANISATION FOR                        RESTRICTED
    CO-OPERATION AND DEVELOPMENT
                                          Paris, drafted: 6th November 1990
    _____
                                            dist.: 15th November 1990
      Centre for Education Research
            and Innovation                            Or. Eng.
    _____

            CERI/EI/90.3



                ENVIRONMENT AND SCHOOL INITIATIVES
                    ACTION RESEARCH SEMINAR

                          June 4-9 1990

                          Frascati, Italy

                Summary and Conclusions of the meeting

                      (Note by the Secretariat)

    _____

    The results of the project were in both cases exhibited in the assembly hall of the school.  The
    exhibition was open to other students, parents and the general public.  Later the exhibitions were
    transported to the city library where they were shown for a couple of weeks.  The school council as
    well as the parents were invited to the opening of the exhibition.  Local newspapers were invited to
    an information meeting during which the representatives of the Ministry of Environment, the
    National Board of General Education and the city of Pori also familiarised themselves with the
    outcome of the project.
```

There are mixed signals coming from the conference group. A lot of people are leaning over talking to their neighbours -- some, obviously, because they cannot hear or understand. I am, in any case, having to read out what is on each slide since people at the back of this very large group simply cannot see. I still sense some of that bemusement and there is still some humour in the group. Some of my slides (this last one, in fact) expose, in some small way, some of the programme leaders and that always buys favour with the 'troops'. But I am trying to read responses to my presentation -- not just for feedback on my performance, but to learn something about these people. Now I am here, on my feet, pointing to the screen, I am talking about the real work and hopes and failures of real people.

This slide almost speaks for itself. It contains two extracts -- one, the cover of a report of an ENSI conference in Frascati; the other an extract from an ENSI case study talking about how the results of a piece of research carried out by children had been reported. The latter extract shows how, at the ground level, information was disseminated as widely as possible -- a travelling exhibition, local newspapers, Ministry of the Environment and more. The first extract, in contrast, which relates to the programme level -- the ENSI policy level -- is marked "Restricted". It is, nonetheless, an action research

132

seminar and it is sponsored by CERI which is paid for by the general public of many countries. *This raises the kind of laughter which tells me the irony is neither lost nor was it previously unnoticed.*

Theorising about ENSI now takes another turn. These two extracts represent windows into ENSI -- ways of knowing about it. The window which presents the practical face of the programme and which exposes to public view the life and work of the less powerful (teachers and pupils) is a relatively open window. The one that might expose the political face of the programme and the work of the relatively more powerful is drawn with the curtain of secrecy. What is the political theory of this programme? What are its political aspirations? What and who can be challenged -- and who is to be protected from public challenge?

Slide 4: An organisational perspective

(from CERI report on Frascati workshop)

AUSTRIA

a) *Organisational Structure*

Eleven schools will form the basic network from different parts of Austria; levels of schools range from elementary to secondary vocational and student's ages are from 6-19 years.

Support personnel include the co-ordinator in the Ministry of Education and two support persons. The budget set aside for this work is $1,000/year/teacher; the salary of the co-ordinator, costs of seminars.

Communication within the network will be organised through three meetings a year to plan activities, exchange information, and for post-event reflection.

AUSTRALIA

a) *Organisational Structure*

Plan to involve seven to twelve schools (students of 11-18 years) in the State of Victoria who are using action-research. The co-ordinator for Australia is involved in policy development in the central curriculum branch for environmental education for the Ministry of Education, Victoria, and promotes professional development activities for teachers as well as curriculum development.

ITALY

a) *Organisational Structure*

The Centro Europeo dell'Educazione (CEDE) is the main co-ordinator of the Italian network of 22 project schools. The CEDE is advised by a Scientific Committee composed of representatives from: the National Research Board, the University of Rome, the Ministry of Education, the Ministry of the Environment, the Inspectorate and from environment associations.

NETHERLANDS

a) *Organisational Structure*

The main thrust of the project is to incorporate environmental education into the core curriculum. The school system and each individual school is responsible, and therefore central efforts consists in creating conditions in which schools can take their own responsibilities. This is known as a "support" function and is carried out by:

Group No. 2 (Denmark, Germany, Japan, Sweden, Switzerland)

Questions discussed were whether societal pressure is towards a conservative or a transforming attitude, how school board and schools gather information, especially regarding the transaction view to the curriculum (the transaction position conceives of education as developing the learner's capacity to solve problems);

In a number of cases, decentralisation can reduce freedom; responsibility for environmental education is shifted to the local authorities and if there is lack of financing or of interest, environmental education will not be encouraged in schools. A general legal framework may be necessary to open schools to society to facilitate environment and school initiatives.

This is, of course, a live presentation I am doing -- but live in more than one way. Much of the presentation is my theorising about what is supposed to be the 'content' I am throwing up on the overhead slides. That process is almost spontaneous -- I recall reasons for selecting these extracts but I had little time to prepare an analysis of them. So I am thinking on my feet -- and thinking aloud to the group about the process of selection of data to use as slides. I have to review my theorising at intervals for it to work.

Data, I explain, is coming in to me as I read through these documents noticing and ignoring bits and pieces. It does not necessarily come in a convenient flow -- as with a story. There are causal relationships, for example, and I find myself looking at effects long before I come across data on causes; there is one half of a political relationship and the other half remains to be discovered. So far I have looked at some of the practical aspects of the programme -- who people are, what they do. I have no sense of what ENSI is as a programme.

This slide shows an extract of an account of the organisational structure of ENSI by country. The first thing I noticed was that the countries are set out in alphabetical order. Although Austria and Italy share a common border, in this document they are separated by Australia. Does this suggest the arbitrary hand of bureaucracy? Is this too rational -- or is it not significant at all for my purposes? It cannot be insignificant -- to construct the document in this way was a deliberate act, I assume.

Visually this information might carry messages. Each country has roughly the same sized paragraph and a similar range of information. They are all reported in English. As I move from Austria (thinking that the word "network" seems to be cropping up a lot in ENSI documentation) to Australia I do so with the same voice in my head. This information appears to be telling me that countries are different but it actually succeeds in telling me that they are basically the same. Here is that same issue about the programme's internationalism. There is a meta-language at play, here, a language that falls between cultures. By this time I am getting a sense of the data I am working with itself falling between the cultures.

Looking at the raw data, kick-starts some analysis. I notice that the first three countries mention Ministries (Education and Environment). I get the sense of a top-heaviness about the programme -- or more evidence for very high level ambitions. That running theme of ambitious scale of people's thinking is again reflected, this time in the Netherlands where the information talks of incorporating environmental education into the core curriculum. This is the inner sanctum of any curriculum and it does not admit non-disciplinary subjects readily. Is there a political strategy for achieving this? Is Environmental Education a contemporary version of a subject discipline?

In Italy, we learn that the main coordinators of the national programme (CEDE) is "advised" by a government 'scientific committee', and now my own prior knowledge and prejudices are brought to bear as I speculate on the role science plays as an authority system backing up the programme.

At the bottom of this slide is an extract from a report of a Paris ENSI conference (headed *Group No. 2*). There is more data on language, here. The English is more or less correct -- but it is very formal. It does not flow well and does not have a natural feel to it. An English person understands it because she understands the words it uses -- not because she understands the underlying attempt at expression. And, too, the raw data raises interesting questions -- prompts me to theorise a little more about the political aspects of the ENSI programme. The phrase "decentralisation can reduce freedom" stands out for me -- it runs counter to many rhetorics both of the left- and right-wings. Where does ENSI stand on democracy -- with strong value placed on local action but equally strong compulsions (apparently) to mix in with Ministries and to play the bigger game.

135

Slide 5:   Case study data

(from ESI Phase 1 case studies)

There was plenty of time to pick reed mace, catch frogs by hand each lunch and talk to a man who was setting his eel traps at the mouth of the stream. The man described how the lake was almost emptied of fish nowadays, whereas formerly a lot of eel were caught in the lake.

A local natural-history description of Godstrup Lake was a valuable source during the course. According to this work the most likely theory is that the origin of the lake is a kettlehole (left by dead ice from the last glacial age). Since the lake is located far west of the supposed main stationary line (limit of the last glaciation) there are two probable geological explanations; *i)* the kettlehole is caused by a local thrust of the ice cap during a temporary cold spell, or *ii)* the main stationary line has been further west than originally supposed.

The doubts concerning the origin of the lake provided us with the opportunity to illustrate for the class that scientific theories are not necessarily final truths, but probable assumptions, which may be changed in the process of acquiring new knowledge.

In the meantime, the centre has grown rapidly. The number of visitors rose from 5,000 (1976) to more than 27,000 in 1987. So it was no longer possible to run the institution only by students. The town took over the financing of a permanent job at the centre and in addition some people were offered temporary jobs who otherwise would be unemployed. In the last years the students and the adults have been expanding their work in the field of nature -- and environment protection and a large part of their time is used for preparing instructional material for teachers and students of other schools to assist them in conducting field work. Five hundred teachers and 3,000 students used this material in 1987.

That the pupils not only obtain knowledge of the actual facts, but also of the possibility of expressing ideas, wishes and utopias.

But the schools involved in WAP are not only "service agencies'; they often obtain valuable attitudinal results, especially the removal of certain mental obstacles for a student's deeper awareness of his power of changing things around him.

Another result we are proud of is involving the local population in environmental reflection, in several phases and at various levels:

Before the students go out into the field, the mayor makes a public announcement stating time schedule, aims of the research and an invitation to the citizens to assist the students.

It was really fund to assume the attitudes of an adult when a town councillor was to be interviewed; it was interesting to discover the old farms; after all, a library means a lot more than boredom, and parents and grandparents know so much about "Amadora ...". Some difficulties arose: What are we going to ask? How are we going to look for the information among so many newspapers and so many books? And what about the nasty neighbour, who refuses to answer our inquiry? And the old noblewoman who had promised to receive us and then didn't? A group of "enlightened" girls had even to abandon their work theme. "Amadora in the romantic literature of the past century" due to the difficulties in obtaining information, and they had to replace it by another theme.

An understanding that the relation between nature and society is not preordained, but that the destiny of nature is determined by the way society administers it. Problems found in the environment are direct or indirect consequences of decisions made in society. Furthermore the pupils must understand that questionable conditions can be changed -- if we so wish.

"It is much nicer with new approaches to teaching. Variation often makes it easier to see new connections. This has made it clear to us that all subjects are part of a greater dimension." They are also pleased with the fact that they have largely been responsible for their own education: "It clearly motivates us if teachers have confidence in us. Then we are far more positive to education in general. All in all project work is too scarce in the curricula. But we also feel that there must be sufficient room for traditional teaching methods".

The pupils are far from happy with the governmental attitudes to pollution:

I relax a little. I am on familiar ground with this slide. If I am a specialist in anything it is in researching and writing case studies. If nothing else I know good questions to ask. The danger, of course, is the same as with any evaluative act. The more relaxed and confident an evaluator feels the more dangerous she becomes because there is a relaxation of self-discipline and self-discipline is sometimes all that stands between an evaluator and a muckraking journalist. The specific danger is that I use this presentation to hold people to account for my own standards of conduct in case study. Anyway, I imagine that the extracts I am using relate to experiences which lie at the heartland of ENSI values and aspirations. Delicate ground, this -- the more so since I do have a general expectation that activities which represent great moral and political investment from adults often depend on children jumping through the right hoops, sometimes making public spectacles of themselves and, generally, being very indulgent indeed of the adults they have to look after.

These are extracts from local case studies that were carried out in what is called "Phase 1 of the programme". There is a range of data here and each extract, for me, raises images of authority. The first two pieces speak of science. Other pieces draw from democratic principles, from systems of moral authority.

Words jump off the page -- at one point the juxtaposition of *"facts"* and *"utopias"* -- the word 'utopia' redolent of visions of benign consensus which, again, seem to permeate ENSI. Schools in one extract are *"service agencies"*. There are neighbours who are *"nasty"* because they refuse "to answer our enquiries"; nature has a *"destiny"*; government has *"attitudes to pollution"*. ENSI appears to promote *"new approaches to teaching"* which seem to include unfamiliar project work -- but pupils appear to be happy to let this live alongside *"traditional teaching methods"*. All this appears to lie as unnoticed and natural on the desk of this programme as bread and butter on my dinner table.

I worry about the status of some of this data. I think some statements are supposed to have been written by pupils, but those statements have more than a resonance of the programme rhetoric. *"It is much nicer with new approaches to teaching. Variation often makes it easier to see new connections."* This paragraph, in particular, has the familiar ring of special pleading -- propaganda, almost. Who wrote it? Here, I assume, is a teacher or a coordinator trying to tell me that the programme is a success -- before I have had an opportunity to make my own mind up about that. I have seen this before -- self-proclaimed success is almost a modern canon of academic life. What is ENSI's stance towards this? What is the relationship between national projects and their governments, and does this affect the kind of information Paris receives from the working end of the programme? If views are subject to manipulation (*if*) so as to put a happy face on this experience what are the realities of pupil experience -- beyond the convenient expressions of satisfaction with adult pedagogical projects?

The comment looking forward to "a student's deeper awareness of his power of changing things around him" is followed by an italicised (why?) comment which may have come from a pupil or a teacher -- "proud of ... environmental reflection ... several phases ... various levels". The aim of enhancing pupils' abilities to change things around them is worthy, clearly, but within what limits? Is it more educational to make students aware of the lack of power they have to change things around them -- after all the politics of the environment that I witness of television almost every day (more evaluation data?) suggest the impotence of citizens in the face of massive corporate and governmental power. What is the ethic of ENSI? How far should I go along with the political romance?

The content of my evaluation case study is looking very complex indeed. It seems to lie (sic?) at a number of levels. There are the words, then something to know about who said them and why, then who reported them and why, and then the political and ethical significance of all of this information. Above all there is a growing unease that my judgement is running unchecked and is forming an ever larger proportion of whatever is represented by the content of my evaluation.

Slide 6: Biographies

(from CARE Prospectus)

John Elliott, another founder member of CARE, is Professor of Education, Dean of the School of Education and Deputy Director of the Centre. Before moving back to CARE in 1984 he was, for some years, tutor in Curriculum Studies at the Cambridge Institute of Education where he designed full-time and part-time in-service courses to support reflective practices in schools. From 1978-80 he directed the SSRC Cambridge Accountability Project, and used case study methods to help schools reflect about the ways they presented themselves to governors, parents, employers and LEAs. During the period 1980-83 he was funded by the Schools Council to support school-based action-research into issues of teaching for understanding in the context of the examination system (the TIQL Project). From 1984 he was seconded to the Home Office Project reviewing and redesigning police probationer training.

I began my teaching career in a secondary modern school in the early 60s as a religious education and biology specialist. The Education Act of 1944 made religion a compulsory curriculum subject. In fact it was the only subject secondary schools were legally obliged to provide. However, the system of public examinations ensured a broad conformity of curriculum provision. The control over the curriculum exerted through public examinations was greatest in the grammar schools. But the content of GCE syllabuses was reflected in the curriculum framework of the secondary moderns. The GCE syllabuses were devised and the examinations set and marked, by a number of university-controlled examination boards.

I learned as a teacher that theories were implicit in all practices, and that theorizing consisted of articulating those 'tacit theories' and subjecting them to critique in free and open professional discourse. I also learned that high-quality professional discourse depends upon the willingness of everyone involved to tolerate a diversity of views and practices. In my school there was certainly an identifiable group of teachers who could be described as 'the innovators'. But we never became a self-contained and exclusive club or an isolated rebel clique, so we never established an impermeable dogmatism.

(from J. Elliott paper on ESI)

I have, of course, approached the documentation with certain biases about the nature of environmental education. These are derived from a general concept of education developed during the course of reflection about my experiences as both a school teacher and teacher educator. I have learned that I can only develop my understanding of educational processes -- the values and principles which define them as educational -- if I do so in dialogue with practical educators. In such dialogue my own ideas and concepts are modified and extended, as indeed hopefully are those of the teachers involved. My account of teachers' concepts of environmental education will inevitably be informed by my own biases about the nature of educational processes. However, I hope that the teachers who participated in the project will recognise the account as in some sense their own.

There are a number of agendas to the next presentation and I wonder how many of them will be as transparent as the slide. John Elliott is sitting in the conference -- finding it as hard as ever, I observe, to play a recessive role. Among the laughter and banter around my presentation his voice is always prominent. His is a big presence. He is one of the programme consultants -- I'm still confused as to precisely what role, but I know that intellectually he is a powerful influence and commands some deference. So he makes for a rich target and an important lesson in evaluation.

In this slide there are three extracts from different versions of John Elliott's biography. In fact, they blur the boundary between biography and autobiography since they were all written by him, though the first is written in the 3rd person. We learn, here, that he is someone who values "dialogue with practical educators" and does so because in these dialogues his "concepts are modified". But we also learn that he is a man who can (and does) stand on a platform as an expert with a weighty record of achievement and experience.

Who are the programme leaders and where do their values come from? It is easier to find data on prominent people in this programme -- that is almost certainly true of all programmes -- and yet the actions and values that are exposed tend to be those of people at the lower reaches of programme activities. Who is important to this programme? Who, indeed, does the programme 'belong' to? Or to put this another way -- who do we have to know about in order to understand ENSI -- and how do we have to know them?

Slide 7: Assessment

(English Assessment strategy for environmental education, Southern examining group, GCSE)

Environment - coursework unit two		Investigation and evaluation of a local environmental issue				
Assessment Objective	Weighting	Mark Range (Use marking guide and tick appropriate range)				Mark
		Level 1	*Level 2*	*Level 3*	*Level 4*	
8. Identify and describe an environmental issue	12	0	1-3	4-6	7-9	10-12	
9. Recognise a variety of views and empathise	28	0	1-7	8-14	15-21	22-28	
10. Show understanding of environmental management	24	0	1-6	7-12	13-18	19-24	
5. Express feelings	12	0	1-3	4-6	7-9	10-12	
6. Analyse feelings	12	0	1-3	4-6	7-9	10-12	
11. Organise and present material	12	0	1-3	4-6	7-9	10-12	
TOTALS	**100**					**/100**

As I present the next slide I have another crisis of confidence. It, too, is sensitive -- sensitive, that is, to people whose sense of personal integrity might easily be challenged by too critical a presentation. It is about assessment. I came across this diagram showing just a fragment of information about assessment from the English context and I have no idea how representative it is of others. I display it quickly and remove it. Then I have second thoughts and replace it. It is, in the end, too important to pass over lightly. Curriculum programmes often contain competing sets of values and interests and they are probably nowhere more exposed than in a juxtaposition between pedagogical and assessment principles.

I know, in any case, that this must be an important part of my evaluation 'contents' because it appears to bring together a number of the questions I have been raising. By now I am beginning to make connections -- to discover contingent relationships between different parts of my data bank. I have questions about the source of values, questions about sources of authority and I have a reasonable sense of the kind of practical activity people are trying to generate at school level. In an assessment scheme I can perceive the resonances of values, authority, the treatment of practical experience. I know my comments will be critical and I apologise in advance. After all, I have no warrant for making a critical evaluation of this programme (other than a pedagogical one) and I have no empirical basis on which to make any informed critique.

Authority is writ large in this diagram -- everything adds up and everything adds up to 100. The values behind this kind of scheme are familiar to me and they are those of technocracy -- (the levels 1 to 4 reflect the absurdities of the English National Curriculum). I have read in this programme documentation about pupils negotiating with their communities, about schools servicing the community, about teachers reviewing their own practices. I have read ambitious plans for revising the relationship between pupils and knowledge and between pupils and their community -- but here the curriculum vision is reduced to nothing more or less than any other curriculum subject. It is measurable against abstract criteria. For reasons which are not at all clear the objective of "expressing feelings" is given only half the weighting (by an unnamed person) of the objective for showing "understanding of environmental management".

Now I am asking myself a question which is, I think, the first substantial evaluation question that has occurred to me. This programme may encourage good environmental practice -- but does it encourage good education? I can make that more specific -- more searching as a question. Is good environment necessarily good education? This seems to be an important question to ask -- especially where some people hold the aim of incorporating environmental education into the core curriculum. Maybe for the first time I feel as though I have something real -- almost artefactual -- to carry with me as an evaluator. I have what I think is a good question. Is this the content of evaluation -- good questions? Is data simply the compost and the seed for the real content?

Slide 8: Conspiracies?

(from Restricted report on Frascati workshop)

4. Networking

20. Both national and international networking are essential tools in the Environment and School Initiatives project, and efficient strategies for facilitating the exchange of information, experiences, people and outcomes is an integral part of the development of the project.

21. The US participants in the project have proposed to host an International Conference on Networking in Nashville, Tennessee in the autumn of 1991 to enable the European, Australian, and Japanese networks to link up with the American network of schools and environmental education centres. These links would be tested for a period of six to eight months, after which another meeting would be held to attempt to evaluate results in Europe.

22. Plans are in process to extend the network to Eastern European countries, and some contacts have been made with Hungary where a network of schools with environmental education projects already exist.

(ER House "Decentralised Evaluation for Norway" in book Evaluation as Policy Making)

The international economic order

As Lundgren notes in his analysis, national governments are no longer totally in control of many aspects of their national lives, particularly their national economies. All countries are now tied into global international trading markets, and economic decisions affecting national life are made in places far away and for reasons other than national benefit. Market economies bring all facets of society into their orbit and have a destabilising effect on society because they dissolve traditional structures and social relations (Gilpin, 1988).

This internationalisation is reflected in calls for education to produce certain types of students and knowledge so that nations can compete successfully in international markets.

The content of my evaluation is becoming a little slippery. I thought it was bits of data -- and then I came to think it was questions. Now I feel myself to be far more critical of this programme -- the more I read of it the more critical I become. I feel myself having to be protective of it -- curbing my judgements because they are becoming too harsh. The content of the experience of this evaluation seems to be full of internal tussles, cognitive conflicts setting opinions against judgements.

This is confirmed to me as I reach the end of my documentation. I have noticed 'networks' more than a few times and here I find a piece actually about them. I read that they are "essential tools" and that they are part of a strategy to extend the programme across the world -- particularly, it seems, to Eastern Europe. This is by no means a dishonourable intention and the worst that can be said of it, perhaps, is that, yet again, it speaks of ambitions which could well run ahead of the capacity to maintain local quality of interactions. I have stored away another question in relation to this which asks about the time-scale of change that people think of inside this programme. It seems to be terribly, unrealistically short.

But I think again about networks. Maybe I am too easily suspicious of rhetorical claims to honourable acts. There are complexities to everything -- what about networking? I recall recently having read something written by Ernest House -- a man whose scepticism reaches Weberian proportions at times. The lower half of the slide is an extract from what I read. It speaks of creeping internationalism and raises the spectre of education systems preparing children for a different kind of world dominance -- one that treats national boundaries with contempt.

The question, by now, is obvious. Is networking -- putting pupils in touch with peers in other parts of the world, creating an international educational agenda -- is this part of this process that House is talking about? It does not have to be deliberate or even understood -- there need be no conspiracy. Just people allowing an historical logic to seep into the logic of their momentary decisions. Does this programme aid the process in which national, cultural issues and experiences are dimmed in the brighter lights of these great global concerns? I have a welter of questions in my mind, now, about the authenticity of some of the disembodied pieces I have been reading. More and more I question the power of language to create the impression (perhaps a myth) of popular movements for environmental improvement and of schools adopting a central role in this international swell. I feel uneasy.

Let me stop this before it gets any further. I am working from documents -- trying to read experience and practice off the page and I am holding a one-sided dialogue with no other voice to challenge mine. I have become a plaintiff and I am thus creating a defendant. This will not do. My mind and my perceptions need some discipline. I know very well that the thoughts and actions of people translate poorly onto paper -- and even worse onto someone else's paper. My judgements, having inflated like a large balloon are fast deflating. They are giving way to a desire for fieldwork. I want to talk to people -- to see behind the honorific fictions created by these literary morsels.

There is an image I often recall at moments like this. Paintings in a catalogue produced, usually, at the highest level of sophistication possible end up with laminated images of great clarity. The pieces of work you see on the canvas rarely live up to them. They are not so crisp -- their colours appear dimmer -- they have less contrast. But it is merely a matter of refocusing the mind-and-eye. The crispness is an illusion -- the richness lies in the ambiguity of the lines. And so with human action.

I am, in a sense, ready to define what will make me content with my evaluation -- comfortable, that is, that I am not doing damage to people's hopes or enhancing their fears. It is anything that will both expand upon these early themes and, at the same time, destroy their clarity. I want to know just who the people are who populate this programme. I want to know why they are here and what they think they are doing. I want to know what it is that they want to do but are prevented from doing. By people this must mean a Minister and a pupil; a professor and a teacher.

I am no longer happy with the term 'content' of evaluation. It is too concrete -- it has already proved too light a term to handle my prejudices and feelings and now it seems too simplistic a term to cope with putting people at the centre of evaluation. Are people the content? Their words and feelings? Or simply the complexities and ambiguities they engender? Is it the notion of 'person' that is the content? I certainly have an evaluation philosophy which seeks to invert the conventional relationship between people and projects -- documenting people's lives and putting projects in that context (rather than the opposite which we almost always do).

A simple answer to the question might be to find a category system for all the various types of data I have used. Then I would say that the content of evaluation is made up of data on:

-- interests,
-- values,
-- political and financial relationships,
-- personal experience,

143

-- educational theories at play,
-- 'moods and mysteries' (as Bob Stake says)
-- dynamics and resistors
-- actions and contexts,
-- rhetorics,
-- methods of organisation and management,
...and so on...

...and so it is. But as I said at the beginning you can barely separate out content from reconstruction -- from the way that content is used and thought about. These things listed don't happen discretely -- they blend and mix and cut across and confuse. They are usually contingent and sometimes exclusive and only make sense, therefore, as elements in an analysis.

In that case you -- the evaluator, that is -- become part of the content just as what you define as the content becomes part of the process of reconstruction. The argument now moves towards a Stenhouse-type solution where what is substantial is process. In this educational equivalent of a non-Euclydian world the most concrete of thoughts and actions are to be held provisional; stated objectives are recognised to be a usurper of intention; and understanding the self is a prerequisite to revealing anything to anyone else. Thinking of the content of evaluation makes us think of how we receive and process data and how our own prior frameworks of thought and experience interact with data. As evaluators we need to be conscious of *how* we are thinking about programmes more than *what* we are thinking. Are we, for example, tying the programme down with our own meanings (with the content of our own experience)? Or do we use our own powers of thought to help release meanings?

I left the presentation there with issues about content unresolved. It had to be so, however, since there was a particular kind of case study that I was aiming at. It was what might be thought of as a collaborative case study where the evaluator serves to bump-start a data generation process and some analysis. I aimed to provide a scaffolding with my case study -- a crude outline of where a building might be erected and some physical assistance with the erection. The rest of the data was there, as it were, in the conference, but in the minds and notebooks and conversations-to-be-held of the participants. They could build the thing -- they might have done so as I was making the presentation.

So the question of content is made problematic for a final time with the addition of one further vector. Others close to the programme have their own content -- and their own cognitive and emotional processes for pulling it together and making meaning from it. As the momentary evaluator of this programme I could have no idea as I left Cromer what that content might be. I had lost what fleeting control I had over my inchoate evaluation. Content, like everything else in evaluation, is also subject to control.

Chapter 8

THE CONDUCT OF EVALUATION

by

May Pettigrew *and* ***Barry MacDonald***
Centre for Applied Research in Education
University of East Anglia
Norwich, United Kingdom

Peel off the surface text of any well thought out principles of procedure for evaluation, and you will uncover a set of values that engage with power relations, politics, people and change. This chapter concerns a particular or, if you like, CARE formulation of some of these issues.

In order to deal with the macro and micro political implications of evaluation, principles of procedure are generally drawn up and presented to participants and negotiated with them. Participants need to understand the purpose of the evaluation and the way it will be conducted. They need to know what rights they will have over the information obtained and how it may be reported. For the evaluator's part, principles of procedure bind her to an agreed form of conduct in exchange for access to, and use of, information. The aim is to minimise risks to individuals or institutions, provide checks and balances on power relationships, facilitate co-operative relationships and provide the bases for fair, accurate and relevant reports.

In the Cromer conference a set of principles of procedure was presented to participants for discussion. They appear at the end of this chapter as Document 1, (you may find it helpful to consider these principles of procedure before reading further). At present, they are being used by a team in CARE who are evaluating the Economic and Social Research Council's, 'Information and Technology in Educational Research (InTER) Initiative. The InTER principles of procedure draw upon an extensive experience of conducting evaluation within CARE. But like all such statements they are tailored to suit this specific evaluation and so represent a particular slant with regard to rights and obligations, as appropriate to the context and constituency of participants.

We begin with two 'tales from the field' recounted to conference participants by Barry MacDonald, in which he reflects upon his experience of doing evaluation. They point to some of the dilemmas and difficulties that evaluators can face; experiences, in other words, that merit consideration when drawing up principles of procedure to govern the conduct of evaluation. Both of his tales are a reminder that evaluation is a consequence laden activity and cannot evade value positions. Nor can it be dislocated from its political context and social and economic implications.

Two tales from the field

First, just trust me I'm the evaluator.

> "I remember my first case study of a school. It was an innovative school, and I wrote a case study and sent it for publication. I anonymised it but I did not consult people in the school. In that instance the school by accident got hold of it and protested strongly. I was brought up to think the researcher was independent and took his data. The only ethical principle was, do not "harm" your subjects. Traditionally schools accepted that. They did not expect to know or interfere. In this case it was an evaluation. The people involved have a big stake in what you say. There are consequences. You may anonymise, but you cannot do it significantly. With evaluation, you are feeding back critical data about employees to employers -- about the powerless to those in authority. Now I saw it was a terrible responsibility. Evaluation is not like research. Research is an abstracted body of knowledge to ultimately influence policy. Evaluation is very different. I had extensive discussions with people in the school and ultimately my evaluation ... and their own account were published, side by side. The result of this experience was that I had to rethink rights and obligations."

It is not just programmes and policies that are at stake but people's livelihoods and self esteem. The account illustrates the requirement that evaluation should show respect for persons, and it is not difficult to formulate some basic principles of procedure that take this value into account. Giving people rights over their own data (but not that of others); guaranteeing confidentiality; and offering to negotiate reports on the basis of their fairness, accuracy and relevance - all reinforce individual autonomy. These principles of procedure are also conducive to the development of co-operative relationships and the validation of accounts. All of these principles are now fairly common practice. However, they do not necessarily safeguard all the interests of the participants. Jenkins (1980) suggests they represent the straightforward approach and side-stepping exit of the "Knights Move" in chess - by securing the trust that gets the evaluator in and subsequently the power that gets the report out to the wider public. This tension between access and accessibility is inevitable in this model of evaluation. Why? Because it wants to safeguard individual rights to autonomy and respect, while simultaneously guaranteeing openness and divergence of views.

The notion of accessibility, however, has wider implications. If, as we maintain, evaluation should function to stimulate public debate about the worth of the programme (and for that matter, the evaluation) its conduct and reporting should be open, responsive to the judgements of non specialists and result in readable, usable accounts. Evaluators, moreover, need to be sensitive to imbalances in power and seek to feed information downwards as well as upwards in the formal or informal hierarchies of power. Here again, it is not only the participants who gain from these procedures: validation of an account by participants, at all levels, is a useful way by which an evaluator can pre-empt any attempt of the sponsor to take control of what is published in the report. The ideal towards which we aspire is, if you like, the democratisation of evaluation. Fine words, but can it work in practice? Let's take the second case, that of 'Bread and Dreams' (1982) as recounted by Barry MacDonald.

146

"This was an evaluation of bilingual education policy in the United States. At the beginning of the '80s we were invited by the Ford Foundation to conduct such an evaluation. The reason was, or the reason given, was that nobody in the United States concerned with that controversial issue, trusted anyone else to do an evaluation of it. It was seen to be so ideologically rooted. Any perspective and any possible evaluation was seen to be partial, in the sense of being either for or against it. So it was thought that it might just be acceptable to bring some people from another country to do an evaluation. Now you may think it is a strange view of impartiality that brings a bunch of white Anglo males into that situation to do such an evaluation, but nevertheless that was the idea.

When I arrived for the first time in the United States to negotiate access for such a study, the Ford Foundation had decided that it would not be acceptable to the Boston Hispanic community, who were to be the focus of it. That proved to be untrue, and I did manage to negotiate access. This was a policy study but we proposed to conduct it ... through the study of one school, a single school, which was in Boston, Massachusetts -- a bilingual school, mainly for Puerto Rican children.

Now, a number of important things happened in the story of that evaluation. The centre piece of the study, as it is of the Report, was a study of a school -- an intimate portrayal of what went on in classrooms, who the people were, who the children were, and what they did. As a result of that we were able to come up with a database for judging the educational justification for bilingual education, and we thought we came up with a fairly conclusive demonstration that it was educationally justifiable. But also, at the same time, we did a study to place that school within the history of civil rights in the United States and within the history of linguistic minority communities, and their efforts to get equality of opportunity in education. The whole Report portrays that school as an outcome of many historical, legislative and cultural determinants. It also looks at local administrative practices and policies, and at policy making in Washington, in a fairly critical way.

Three points here. One is that it is not terribly difficult to look at what's going on in the school, relate that to every level in the system and see how appropriate that is; and in some senses this is inescapable for understanding what is happening at the school level. But let me take each point at a time. When we first drafted the school study, and we gave it back to the school, the school was disappointed with that in a number of ways. One of the important things about their disappointment with the draft was that it was not partial enough, it did not simply say that the school was absolutely wonderful and without problems. Now the Hispanic people, the bilingual activists, were expecting and hoped for that kind of allegiance from us, and in a sense, thought that they had got that promise from me. And when they said, "*Yes, we will let you in because we trust you*" -- that is what they meant. Another important reaction to the draft of the study was that people in the school said, "*This is not our school, this is cold -- that is not how we feel about what we are doing.*" What was missing was the dynamics. What was missing was the joy, the happiness, the dynamics of the relationships between adults and children in the school. At that point we said, "*Yes, OK, fine*", and we brought Saville Kushner in, and said to Saville, "*Go and collect the dynamics*", which he did. And we put that into our account of the school, and that consisted of a whole variety of kinds of data. It included, for instance, an account of a school picnic, in which the adults and the children were out together, and things like that. Before he did this, there had been a missing dimension. They had been saying, "*you are not showing what this means to the people in the situation*". So that the emotional life of the school had been missing, in a sense.

So that was one interesting point about that. The other one was that when we came to present -- note the title -- Bread and Dreams -- we did make very effectively, we thought, the educational case for bilingual schooling. At the same time we described the bilingual movement as an economic movement, (the 'Bread' in the title) in two senses: in the educational sense it was, of course, a means of giving disadvantaged children access to the market -- to jobs and occupations. In another sense, bilingual education itself provided an economy of jobs for which linguistic minorities were better qualified than those who presently held most of the jobs in the education system. Now, when I went about negotiating the draft account of that aspect of the report, it was not just the teachers and the school who felt let down, it was people - activists, or representatives of that movement - at every level up to and including Washington. And they said, "*OK, it ...*

...is correct, but it will kill us. The economic argument, the jobs argument, that is where the threat to the majority is seen to be, the cost. If you put that in, that is what they will pick out. That is what they will choose, that is what they will select and that is what they will use against us." And, of course, at that time, Reagan was in power. They said, "*Why couldn't you just stick to the educational argument, and leave all the rest of it out?*" Now, we felt that we could not do that. But we did know that what they were saying was right -- that it would be used selectively. We still chose to do it, and we still chose to publish in the way that we have. But the thing is there is no escape from the responsibility of making that decision, and that I think is the point. There is not a formula, there is not a model, or a recipe, which lets you escape from personal responsibility for what you do in this particular field -- there is no absolution, and it is very difficult to say you were right, or you were wrong. The arguments for saying, in this case, we were right tended to be long-term arguments; the arguments for saying we were wrong tended to be short-term arguments. In the end, every one of us has to decide what kind of reality, and how much reality, are you actually going to portray in an evaluation report? And you have to take responsibility for that. I would say that the more that responsibility is shared the less badly you might feel about it, but nevertheless, it does get down to that question: how much of the reality which you know are you going to put into an evaluation report? In that sense I am saying, there is not a difference between insider and outsider in terms of those responsibilities, both of us face that kind of dilemma".

Essentially, there are two competing values at stake here: the rights of individuals to protection, privacy and respect and the rights of wider audiences to information which will render publicly funded programmes accountable. Irrespective of the degree to which decisions about the evaluation are made jointly with participants, evaluators are in the end subject to their own judgements based on their values. The basic tension is illustrated in the above account of Bread and Dreams and we can see in it something of the difficult relationship between trust, obligation and control. The evaluators gained access because the school and the political supporters of bilingual education trusted them. No doubt they obtained that trust through negotiating principles of conduct that assured people in the school of their rights to have a say in how their work would be represented in the report. The principles of procedure conveyed this by granting individuals negotiating rights over their own data and the school as a whole over the way it was portrayed. The individual's or the school's rights to control ended there; no one group had rights over how other groups were represented and this proviso is generally indicated in statements of principles of procedure. Ultimately, though, evaluators are faced with moral choices about which of competing values should have priority. Every evaluation is a pragmatic activity situated in context. There are always competing interests and values and no set of principles of procedure can release the evaluator from the responsibility of making and living with decisions. Here, the value of serving the long term public interest held sway over protecting the interests of the bilingual education constituency.

The decision to report the economic benefits to the Hispanic community was premised upon a theory of change; rather simplistically put, this theory views an informed electorate as the ultimate and proper arbiter of social policy and provision. The role of evaluation of publicly funded programmes and policies is to service the public's information needs and it is by this means that social justice will be

148

demanded and delivered. An electorate which has all necessary and relevant information is, in principle, able to exercise its democratic rights through the ballot box or at least offer a potential check on government misuse of power. It may also pursue a case by lobbying elected politicians: in this sense the public's right to know is the hallmark of a just society, and this will be served, not by advocacy in evaluation, but by impartiality. Hence in the Bread and Dreams study the evaluator decided to risk giving ground to political prejudice in the interests of supporting wider and better informed debate.

The value of serving public accountability is a strong one in the CARE model of evaluation. So too is that of respect for individual autonomy. Other values can be inferred from the account above such as accessibility of process and products and the idea of the evaluator as broker of information across differential power groups (see MacDonald 1976). Perhaps these assume particular significance in the CARE model, because of the traditions and operation of democracy in the UK. For evaluators conducting their work elsewhere, values may rest on somewhat different premises about how democracy works in their own context. Lets look at the British political system and consider a few assumptions about its origins and how they influence the workings of democracy. Britain has a rather paternalistic social history which invests the established elites with a degree of, almost feudal, responsibility for the welfare of the underclasses. The democratic tradition is a strong one but the executive draws back from too much openness: secrecy abounds. Utilitarianism has been particularly influential and goes some way to explaining a resistance to intellectualism. Can attempts to engage some of these features of the British political system be seen in the values underpinning the CARE model of evaluation? Paternalism and expectations that people should defer to authority might prompt an evaluator to try and facilitate individuals' autonomy and protect them from mistreatment by the powerful. Giving them rights over their own data, and over how that information is represented, extends to the powerless the rights to secrecy which are already assumed by the powerful. An aspiration that reports should be accessible to non specialist audiences, while not explicitly anti-intellectual, is not incompatible with such a stance. It also, of course, puts a check on the covert exercise of power.

What is interesting is to ask what happens to an evaluation methodology of this kind when it is transported into a different cultural setting, premised upon a different form of democracy? So the question here is, whose democracy mattered in this evaluation of bilingual schooling? Was it the one the evaluators found in Boston or the one they left behind them? In the British system, and particularly, in the English one, with its paternalistic tradition, would the same dilemmas have emerged? If an evaluation of a comparable programme in Britain reported that it resulted in economic advantages to an ethnic minority group, it is hard to imagine that this could be used by right wing interest groups to fuel their political armoury. The established élites in Britain still make their gestures, however hollow, to a notion of obligation for the welfare of the less advantaged. Political capital might be made out of cultural innuendoes based on race, culture or social class, but not out of an economic argument. Why else do the Welsh get away with bilingual education provision throughout the principality?

Questions from practical experience of conducting evaluation

These two tales from the field raise a very wide range of issues common to the conduct of evaluations. But evaluators are always being taken by surprise, as new issues emerge and old ones re-appear in new guises. In the second half of the chapter we want to reflect on possible answers to a small number of very practical problems which we know from experience can be difficult to handle.

What is the relationship between school study and policy study?

In the tale of Bread and Dreams the evaluators decided to conduct a policy study "through the study of a single school." This approach is grounded in an understanding of the reciprocal relationship between the microcosm of the school and the macrocosm of society. Schools are embedded in their wider social and policy context: so the action, the experiences, the 'dynamics' of schools can be set within this frame. But the opposite is also true: a case study of a school can be a case study of society. There are, moreover, obligations to portray this 'lived experience', both to those under study and to the wider audiences of the report. People need a vicarious 'feel' for the case in all its complexity if they are to make judgements and to learn from the programme. And so, the evaluator has an obligation to be as representative as possible of the views and experiences of the diverse interests groups in the programme or case.

In the case of Bread and Dreams the aspiration to represent the plural interests was clearly problematic. Hence the dilemma over presenting the economic benefits of bilingual education. Failure to be representative can though, be a consequence of the use of principles of procedure. It is important to explain that some group views were excluded from the Bread and Dreams account in a direct form. If participants act upon their rights to withhold their data from the account the ideal of representativeness can be undermined.

In conducting a policy analysis there is a danger which is not always appreciated. It stems from the latent power of the evaluator, and the implications if she chooses to vest this power in establishing relationships with those who wield political influence and budgetary control. A policy analysis focused mainly or exclusively at this level might reinforce a top down relationship between policy and practice. To overcome this problem, the evaluation may be conceived of in layers. The centre is what happens in schools which might be portrayed by action research. The outer layers are there to support the action research and need to grow with the movement: infrastructures should grow with school work. An evaluation might, therefore, be conducted at more than one level, so that it explores and portrays both the potential development in the schools and the potential development in the infrastructure.

This relationship between school-focused evaluation and policy evaluation is interesting. A school-focused evaluation looks at how well the 'idea' of this programme is being realised in schools. It can answer questions like: 'What kinds of forces of support does the initiative attract?' 'What constraints surround it (for example, attitudinal or organizational constraints, etc.)?' You can ask the question, 'What is stopping ENSI?' The obstacles may be at different levels. There are **always** implications for policy in evaluation, because we must always ask, 'At what level could action be taken to get the conditions required to permit the programme to flourish?' This is why evaluation reports are contentious. The form of reporting can help to handle these tensions but it can never screen them out completely. For example, one thing the evaluation can do is to describe the situations and activities in the programme. Description is, in any case, more or less a basic requirement of representing the case. But description is not easy or unproblematic. It is political and highly contentious: because the effect of good description is to prevent those at a distance from over-simplifying the issues and problems which engage those responsible for carrying out the programme.

How can evaluators set about negotiating the conduct of evaluation?

Written statements of principle of procedure are one thing; the degree to which their implications can effectively be explained is quite another. Often participants will not fully appreciate either the significance or the potential consequences of involvement in an evaluation. No evaluator is ever entirely 'off duty' and although what is overheard or discussed in social situations might not be quoted directly, all data, however obtained, will inform the evaluation. Participants cannot anticipate how the evaluator will construe their meanings and actions. There are practical ways of facilitating discussion about evaluation procedures. It is good idea to show participants appropriate examples of previous evaluation reports. If this is not possible, a small report, written as early in the evaluation phase, as possible and fed back to participants fast, will come as a shock. But this will provide the conditions for full and frank discussion. The principles of procedure may have to be re-negotiated. They may need continuous negotiation especially if the unexpected arises. The important point to recognise, is that they are a means of reducing uncertainty and of binding the evaluator. Especially in the case of insider evaluation, they are an adjunct to the relationship of evaluation and project, not its unalterable contract.

There are some additional difficulties in the use of principles of procedure. They are very resource consuming. There is the time and effort required for transcribing, returning and in the light of participant comment, amending interview data or feedback reports. Transcription of interviews may have to go by the board. Where the evaluation is embroiled in conflict (and this is not unusual) or as in the case of many of the ENSI evaluators, a change in role has to be continuously negotiated, principles of procedure may come under strain. It is important to balance what is desirable with what is necessary with what is possible.

How can evaluations address issues of imbalances in power?

Evaluations commissioned by government ministries or agencies are prey to attempts by the sponsor to control the evaluation agenda, its conduct and reporting. In Britain the standard terms of contract that are issued by Government departments for the commissioning of external evaluation and research are highly restrictive. All such contracts control publication rights, most include controls over methodology and some assume complete control over all aspects of the work. We have now reached a point where external, independent evaluation of publicly funded programmes is not admissible, if paid for from the public purse administered directly by Government departments. In Britain and elsewhere there is a growing trend in ministries to establish in-house evaluation units. Evaluation abounds but is increasingly confined within the corridors of power. It has become a powerful means of getting information out of the system and maximising information at the centre. Little information is going the other way. In these circumstances it becomes more important to build in some barriers and to develop the theory of evaluation from a technical service to that of public watchdog.

Some ENSI evaluators are based in universities or research centres, others work with education ministries. All will face, albeit in different contexts and to different degrees, the problems of negotiating their report with those who are either more or less powerful than themselves. The kind of principles of procedure which are important in establishing the rights and controls of the less powerful also serve to limit the control of the sponsors over the evaluation data and report: at a purely pragmatic level it is easier to argue a case on the grounds that you are bound by ethical agreements to programme participants than simply to say that you do not want to do as the sponsor asks. You can say, "I will do my best but other people's questions have to be answered in order to get their co-operation." Co-operation of the participants is essential to ensure the validity of the data, which means that the validity of the evaluation depends upon abiding by ethically sound principles of procedure. This is also a powerful argument for ensuring that participants rights are assured. Many civil servants or ministry officials, who have responsibilities in the area of public service provision, are becoming involved in evaluating the impact of policy at grassroots level and are being asked to report their findings to their superiors. One difficulty is that their work can invoke suspicions of surveillance and limit their opportunity to access data. The concept of mediating between levels of power, and negotiating reports with those who are evaluated, makes sense in these conditions. Principles of procedure can be seen as appropriate by officials who need ways of facilitating co-operation and increasing the validity of their accounts. There are alternatives to relying on power and the assumptions of power.

What special issues do insiders have to take into account when conducting evaluation?

ENSI participants face multiple demands as they approach the task of evaluating the project. The reports have to serve diverse purposes; first their is the obligation to the schools to feedback formatively and assist the development of the initiative. Many of the evaluators in the project are pedagogic support persons who have been involved in actively supporting the work of teachers on the ground. Their role has been both that of advocate and facilitator. As insiders, they have to switch hats to execute an evaluation function. This is in the interests of producing a summative account which informs relevant groups in participating countries, OECD itself, their own ministries, the wider public as well as the schools themselves. Theirs is a particularly difficult task.

Unless carefully negotiated, the move from supporter to evaluator could be seen as a betrayal of trust. Principles of procedure may help to establish formal limits for the evaluation but in the interpersonal relationships through which they are enacted, there is a need for vigilance. The evaluator is a role, not a friend. Yet insider evaluators already have access to sensitive information, indeed they have unique access to data in a complex situation and have already learned much from working in a research support mode with participants. They have worked with the difficulties as well as the successes as teachers struggle to realise an innovative practice. Teachers, however, being at the bottom of the power structure are particularly vulnerable to criticism of their work. But for the evaluator, being risk averse is no solution. A glossy picture will limit credibility of the evaluation and reduce its impact on policy provision. It will limit public understanding and its means to exercise leverage on decision making. And it will limit the capacity of the teachers themselves to learn from the experience of innovation in their own and other's contexts. CARE is an external evaluation agency and aspires to co-operative not collaborative relationships with participants. Insiders, such as those evaluating ENSI projects, cannot be so independent ; decisions about how to represent the project have to be taken collectively with participants. The task is to negotiate agreement that the risks of evaluation are worth taking in order to secure wider gains.

152

DOCUMENT 1

THE INTER POLICY EVALUATION -- PRINCIPLES AND PROCEDURES

by

Barry MacDonald *and* **Ian Stronach**

Centre for Applied Research in Education,
University of East Anglia

The conduct of the evaluation: principles and procedures

Evaluation that intends to be formative within a development Programme, as well as informative for outside audiences, has to develop a relationship with the Programme and its associated Projects that is collaborative, critical, and constructive. Much of the formative potential relies on the quality of this dialogue between participants and evaluators; that is, open, equal, tolerant, and responsive exchanges of information and interpretation. Within such a climate, evaluation can both educate and be educated.

It is the intention of the evaluators to try to develop those sorts of relationships, and the kinds of trust and respect on which they rest. But such conditions do not happen by chance, are not endemic to academic culture, and are not ever realisable in their entirety. The extent of their realisation will depend mainly on our behaviour in the field, and on our perceived competence in carrying out and reporting research in a way that is timely, relevant and challenging. Nevertheless, a formal statement of principles and procedures provides a basis on which collaboration can develop, in that it places the evaluation under a set of obligation intended to safeguard both the interests of the Programme participants, and the viability of the evaluation.

The following protocols are proposed as a framework for the collection, use, and release of evaluative data.

1. The evaluators will assume that they can freely approach any individual, group or institution involved in any way with the Programme.

2. The evaluators will assume that they can attend all formal meetings related to the development of the overall InTER Programme, but will negotiate terms and conditions of access to invitational meetings organised by individual Research Centres to further their InTER aspirations, and to the sites of research activities.

3. The evaluators will seek access to all documents, materials, opinions and practices relevant to the Programme's activities. No private documents or materials will be examined or copied without authorisation, and copies of confidential information will be held in locked files until released, returned or destroyed.

4. Respondents will be offered anonymity where they consider it appropriate, as will institutions. Where information appears in effectively anonymised form, its use will require no special authorisation from the individuals or institutions concerned.

If it is felt necessary to further protect the identity of any respondent or institution, the evaluation may seek permission to fictionalise non-essential aspects of accounts in order to protect sources. Where such reporting occurs, it will be stated in the text.

Nevertheless, the evaluators are committed to open discussion and reporting, and will normally seek to negotiate accounts which acknowledge the identity of individuals and institutions.

5. No individual will have privileged access to the evaluation data unless that individual is the sole source of data (as, for instance, interview data). Nor may any individual proscribe the use of another person's contributions to the evaluation.

6. The evaluators will treat everything seen or heard that is relevant to the Programme as possible data. There will be no 'off-the-record' exchanges.

7. The evaluators will seek the permission of individual respondents to create or use audio or video records.

8. Evaluative data based on interviews, meetings and correspondence, which is intended for attributed use, will be referred to respondents for comment at or before the production of a draft report. Such comments will be used to improve both the data base and the interpretation.

9. Participants whose activities are directly subject to reporting will be invited to comment on draft reports in order to improve their fairness, accuracy and relevance. Such comments will be taken into account in improving the final version. Participants in the Programme will have the right to insist that a final report which concerns their role includes whatever qualification and objection they require.

10. Reports will attempt to include, fully and fairly, the perspectives of Programme participants, and to make explicit the range of opinion concerning any major issue. Where the evaluators feel able to offer judgements in such areas, they undertake to also represent alternative interpretations expressed in the field, or suggested by the data.

11. It is the understanding of the evaluators and their sponsors that evaluation will result in public reporting, and in a dissemination of findings to the range of interested parties. Respondents will be made aware of the anticipated audience of each report.

References

JENKINS, D. (1980), 'An Adversary's Account of Safari's Ethics of Case Study' in H.Simons (ed.) *Towards a Science of the Singular*. Centre for Applied Research in Education, Norwich, UK.

MCDONALD, B. (1976), 'Evaluation and the Control of Education' in D.Tawney (Ed.) *Curriculum Evaluation Today: trends and implications*, Schools Council Research Studies. Macmillan, London.

MCDONALD, B. et al, (1982), *Bread and Dreams: a case study of bilingual schooling in the USA*. Centre for Applied Research in Education, Norwich, UK.

Chapter 9

INTERVIEWING IN CASE STUDY EVALUATION[1]

by

Barry MacDonald
Centre for Applied Research in Education
University of East Anglia
Norwich, United Kingdom

As evaluators we are usually pushed for time and resources, and these constraints are largely responsible for the peculiar features of the evolving tradition of case study in evaluation. We can't afford the kind of lengthy immersion in programme action sites that has characterised and shaped other ethnographic traditions. We go for condensed fieldwork, short sharp bursts of data gathering leading to negotiable accounts of social action in situ. Negotiation is crucial, not just because the constraints entail problems of validity and adequacy, but because our reports may damage the interests of those whose work we represent. The context is evaluative, the intent (ours or someone else's) to judge. The combination of logistic limitations and threatening purpose makes for heavy methodological reliance upon interviewing as the principal mode of data gathering. Compared with observations, interviews are easier to obtain, easier to do, easier to process and easier to negotiate.

But the use of the interview exacerbates a problem that is in any case a worrying feature of case study evaluations, the tendency of such studies to be over-protective of the institutions and practices of which judgement is required. Case study is a social process, imposing upon its users the social obligations of a guest. Interviewing is even more demanding, since it brings into play the values and expectations associated with interpersonal relationships. Few of us would deny that, in seeking access to the case and in cultivating the cooperation of its residents we de-emphasise the evaluative purpose and exploit whatever personal qualities we can muster in order to "sell" our presence and so make good our mission.

This brings me close to my point. The difficulties of negotiating and maintaining the cooperation of the residents, reinforced by our natural reluctance to engage in ad hominem evaluation, involve us in two (usually implicit) promises to the interviewee, both designed to ease our path by making him or her feel more comfortable. The first is that we have not come to evaluate the individual, but to evaluate the activities in which s/he is engaged and for which many others share responsibility. So far so good - we do not see ourselves surely as the hounds of individual retribution. It is the second "promise" that makes the keeping of the first fatally undermining to our mission. We make it clear that the interview is an opportunity for persons to defend their practice to those who seek to judge it. We are their agents, their means of representation to the outside world.

---

[1]   The original version of this article was written by Mac Donald et al. (1981), Evaluators at Work: Report of a Workshop, for IFAPLAN, Cologne.

There is a lot to be said for these promises. Our audiences are almost always more interested in the strengths and weaknesses of the programme than they are in the performances of those employed by them. And the people in the case have a right to be heard and a right to defend what they do and how they do it. But, and it is a considerable 'but', we commit ourselves and our interviewees to a process of enquiry and reporting that is conservative, not just of persons, but of institutions and practices. Such case studies are insufficiently evaluative to serve the needs of review.

In so far as my argument so far is persuasive enough to merit further exploration, I want to argue further that the evaluative purpose is in any case poorly served by both traditional and contemporary approaches to interviewing, and that any effort to improve the evaluative utility of the case study should start from a reappraisal of interviewing practice and possibilities. What follows is conceived as a contribution towards such a reappraisal. My goal is to reach a conception of the interview that permits the reasonable rights of the interviewee to be met without undermining the evaluation purpose. In my view this calls for effective means of shifting the interviewee from a defensive to an evaluative posture. In other words I see some form of self-evaluation as the alternative to the kind of self-justification that our approaches tend to evoke, and I believe we need to evolve new approaches to the interview in order to achieve this change.

In case study evaluation, there is a need to get away from the kind of role-locked encounter that is fostered by conventional approaches to interviewing. Such approaches range from the animate questionnaire, where through a simple stimulus/response process the blanks in a pre-structured form are filled in, to the so-called unstructured interview in which the interviewer continuously processes what he is told and writes his edition in a notebook. In this latter approach the helpful, nervous, or impatient interviewee responds to the processing problem in a number of ways; by being as articulate and succinct as possible, by slowing the pace of his responses to the pace of the writer, by noting and acting upon what stimulates or fails to stimulate the interviewer to write, by adopting conservative assumptions about which of the thoughts that come to him are likely to be relevant and useful, and editing his thoughts accordingly. For his part the interviewer, compelled by the imperative of instant codification to rely upon familiar categories, selects and marshals the data in response to a matrix in his head. Inevitably, and despite the best efforts of the interviewee to aid the process of conversion from spoken to written discourse, slippage occurs. Incomplete statements and thoughts get rounded out, complexities of tone and non-verbal communication reduced to single word indices. Case study interviewers who adopt any of these pre-processed or continuous processing approaches to the interview should give some attention to their coiffure, since the interviewee spends a lot of his time contemplating the top of the interviewer's head.

The manifest instrumentality of such encounters limits their power to evoke the personal experience of public life. The concept of the person embodied in such interactions is inescapably a diminished one, at worst a category within a known range, at best a mixed bag of dross and ore from which the nuggets can readily be extracted. The fact that most people are willing to play such roles simply means that they accept the instrumental purpose but withhold their persons from its probing; their uniqueness, wholeness, mystery, essential unknowability are not at stake. The inherent reductionism of the procedures invites, and usually gets, the immediately negotiable account.

This will do for some case study purposes; we don't always need access to the person behind the account. Much of the time we are usefully gathering data that shows how things look, what people do and what they readily say about what they do. They see us, rightly, as agents (direct of indirect, advertent or inadvertent) of accountability, and this reinforces their common impulse to defend and justify what we see them doing. So the accounts they give us aspire to plausibility and acceptability. Good. We need such accounts - they are expected by our audiences and they reflect the terms by which the case residents agree to be judged or accept they will be understood.

We could therefore, and often do, stop there. We may have done enough to inform people about the case, to reveal some important discrepancies between observation and explanation, to stimulate reflection, to provide a reasonable basis for reviewing roles, goals, resources and rewards. A basis for improvement, rearrangement, modification, amelioration. Seldom, however, a basis for significant change, even though we continue to live in the midst of significant failure. Why so?

We fail in our work to separate persons from practices clearly enough to understand, or enable others to understand, the nature of the compromises that make up our public institutions. In so doing we fail in our primary purpose - to reveal educational possibilities. We have a sense of our own possibilities, an understanding of our own compromises with circumstance, that is rarely matched in our accounts of others.

So much for the problem. What does the solution look like? I don't have time here to elaborate in any detail an alternative, but my own experience of interviewing, in a style which has evolved over a number of years, offers some pointers to a way ahead.

First, the technology. Let's get rid of the notebook, for the reasons given. We still need to document though, and my preference is for the unobtrusive tape recorder, for reasons which are important to the development of the interviewee as evaluator. It allows me to listen to everything that's said, to observe the whole communication continuously, to pick up non-verbal clues, interpreting pauses for instance rather grasping the opportunity they afford to make notes, to respond facially rather than verbally, to post edit and categorise, and above all to develop a person to person dynamic.

Secondly, let us concentrate upon the interviewee as a person rather than as a role incumbent, and use the interview as a means to explore the relationship between people and the jobs they happen to be doing. Rob Walker and I once ran a weekend conference for young teachers on the theme "To what extent is the person you are the teacher you are?" The result was an astonishingly penetrative evaluation by the participants of their own institutions and practices. This question could and should, in my view, be the basis of a much more personalised approach to interviewing in which the person being interviewed is invited and encouraged to take an "outsider's" view of his professional situation and subject it to evaluative scrutiny. Lawrence Stenhouse argued that the only ideas one can objectively evaluate are one's own, and this provocative statement could be put to the test in an interview which continuously focuses on the interface between persons and their professional roles.

Finally, let us be careful when we are negotiating access to the people in the case, that we communicate clearly this concept of a shared task in the evaluative process. Let us say to them that we assume that all social action is a compromise of some kind between values, interests and circumstances, and that our task, and theirs, is not to defend that compromise but to understand its precise structure. This is not a promise, but an invitation to locate the evaluative act where the action is. I think this may be a way forward.

Chapter 10

MAKING THE MOST OF JUDGEMENT DATA

by

Nigel Norris
Centre for Applied Research in Education
University of East Anglia
Norwich, United Kingdom

What is judgement data?

The value of educational activities is set by people. It is people who value educational activities not criteria or standards or checklists. Description and judgement are two basic and inter-related activities in evaluation. We need to know what it is that is being judged, what is the character of an educational programme. And we should not assume that it has a single character because the meaning of an educational programme, what it is, will depend on the relationship between the observer or participant and the programme. What a programme is depends on your perspective; slightly vary the perspective and the programme will vary too.

A central issue in the political theory of evaluation is who should judge the worth or merit of an educational programme:

> Is it the responsibility of the evaluator to pass judgement on the value of an educational programme?

> Should the evaluator refrain from making judgements and instead provide data on the match between programme objectives and learning outcomes?

> Should the evaluator collect, record and analyse the judgements of others about the nature and value of an educational programme?

It is the last of these I want to focus on today - collecting, recording and analysing judgements about the nature and value of an educational programme.

Judgement is a complex business and it can be as much about the exercise of prejudice as it is about the exercise of a critical and informed intelligence. Prejudices about a programme - uninformed judgements - are an important source of data; indeed they may be influential in shaping how a programme is seen and whether it is valued. Prejudices as well as informed critical judgements are part of the matrix of judgement data we should collect about a programme.

Critical and informed judgements are likely to reflect different kinds of comparison and valuing. Comparisons are often made between actual and intended outcomes to yield judgements about the success of a programme at meeting its objectives. As a programme develops participants make claims about it and these can form the basis of a comparison with what actually happens. One project might be compared with another so as to highlight different values, different interpretations of educational opportunities within the programme, different contexts of operation or different outcomes and degrees of success. A programme like environmental education might be contrasted with other forms of curriculum provision to illuminate what is unique about the subject matter and pedagogy, and to explore its sources of legitimacy. Another source of comparative judgement about a programme is the literature on innovation offering the possibility of judging the programme in relation to theories of change. Judgements about the worth of educational programmes are also founded on comparisons with different views of education or different expressions of educational value. When making judgements, of course, other more personal values and experiences also play a part. Both the personal values of evaluator and other programme participants are an important factor determining what is significant and how it is judged.

Collecting judgement data

Many people come in contact with an educational programme: teachers, children, parents, administrators, project personnel, programme managers, inspectors, advisers, visitors and others in the community. When they come in contact with an educational programme participants and observers make judgements about its nature and values and this represents an important source of data for an evaluation. In addition to observing the processes of judgement that occur naturally in and around a project, evidence of the values and worth of a programme can be deliberately elicited through the use of expert reviewers, evaluation seminars involving participants, interviews and questionnaires.

When collecting judgement data it is important to understand the comparative basis of judgement and it is difficult to get at this through observation or questionnaires alone. We want to know not just how people value a programme, not just what they see as worthwhile, but also why. Judgement data need to be contextualised and in order to locate and understand judgements we need to know who made them, when they made them and under what circumstances.

There are many ways of collecting judgement data. Particular methods need to be selected according to purpose and opportunity. Some of the key questions to address are: What do I want to know? Why do I want to know it? How best to collect data given the opportunities and resources available? What will be the impact of my role on the quality of data?

Recording judgement data

How data is to be recorded in an important consideration in any evaluation. Typically data is recorded in the form of notes, precoded or pre-structured questionnaires or schedules, video tapes, audio-tapes, interview transcripts, collections of documents and other written evidence. The more complete or detailed the record the more time is likely to be needed for analysis and reporting. Selective recording can be a source of bias, for example recording only those judgements that are consonant with ones own.

Ideally when recording judgement data we want to know about the context in which judgements are being made and we want to know something about the experiences on which the judgements are based. We want to know as much about the judge and their judgements as time and resources will allow. And these matters should, where possible, form part of the record.

162

Analysing and using judgement data

A key issue in the analysis of judgement data is the extent to which the evaluator uses the data to forge a synthesis of values so as to make a definitive statement about the programme or project.

An analysis of judgements that attempts to provide an overarching and convergent account of the programme is likely to focus on the frequency of certain kinds of judgement and to set aside the unusual or discordant. In this form of analysis the evaluator literally constructs the programme out of the dominant conceptions of its nature and values. An analysis of judgement data that aims to represent judgements in the context of their situational valuings rather than capture the essence of the programme is likely to focus on the divergence of values leaving the reader to construct the programme.

Judgements about a programme are located in time and space. They are elicited in a particular context or by a specific method, or they are occasioned by a specific event. Judgements are related to the experience someone has of the programme and of other programmes like it. It matters when a judgement is made. Judgements made at the start of the programme are likely to focus on promise or prediction whereas judgements made when things have started happening are more likely to focus on the problems of implementation. The judgements of teachers and pupils about a programme often reflect their competence and confidence in working in new ways. It is important, therefore, to try and collect judgement data over time and to note how judgements vary as understanding about the programme change.

It is important to distinguish between judgements that revolve around empirical claims and those that do not. Judgements that rest on empirical claims can be related to other kinds of evidence, they can be tested against what is known. For example, the judgement that projects which take children out of school make it more difficult for them to settle to their "normal lessons" and are therefore a bad thing, is in part an empirical claim.

The collection and analysis of judgement data provides one way of combining the advantages of insider and outside evaluations. Insiders with evaluative responsibilities can look to outsiders to provide different bases for judgement and different perspectives on the project. Outsiders can collect and represent the judgements of insiders who are closer to the reality of the programme than they themselves are.

Who values what about a programme? Why? And on the basis of what Experience? Judgement data that is de-contextualised may be easy to use but it is difficult to understand. For example, knowing how many people think that a project failed to realised its potential tells us little about why and how to change things for the better. One of the advantages of case study is that it creates a context for reporting judgements and provides a context for their interpretation. If individual project-based evaluations are going to provide data for a cumulative evaluation, then case study might preserve the particularity of projects and judgements about them while offering some means of looking at the programme as a whole.

Some issues to be going on with

1. Collecting and selecting judgement data is a form of sampling and as such is prone to bias. Does this require monitoring or procedures to identify sources of bias?

2. Can you represent the range of judgements about a project across participants and over time? If not how will this alter what you can say about a project?

3. How are people's judgements to be represented or used? Whose words will predominate? Whose interpretations will be used to construct an account of the project?

4. When the less powerful make judgements about the performance of the more powerful they are potentially vulnerable. What are you going to do about this?

5. Are some people's judgements more important than others? Where should efforts be concentrated? Whose judgements are essential to your purposes?

6. How is judgement data going to be reported? Are judgements going to be described or analysed? Used to construct a meta-account or reported directly?

7. What is the relationship in the evaluation between description and judgement?

Chapter 11

REPORTING EVALUATIONS

by

Bridget Somekh, Richard Davies and Maggie MacLure
Centre for Applied Research in Education
University of East Anglia
Norwich, United Kingdom

This chapter is based upon a presentation by Richard Davies and Maggie MacLure, which was in the form of a dialogue followed by a discussion with the conference participants. The chapter is written as a series of questions and reflections, to give something of the style of the original presentation. The second part of the chapter focuses on different styles of reporting, through an examination of four short extracts from evaluation reports.

The content of evaluation reports

Reporting is important for several reasons. It is the means by which the work of a Programme is made public and is almost always a contractual obligation. In addition, reporting has a particular importance within the Programme itself, making it possible for individual participants to get an overview. In ENSI, reporting offered the possibility of exchanging accounts between countries in a way which was mutually supportive.

Decisions about the content of an evaluation report are closely related to the overall purpose of the report. When it comes to a report on Environmental Education, the nature of the content may not be clear, because of differences of opinion as to its purpose. For example, in Environmental Education circles, some people reject what they regard as theoretical knowledge. The following statement was recently overheard at a conference: "Knowledge causes acid rain. Let's have action, not knowledge."

It may be possible to illuminate the issues surrounding this question of content, in general terms, by reflecting upon some actual examples of reporting. What are the purposes which emerge for a writer in the process of selecting the content of a report?

We begin with the case of the Interactive Video In Schools Programme (IVIS) for which Richard Davies was a member of the evaluation team. It was an evaluation of a programme of technological innovation that began in 1986. The report was completed in September 1988. The programme concerned itself with the design, production and development-in-use of interactive video in schools, a new technology which was perceived to have educational potential. The national programme was multi-site, insofar as it consisted of eight separate projects based in Northern Ireland, Scotland and England. Each site had very different resources, structures and personnel, curricula concerns, production facilities and so forth. The evaluation team had to develop a report that accounted for all the projects - both for their differences and for their common experiences. The evaluation was funded by the British government Department of Trade and Industry (DTI) and ran for 18 months.

Who was the report addressed to?

It is now a general rule in government departments in Britain, that all venture capital, or risk capital, must be evaluated. Programmes like IVIS or ENSI are regarded as risk capital - that is, as investments in possibilities which are judged worthy of support but have, of necessity, uncertain outcomes. There is a contractual obligation to write a report which has a formal purpose in terms of the government department's accountability for spending public money.

IVIS was a programme in which there was very little action in the schools, so that the evaluation had the potential to cause serious embarrassment for the government department that funded it.

A related issue was that the IVIS programme was difficult to evaluate:

-- logistically, because it spread over a wide geographical area and incorporated eight semi-autonomous projects;

-- technologically, because interactive video was new and untried and was subject to delays in production and failures in operation;

-- educationally, because there was much less use of the technology in the schools than the evaluators had anticipated.

As a result there was less hard data on the technology's effectiveness than the sponsors or evaluators had expected they would be able to collect.

For the CARE evaluation team, the primary audience for the IVIS evaluation report was the participants in the Programme. The contractual audience was the government department which funded IVIS, but the primary audience was the participants. Our approach to evaluation emphasises the process rather than the products: we know from experience that reports may have very little impact, but the conduct of the evaluation, if conceived properly and carried out fairly, can interact supportively with the development work of a Programme. If there are two reports, one of them interim and one final, the interim report tends to be more influential, and the earlier it is produced the more effective it is, since the constituency is still open to influence and its membership is not fixed. For example, at the policy level an interim report is feeding into decisions yet to be made. Theoretically the programme should be finished and the evaluation report delivered to the sponsor before any decisions are made, but in reality the decisions are usually made before the final evaluation report is completed.

Were there any constraints placed upon the authors' freedom in deciding what to include in the report?

At the formal level, the IVIS evaluators' freedom of reporting was severely limited. The Department of Trade and Industry retains very tight control, because of the kind of projects it normally sponsors: its contracts are drawn up with a view to owning technical and commercial products which may result from a project's work. The contract was written in rather obscure, legal language and was concerned with stopping people from making private profit out of public funds. In addition, the evaluators obtained a private assurance of good faith with regard to publication and dissemination. This 'letter of intent' did not provide a satisfactory resolution of the problem, but it was better than nothing.

In addition, there were the usual constraints connected with the status of the report as a public account. There are important ethical principles which have to be taken into consideration with respect to the construction of public accounts. The rights of individuals and groups have to be respected, but these must be balanced against the public's right of access to information. To some extent the report could be anonymised, but in reality it was always going to be possible to identify the particular projects and individuals portrayed in the case studies and examples. This kind of information had, therefore, to be cleared with the individuals concerned, who were asked *a)* if they considered the report to be a fair representation of their work and *b)* if they were happy about the way in which they had been portrayed. The evaluators then had a responsibility to make any changes which were requested in such a way that the honesty and integrity of the report was not lost. Sometimes this was best done by incorporating an alternative 'minority view' alongside the original piece under dispute.

There was also a consideration of fairness. The evaluators had to ensure that each project felt adequately represented. In some senses this was a political issue, in that projects were drawn from different parts of Britain and each had to be given equal representation.

How does an evaluator write a report based on information from many sites? In IVIS, the schools discussed were disparate, but the evaluators had to impose an order for the purpose of reporting. Was this feasible? If so, how did they do it?

The evaluators began by creating a format under a number of category headings loosely based on those used in the SAFARI programme (1974). These included: location, aims, descriptions of the curriculum package, some account of the resources available, and a very brief history of progress of each project. Within that overall format other headings could be used to reflect the individuality of a project's work, where items or categories did not fit. The strategy was to use one common format to structure the report, but to allow room to include local differences. This was a compromise solution: it made the writing of the report possible, but it was still difficult to ensure that justice was done to each project.

There was a danger of over-simplifying in order to achieve a level of generality. Within each section there was some sacrifice of the complexity contained in individual accounts. However, some measure of complexity was an aggregate result of reading all eight. The diversity was a feature of the whole, whereas the individual accounts were very condensed and suffered as a result.

Were there different cultures? The report imposed an apparently neutral framework, but did each school have a distinct culture, and, if so, did interactive video have a different meaning in each culture, so that children in each school had different expectations?

In writing multi-site studies it is difficult to retain the distinctiveness of individual sites and still say something which applies across cultures. The IVIS report did not include a discussion of cultural diversity in each site but tried to deal with the issue in two sections called 'Overview' and 'The context of innovation'. For example, in one paragraph the authors noted that in Scotland there was considerable interest in Environmental Education, which was not matched by a similar interest in England at the time. In the next paragraph they went on to discuss a particular school in southern England, involved in the primary science project, and look at the way this school dealt with environmental issues, in a different national context. This was a descriptive, discursive account of diversity integrated with the general argument about what was characteristic about the programme. Each section of the report had a distinctive character with distinctive purposes. In this way the authors hoped that in aggregate the whole report would represent something of the programme's cultural complexity and diversity.

This is an important issue, because culture is a significant determinant of the uptake of the innovation. It is not really possible to understand what is going on in a classroom, or a school, without reference to its culture. The report included six mini case studies: three of primary schools, three of secondary schools. They included as rich a description as possible of the local conditions of the school, built around factors which the evaluators and programme participants considered significant. What was important was to represent the uniqueness of each situation and to make the account readable. This was intended to enable readers to locate the common features in the generalised section of the report to a context which was close to their own experience. The success of this aspect of the report can only be judged in terms of the readers' responses.

Culture is not just a feature of national differences between IVIS schools in Scotland and England, or ENSI schools in Austria and the United States, nor even just a feature of differences between schools. Culture is everywhere and it is always essential to understand how culture produces meaning. In a sense the problem in writing reports of multi-site programmes is the same problem of reductionism endemic in making any generalisation in research in the social sciences.

How do we choose the criteria for judging a programme? Since the criteria are grounded in questions of values, who should decide what they should be?

Recently, the British Government has begun to commission large firms of management consultants to undertake evaluations of educational and organisational innovations. Since they come from the world of management, the indicators they value and feel confident they can use may not be in tune with the kind of indicators valued by the education profession. This presents a problem. The methodology we are discussing here is based on the assumption that the best understandings of an innovation are held by the participants. The important thing for an external evaluator - or for a single internal evaluator - is to understand why people prioritise things differently in different places. That can only be done by inferring those priorities from observing people's actions and asking 'why is that aspect of this initiative so important to you?' The answer will often be rooted in that particular cultural context and the values of the individual.

The value-laden nature of evaluation criteria is a potential cause of tension between evaluators and project participants. In the ENSI programme, the pedagogic support people usually worked with six or seven schools. When they came to writing an evaluation report they unavoidably saw some schools as better than others in terms of what they believed the project should be achieving. They had a problem deciding how to represent the work of all those schools, given that they had a support role as well as an evaluation role. This problem was related to the issue of representing cultural diversity: ****it was important that they understood the values and aims of all the teachers concerned and did not make the mistake of believing their own criteria to be neutral and unproblematic.

In the IVIS project, Richard Davies' had only one formal role, that of external evaluator, but over the course of the eighteen months visiting schools he developed an informal support role. Teachers were experiencing considerable difficulty in operating the technology and he could not achieve some of the aims of the evaluation unless the interactive video discs were being used. In order to judge the educational potential of interactive video he frequently found himself in the position of supporting teachers. In practice, the evaluators reduced the extent of Richard's role conflict by taking the stance that it was the programme as a whole and the technology, rather than the schools or the teachers, which was being evaluated. They focused on the funding of the programme and issues relating to implementation of the IV innovation in the schools; the schools were primarily the domains within which a key variable was being evaluated - namely new technology. Teachers were extremely anxious at the beginning because they knew they were having difficulty with the technology and they thought Richard was there as a judge of what they were doing, but through the working procedures he adopted he was able to allay their fears and work with them more collaboratively.

168

How can an evaluator separate the teacher from the innovation in the way suggested? If an evaluator is interested in studying the innovation in terms of its implementation patterns, and wishes to understand those in a contextualised way, then surely he or she is unavoidably evaluating the context.

In a project such as IVIS the evaluator has to take a complex, multi-dimensional approach: the teachers' experience of the innovation, their ideas, and even the evaluator's relationship with the teachers are all, to a certain extent, the material of the evaluation. But part of the context of IVIS was that the innovation had been imposed upon the teachers: it had been brought into their classrooms. That made a difference. The teachers were an important means by which the innovation was undertaken, but they were not responsible for it. The evaluation report contextualised the innovation by presenting some of the uses and practices of interactive video in particular classrooms; this included a negotiated account of the particular teacher's own experience and perceptions of how the innovation was going ahead. Inevitably, there was *some* ambiguity of roles, but primarily Richard did not feel that he was there to evaluate the teachers. He was there to obtain, with the help of the teacher, as full an understanding as possible of what the experience had been like, and what had been the principle educational and implementational issues.

In one sense the IVIS evaluation report did not fully contextualise the innovation. For example, it did not include any description of the professional lives of the teachers within their context. Judgements had to be made about what to include in the report and what to leave out. In that sense it was an economical contextualisation, limited by considerations of the length of the report. The impact of any innovation is strongly influenced by aspects of the school's structure, such as time-tabling, and curriculum traditions (for example, the importance placed upon knowledge of the subject disciplines, as opposed to knowledge construction through individual and collaborative enquiry). But the evaluation itself takes place within a context and has restraints built into it. The IVIS evaluators did not have the time or the funding to be able to undertake a fully contextualised account. The mini case studies included in the report were conceived as the beginnings of a data base that could be shared amongst teachers, as illustrations of what the innovation had been like in the classroom.

It is not only a question of deciding *how much* contextualisation to include in an evaluation report: there is also the question of *what aspects* of the context should be reported. Different evaluations have different emphases. IVIS was very different from the ENSI Programme where there was a lot happening in the schools and their local communities. Little was happening in the IVIS classrooms because the curriculum packages were incomplete - the technology was not working. The many problems were all rooted in the way in which the programme had been conceived and organised. So the IVIS report placed emphasis on contextualising the policy making and decision making that led to there being a large super structure but very little innovation in the schools.

Are there any problems when the report needs to include a detailed evaluation of the work of individual teachers and schools?

In the case of IVIS the personality of the teacher and his or her professional biography were not an important context, because it really became a programme dissociated from the person of the teachers, but in the case of ENSI many of the teachers involved brought personal conviction to what they were doing, and this created a completely different situation for the evaluation. The more that, as individuals, our personal identity is involved in what we do, the less it is possible for us to accept evaluation. We cannot put ourselves in question, in a fundamental sense, without deep trauma. So in order to accept evaluation (either self-evaluation or external evaluation) it is necessary for us to develop an experimental attitude to what we are doing. In this way we can achieve a certain distancing between our selves - the core of our identity - and what we do and can observe. Cultivating an experimental attitude towards the innovation, in the teachers, was an important part of the ENSI evaluation. Evaluations which do not take this into account risk alienating teachers, who will then typically distance themselves from the report by

169

rejecting many of its findings. Whatever the uses of this style of evaluation, they are not formative, and may actually be destructive of further development.

The style of evaluation reports

This second half of the chapter will explore the relationship between written style and the impact of a report. The following three extracts from evaluation reports (written by CARE researchers) give an indication of the variety of possible styles, and enable us to discuss the range of responses they evoked from readers.

Extract 1

The evaluator was in conversation with students from the MPCS Project and they were questioning him about the way the evaluation worked. How would it report? Would there be, at the end of a long three years, a lengthy and unreadable report? The response (not at all frivolous) was that the more successful the evaluation, the shorter the report - the best final report would be a simple but all-encapsulating phrase. Some weeks later the evaluator was sitting with the Project Director in a bar around the corner from the Guildhall and a regular dropping-in place for students. Simon, a singing student on MPCS, came in for a quick drink before going off to hear a concert being given by singing students on the Jazz course. "Simon", shouted Peter across the bar "will you be joining the course again next year?" Simon hesitated. "I don't think so, Peter. I might have a chance of getting on to the Opera course". (An advanced course and a prestigious opportunity). "Oh, Simon,", Peter teased, "I thought you were committed to this innovation - I thought you'd abandoned the star system!" Simon leaned over sideways as he reached for his pint at the bar - "well, there you are. You see you're not just fighting the institution, you're fighting the dream."

Extract 2

What is clear in our view is the need for better support structures at Force level, more effective monitoring and feedback of probationer experience into formal course provision at both the initial (and subsequent) stages of the centrally planned curriculum. We close this account with two profiles of probationer experience which may help to remind us of how much variation lies behind generalisation. We have chosen these particular probationers because they illustrate the difficulties of responding to variation of many different, but very human kinds.

First Probationer:

Lack of local knowledge hit me very hard. You come from the DTC with a knowledge of all these offences but find that the public really want to know the name of a good fish restaurant, antiques shop, etc...

I am surprised that as regards *paperwork* there are no hard and fast rules. Everybody seems to have their own way of doing things. If I were to ask two different people I would be told two different ways of doing things - all to the same end, though.

Things are not black and white outside. The spirit of the law comes into it. You come out from DTC full of enthusiasm, raring to go. But it's not like that. There is a need for discretion much more than we were led to believe.

Extract 3

Epilogue/Dialogue

...a book is not a closed system(...) but an event in a real, complex, cultural situation. How it is read (misread or not read) is an integral part of that event.
(A. Sheridan 'Michel Foucault: the will to truth')

Well, what kind of an 'event' do we want this report to be? It is certain that we want the report to help us move from monologue (for how else can a text declare itself?) to dialogue (for how else can evaluators learn the missing stories, the neglected interpretations, the plain errors of fact..?). We see that move as a necessity rather than an appendix - we want to 'break' the text that we have made so that we can go beyond it in our understanding. After all, this was a first account from the evaluation. It was only a series of experiments in story and theory - certainly no definitive history - and of course we can do better if we can generate further comment and criticism. So we want this to be an educational event, for ourselves, as for others: we want (already) to reconstruct the account, and undermine the way in which the singularity of the account-as-text undermines the plurality of the stories and theories we have represented.

How are the author's values revealed in a report?

Written style can be a means of clarifying the author's values, or at least appearing to do so. An author's values are never explicit, but there are stylistic techniques which create an illusion of neutrality. In evaluations there is always an issue of self-confirmation: an evaluator inevitably comes to the evaluation with a set of expectations and beliefs and there is a danger that the report may do little more than confirm those beliefs. For example, an evaluator might hold the tacit hypothesis that the best evaluations all analyse failures - and this might lead to him or her writing a report which concentrates on explaining the way in which failure came about. To avoid this trap, evaluators need to be open to other perspectives and other theories and that is a very difficult task, both for an external evaluator and for an insider.

One aspect of the problem is that the author's values may be hidden by the style of writing. Extract Three is a kind of reflection on the aims of the report and its style, and Extract Two makes generalised statements. In both cases the author's values are not made explicit: in the first case because the tone is ironic and detached, and its impact upon the reader is indirect; in the second because the tone is neutral and measured, so that the reader is distracted from considering whether the generalisation is self-confirming.

What is the impact of the report's style on the reader?

Extract Three is fairly representative of the report from which it comes. It is taken from the final page and is a reflection on the report itself. It evoked a strong response at the Cromer conference. One person did not like it but was not, at first, sure why. Was it manipulative? Well, perhaps it was more that the author seemed to be trying to create "an artificially anti-authoritarian report". The report was written for an audience of university academics, some of whom responded to it along the lines: "It is very clever, and we admire it, but it is not very useful." It appealed to the values of this audience, because it avoided the simplification of definite answers and adopted a postmodern reflexivity which was, in itself, of interest to academics at the time. When this report was first written it was not what was expected, but with the passage of time it has become more familiar and therefore increased its appeal to a wider audience. Of course, it is a generalisation to say that no one found it useful - some did find it useful and relevant - but, nevertheless, as a style of reporting, this was a closed system. Readers found it difficult to get into the report. There was ambivalence. Some felt it is was too detached but others objected on precisely the opposite grounds, that it was too intrusive, trying to "pull them in". One person felt "seduced" by the narratives in the text. So, the issue of the style of reporting is a complex one. There is often a rather simplistic assumption that scientific language is neutral and that discursive or narrative writing is either manipulative or subjective. But it is worth asking if there is any such thing as 'neutral' language that speaks direct to the reader without creating layers of meaning in between.

One person at Cromer felt Extract Two was more persuasive because of its clarity. Its style states what kind of evaluation it is conveying: it seems to say that this is a professional job, which claims authority for the value judgements it puts forward by drawing on the collective data and examples. For this reader, there was a clarity and professionalism about the report which was convincing and made him want to read more, whereas he said he was put off by the lack of these qualities in the other extracts.

Extract One comes from a report which was written for students, teachers and inspectors in the field of music and music education. It was very well received because it was consonant with the culture into which it was delivered. At the conference, one participant felt that this extract shared some of the features of a teacher's case study, using quotations from the students' diaries, and giving a vivid picture of events. The reader is free to accept the picture or not, but from the start, this extract is easy to read.

How important is it to adopt the language of the expected audience?

For one person, the strong impact of Extract One resulted from the author's awareness of the power of the metaphor in the last sentence. Whether the author had quoted exactly from data, or made a slight alteration to what was actually said, did not matter. The metaphor encapsulated the problems experienced by those involved in this innovatory music education programme. The choice of metaphor was a significant part of the author's search for the language of the professional group he was addressing. If a psychotherapist uses the wrong language the patient will reject the therapy, and the same is true of the audience of reports. The person who particularly liked this metaphor was encountering a particular problem in writing curriculum designs in ENSI. He found that when he used an academic style the "nature lovers" began to drop out saying, "This is horrible", but equally the "academics" reacted negatively if the style was too informal.

As a result of this need to suit language to reader, it is very difficult to write for multiple audiences. The authors of the ENSI project reports were faced with trying to satisfy a number of different constituencies, for example: nature lovers, those who believed in behaviour modification, action researchers, and the whole community of teachers (in their own country and other countries). It was clearly going to be very difficult to strike the right style. One conference participant felt that it would not be possible - and "if it is not possible, probably it is not desirable". For another participant it was not a matter of being in sympathy with the readers, because he preferred to remain more detached; he wanted "not to persuade them to take over my conclusions, but to think with me". But this meant that he had to "get into their language". A report written in Dutch could not be read by those who did not speak Dutch, but this was only an extreme example of a more general phenomenon. He believed that every report is written in a language which includes some readers and excludes others.

In what ways can a report be written to be persuasive?

The persuasiveness of a report is closely related to questions of language and style, but it is worth mentioning two additional points which arise from the examples.

First, it is often important to create a sense of "being there" by the richness of contextual detail included in the report (Geertz, 1988). Of course this is also a means of claiming eye witness authority over the reader. The text is constructed to suggest to the reader, 'look, trust me, I was there." It could be argued that although the first extract looks more accessible and detailed it is just as much a construction of its author as either of the other two extracts.

That said, evaluation reports aspire to accessibility. This has implications for the kind of access to data which the evaluator needs to negotiate with participants. In Chapter 8 we explained the distinction between "on-the-record" and "off-the-record" data. It is clear that the persuasiveness of Extract One is very dependent on acceptance by the participants that *everything* is on-the-record, and can be drawn upon in the report. To create this style of reporting, the evaluator needed to draw on informal data such as coffee-bar conversations, which here seem to be crucial in communicating the essential meanings of the Programme.

The second point relates to variation in style and format. People might say, "Why should such wide variations of style occur in reports emanating from one small Centre in evaluation?" The variation is deliberate and springs from our realisation that most evaluations are never read because they are too dull; we experiment with different styles of reporting to see if we can increase the attractiveness and readability of reports. A novel style and format is particularly important when trying to reach audiences who do not normally handle things like evaluation reports. On the other hand, such reports can receive very mixed responses. In one CARE evaluation study, of an innovatory technology-mediated curriculum, the interim report was written as a comic strip. The audience included the pupils in the schools who found the report accessible and interesting. But the official response of the schools was to reject the report because senior members of staff were scandalised: they could not conceive of serious information presented in comic-strip form. Video reports are effective because they give people access to the activities in a project, with less intervention from the evaluator, in terms of selection and interpretation, than is the case with any other form of reporting. They are persuasive because they create a strong sense of "being there". But these too have their disadvantages. Video reports create production problems: the quality of the image, and in particular of the sound-track, needs to be high to make an impact on audiences used to the standards of commercial television.

In what other ways might the expected audience influence the language of the report?

There are difficult dilemmas arising from this question of readability. There is often a tendency for sponsors to expect reports to be written in a restricted form - what one might call "de-eroticised" reporting. A programme such as ENSI, funded by the OECD, is likely to face this kind of restriction - and pressure may be brought to bear upon individuals to ensure that they report in a conventional form and language. When this came up for discussion at the conference, one person suggested that it might be a definite strategy. In his view many official reports of the European Community were unreadable ("You do not know who wrote them, the life is taken out of the language") and this appeared to be as a result of deliberate editing ("I have read things I wrote, which other people have edited, and I didn't recognise the report.").

This editing of reports to produce a uniform, neutral style can be a particular problem in the case of reports written for an international audience, the majority of whom will not be reading it in their first language. Different international organisations use different levels of language. In the view of one participant at the Cromer conference, OECD reports are among the most difficult to read in terms of language, whereas Council of Europe reports are easier to read. This can be understood if the purpose of the report is more widely construed. The kind of words used is of great importance if the primary consideration is that people should be able to understand the report. However, reports can have other purposes. They may have more significance as artifacts. If this is the case, the kind of language used may depend on the self-image of the international organisation. The OECD sees itself as a scientific organisation which applies scientific methods to research in economics and the social sciences, so we can infer that it gravitates towards a technicist style and form in an attempt to present knowledge in a neutral 'scientific' language. The question then becomes not whether reports are read, but 'what are the status implications, and authority implications, behind the form of the language that is used?' The relative ease in reading Council of Europe reports may be because it does not have the same need to build up its status as an authoritative, scientific organisation. The style of reporting has become a question of the image of the organisation.

Another dilemma is over length. If we want people to read evaluation reports then the shorter they are the better, but on the other hand, the shorter they are the more lifeless they tend to become. Perhaps, the best solution is to have several reports at different levels of length and detail, so that people can have one-page summaries, six-page summaries and 200-page supporting documents. The hope is that they will look at the summaries and at least dip into the full report, either to validate the summary or simply to find out more. This is a matter of judgement and responsibility. One evaluation carried out at CARE produced a series of case study accounts for a committee charged with making decisions about the future of a number of projects. With difficulty, the length of each case-study was reduced to between 10 and 15 pages, without losing the complexity and without waiving the participants' rights to negotiate the accounts (to ensure that the reports were adequate representations of those projects upon which people could make decisions about their value). When a member of the committee still complained, saying, "I sit on 74 other Committees as well as this one. I cannot read this", the evaluators' answer was, "We serve the judgement, not the judge." The authors of evaluation reports have to take into consideration that decision-makers are busy people, but ultimately, if they are unable to read reports which have been made as succinct as possible, it is arguable that they should not be making decisions. Of course, this line of reasoning does not appeal to those concerned.

A third dilemma relates to the sponsor's need to maintain the kind of image which will secure its funding. Perhaps decision-makers would read reports if they were interesting, regardless of the length, but this would require an open style of reporting which would expose the organisation to possible criticism.

Can teachers in different countries benefit from exchanging their writing? How does the writing stage compare with the final product in terms of the participants' and the sponsors' learning?

What is the chance that a report from Finland will be read by a teacher in Italy? Teachers in the programme have a degree of cultural tolerance, but there is a need for an international programme such as ENSI to create a common language. A good starting point, drawing on Extract Two, might be to find some good metaphors, as the first step in generating a common language and discourse. It is not only a question of language, but also one of authenticity - the report may depend for its life upon the kind of examples that are included and the way in which they are presented. The next step might be to establish some ground rules for the format of reporting. In the first phase of ENSI John Elliott set out a framework for writing case studies, and many teachers wrote reports with a strong narrative thread. These were readable and informative, and could provide a starting point in discussions leading to an agreed format for the evaluation reports. However, some teachers may need a lot of support to write case studies of this kind, depending on the cultural context in which they are working (in terms of both subject discipline and nationality).

It is not only the style of reporting which is important. Unless a report has some function for the reader, relating in some way to a shared concern, the only reason for reading it is as one reads a novel. This makes big demands on the skill of the writer in creating a text which compels attention. However, if a report has a function for the reader, in the sense that it contains important information, it becomes readable even if it is not vividly written. As authors, we have to think about the function of the report in the whole context of our work. It is a plausible hypothesis that one of the reasons why final reports are so rarely read is that the content is not seen as important by those who commission them. What is important is only that they have asked someone to conduct an evaluation, because that establishes their accountability for the spending of public money. They don't feel in any way obliged to draw consequences out of the report. It is not read, because it is not really functional. On the other hand, if the report does not have apparent status and authority it may not fulfil its purpose in terms of accountability.

These multiple purposes of the evaluation mean that the most important interaction and communication between people happens *during* the writing stage, rather than after the report is written. At this stage people feel obliged to listen to each other. The writers feel acknowledged because in the course of writing they can offer something from their own experience, and the readers have a purpose in that there is a possibility of influencing the report through their advice. Interaction at the writing stage is a learning process, by comparison with which the end product is relatively unimportant.

What is the role of theory in an evaluation report?

However descriptive an evaluation report, it will still be informed by theory in the selection, ordering and tone of its presentation. Some of this will be contextual; that is the theories that emerge through the study of *this* case, or *this* programme. But is there an argument for setting the report within more explicit or abstract theoretical analyses? People will often say it will not appeal to sponsors and that they dislike reading 'academic knowledge' in a report because it appears arcane, spuriously authoritative and alienating for those who are not part of the culture of the knowledge club from which it is derived. However those who are in such a 'knowledge club' may be important interest groups for the evaluation. Representing their knowledge provides the opportunity for insight into the rationales and theories that inform their actions. The evaluation of the British Government's Training Agency 'Standards Programme' is a clear example. This evaluation was conducted by Maggie MacLure and Nigel Norris and focused upon the question, 'How is knowledge handled within the competency based model, when deriving occupational standards across the professions?' They found that different groups privileged different kinds of knowledge. By analysing these knowledge frameworks and conveying the diversity of views, the evaluation acted as a mediator across these different groups. Each party had supposed, incorrectly, that they had previously understood the motives of others. The report emphasised the need for each of the groups - the educators, professionals and trainers - to trade conceptions of knowledge.

Because knowledge frameworks are customised to different groups in this way, representing theoretical knowledge can help to contextualise the meanings behind people's actions. This is as true for environmental education as for any other field. At the beginning of this chapter we quoted a comment overheard at a conference on Environmental Education: "Knowledge causes acid rain. Let's have action, not knowledge." Paradoxically, this is a statement of a theoretical position. People reading this in an evaluation report would need to know the premises upon which this demand for action is based. The task for the evaluator is to excavate and represent such tacit theories. Politics and action in the environment are matters of complexity and contention. Evaluation should facilitate a concern to reach for deeper understandings and engage in a process of enquiry. The purpose of an evaluation report should be to stimulate reflection and debate, not foreclose upon it. In the words of TS Elliot (1963):

We shall not cease from exploration
And the end of all our exploring
Will be to arrive where we started
And know the place for the first time.

References

ELIOT, T.S. (1963), "The Four Quartets", In *Collected Poems 1909-1962*, Faber and Faber: London.

GEERTZ, C. (1988), *Works and Lives: the anthropologist as author*, Polity Press: Cambridge UK.

MACDONALD, B., Walker, R. (1974), SAFARI - Innovation Evaluation Research and the Problem of Control, SAFARI - Workshop Curriculum No 1, CARE, University of East Anglia.

SHERIDAN, A. (1980), *Michel Foucault: the will to truth*, Tavistock: London.

APPENDIX

LIST OF PARTICIPANTS

Australia

Ian Robottom
School of Education
Deakin University
Geelong
Victoria 3217

Austria

Günther Pfaffenwimmer
Ministry of Education and Arts
Minoritenplatz 5
A-1014 Vienna

Peter Posch
University of Klagenfurt
Universitätstraße 67
A-9022 Klagenfurt

Franz Rauch
University of Klagenfurt
Universitätstraße 67
A-9022 Klagenfurt

Belgium

Claude Bustin
Centre d'auto-formation et de formation continuee
Rue Grégoire Bodard, 1
B-4500 Huy

Dirk Coolsaet
HPIGO Lier
Berlaarsestraat 31
B-2500 Lier

Luc Henau
Inspecteur de géographie
Rerum-novarumstraat, 4
B-8370 Blankenberge

Denmark	Christian Christensen Royal Danish School of Educational Studies Emdrupvej 101 DK-2400 Copenhagen NV
Finland	Reijo Laukkanen Counsellor of Education National Board of Education Hakaniemenkatu 2 SF-00530 Helsinki
	Kyosti Kurtakko Professor, University of Lapland Post Box 122 SF-96100 Rovaniemi
France	Maryse Clary IUFM d'Aix-Marseille 23 rue Eugène Cas F-13000 Marseille
Germany	Dietmar Bolscho Universität Hannover Fachbereich Erziehungswissenschaften 1 Bismarckstraße 2 D-3000 Hannover 1
Hungary	Judith Szunyogh Senior Adviser Institute for Environment Management Department of Education 1369 Pf 352 Alkotmàny u 29 H-1054 Budapest V
	Emoke Mohi Ministry of Environment
Eire & Ulster	John Medlycott Curriculum Development Unit Sundrive Road Dublin 12 Co Dublin

Italy	Michela Mayer
	Centro Europeo dell'Educazione (CEDE)
	Villa Falconieri
	I-00044 Frascati
	Bruno Losito
	Centro Europeo dell'Educazione (CEDE)
	Villa Falconieri
	I-00044 Frascati
Japan	Noviyuki Nasu
	University of the Air
	2-11 Wakaba
	260 Chiba
	Kazuo Watanabe
	Senior Specialist
	International Affairs
	Planning Division
	Ministry of Education
	2-2 Kasumigaseki 3-chome
	Chiyoda-ku
	Tokyo
Netherlands	Maarten Pieters
	National Institute for Curriculum Development SLO
	P O Box 2041
	NL-7500 CA Enschede
	Bert Van Beek
	KPC Innovation Institute
Norway	Astrid Sandas
	The Royal Norwegian Ministry of Education and Research
	P O Box 8119 Dep
	N-0032 Oslo 1
	Per Bjorn Foros
	Trondheim College of Education
	Rotvoll Allé
	N-7000 Trondheim
Portugal	Odete Sousa Martins
	DGEBS (Direccao Geral dos Ensinos Basico e Secondario)
	Av 24 de Julho, n_ 140
	P-1391 Lisboa Codex

Slovenia

Barica Marentic Pozarnik
Univerza Edvarda Kardelja
v Ljubljani
Filozofska Fakulteta
Askerceva 12
61001 Ljubljana

Majda Skerbinek
Univerza Edvarda Kardelja
v Ljubljani
Filozofska Fakulteta
Askerceva 12
61001 Ljubljana

Spain

Ramon Lara Tebar
Universidad Complutense
Av Filipinas 3
E-28003 Madrid

Sweden

Harriet Axelsson
Institute for Education
University of Gothenburg
Box 1010
S-43126 Mölndal

Olle Nordgren
Swedish National Board of Education
Karlavagen 108
S-10642 Stockholm

Switzerland

Regula Kyburz-Graber
Universität Zürich
Abt Umweltnaturwissenschaften XB
ETH-Zentrum
CH-8092 Zürich

United Kingdom

Colin McAndrew
SCC
Gardyne Road
Broughty Ferry
Dundee DD5 1NY

United States

John R Paulk
Tennessee Valley Authority
415 Walnut Street
LB 1N
Knoxville TN 37902-1499

Lynn Michael Hodges
Tennessee Valley Authority
Forestry Building TVA
Norris TN 37828

Members of CARE

Richard Davies
John Elliott
Saville Kushner
Maggie Maclure
Barry MacDonald
Anne McKee
Nigel Norris
May Pettigrew
Lucila Recart
Bridget Somekh
University of East Anglia
Centre for Applied Research in Education (CARE)
School of Education
Norwich   NR4 7TJ

Secretariat OECD/CERI

Kathleen Kelley
2 Rue du Conseiller Collignon
F-75116 Paris

Catherine Beattie
c/o OECD/CERI

Acronyms

A-R	Action research
CARE	Centre for Applied Research in Education
CERI	Centre for Educational Research and Innovation
DTC	District Training Centre
DTI	Department of Trade and Industry
EE	Environmental education
ENSI	Environment and School Initiatives
HCP	Humanities Curriculum Project
INSET	Inservice training
IV	Interactive video
IVIS	Interactive Video In Schools Programme
IT	Information technology
LEA	Local education authority
MPCS	Music, Performance and Communication Skills
OECD	Organisation for Economic Co-operation and Development
PALM	Pupil Autonomy in Learning with Microcomputers Project
SAFARI	Success and Failure and Recent Innovation
WWF	World Wide Fund for Nature

MAIN SALES OUTLETS OF OECD PUBLICATIONS
PRINCIPAUX POINTS DE VENTE DES PUBLICATIONS DE L'OCDE

ARGENTINA – ARGENTINE
Carlos Hirsch S.R.L.
Galería Güemes, Florida 165, 4° Piso
1333 Buenos Aires   Tel. (1) 331.1787 y 331.2391
Telefax: (1) 331.1787

AUSTRALIA – AUSTRALIE
D.A. Information Services
648 Whitehorse Road, P.O.B 163
Mitcham, Victoria 3132   Tel. (03) 873.4411
Telefax: (03) 873.5679

AUSTRIA – AUTRICHE
Gerold & Co.
Graben 31
Wien I   Tel. (0222) 533.50.14

BELGIUM – BELGIQUE
Jean De Lannoy
Avenue du Roi 202
B-1060 Bruxelles   Tel. (02) 538.51.69/538.08.41
Telefax: (02) 538.08.41

CANADA
Renouf Publishing Company Ltd.
1294 Algoma Road
Ottawa, ON K1B 3W8   Tel. (613) 741.4333
Telefax: (613) 741.5439
Stores:
61 Sparks Street
Ottawa, ON K1P 5R1   Tel. (613) 238.8985
211 Yonge Street
Toronto, ON M5B 1M4   Tel. (416) 363.3171
Telefax: (416)363.59.63

Les Éditions La Liberté Inc.
3020 Chemin Sainte-Foy
Sainte-Foy, PQ G1X 3V6   Tel. (418) 658.3763
Telefax: (418) 658.3763

Federal Publications Inc.
165 University Avenue, Suite 701
Toronto, ON M5H 3B8   Tel. (416) 860.1611
Telefax: (416) 860.1608

Les Publications Fédérales
1185 Université
Montréal, QC H3B 3A7   Tel. (514) 954.1633
Telefax : (514) 954.1635

CHINA – CHINE
China National Publications Import
Export Corporation (CNPIEC)
16 Gongti E. Road, Chaoyang District
P.O. Box 88 or 50
Beijing 100704 PR   Tel. (01) 506.6688
Telefax: (01) 506.3101

DENMARK – DANEMARK
Munksgaard Book and Subscription Service
35, Nørre Søgade, P.O. Box 2148
DK-1016 København K   Tel. (33) 12.85.70
Telefax: (33) 12.93.87

FINLAND – FINLANDE
Akateeminen Kirjakauppa
Keskuskatu 1, P.O. Box 128
00100 Helsinki

Subscription Services/Agence d'abonnements :
P.O. Box 23
00371 Helsinki   Tel. (358 0) 12141
Telefax: (358 0) 121.4450

FRANCE
OECD/OCDE
Mail Orders/Commandes par correspondance:
2, rue André-Pascal
75775 Paris Cedex 16   Tel. (33-1) 45.24.82.00
Telefax: (33-1) 49.10.42.76
Telex: 640048 OCDE

OECD Bookshop/Librairie de l'OCDE :
33, rue Octave-Feuillet
75016 Paris   Tel. (33-1) 45.24.81.67
(33-1) 45.24.81.81

Documentation Française
29, quai Voltaire
75007 Paris   Tel. 40.15.70.00

Gibert Jeune (Droit-Économie)
6, place Saint-Michel
75006 Paris   Tel. 43.25.91.19

Librairie du Commerce International
10, avenue d'Iéna
75016 Paris   Tel. 40.73.34.60

Librairie Dunod
Université Paris-Dauphine
Place du Maréchal de Lattre de Tassigny
75016 Paris   Tel. (1) 44.05.40.13

Librairie Lavoisier
11, rue Lavoisier
75008 Paris   Tel. 42.65.39.95

Librairie L.G.D.J. - Montchrestien
20, rue Soufflot
75005 Paris   Tel. 46.33.89.85

Librairie des Sciences Politiques
30, rue Saint-Guillaume
75007 Paris   Tel. 45.48.36.02

P.U.F.
49, boulevard Saint-Michel
75005 Paris   Tel. 43.25.83.40

Librairie de l'Université
12a, rue Nazareth
13100 Aix-en-Provence   Tel. (16) 42.26.18.08

Documentation Française
165, rue Garibaldi
69003 Lyon   Tel. (16) 78.63.32.23

Librairie Decitre
29, place Bellecour
69002 Lyon   Tel. (16) 72.40.54.54

GERMANY – ALLEMAGNE
OECD Publications and Information Centre
August-Bebel-Allee 6
D-53175 Bonn   Tel. (0228) 959.120
Telefax: (0228) 959.12.17

GREECE – GRÈCE
Librairie Kauffmann
Mavrokordatou 9
106 78 Athens   Tel. (01) 32.55.321
Telefax: (01) 36.33.967

HONG-KONG
Swindon Book Co. Ltd.
13–15 Lock Road
Kowloon, Hong Kong   Tel. 366.80.31
Telefax: 739.49.75

HUNGARY – HONGRIE
Euro Info Service
Margitsziget, Európa Ház
1138 Budapest   Tel. (1) 111.62.16
Telefax : (1) 111.60.61

ICELAND – ISLANDE
Mál Mog Menning
Laugavegi 18, Pósthólf 392
121 Reykjavik   Tel. 162.35.23

INDIA – INDE
Oxford Book and Stationery Co.
Scindia House
New Delhi 110001   Tel.(11) 331.5896/5308
Telefax: (11) 332.5993
17 Park Street
Calcutta 700016   Tel. 240832

INDONESIA – INDONÉSIE
Pdii-Lipi
P.O. Box 269/JKSMG/88
Jakarta 12790   Tel. 583467
Telex: 62 875

IRELAND – IRLANDE
TDC Publishers – Library Suppliers
12 North Frederick Street
Dublin 1   Tel. (01) 874.48.35
Telefax: (01) 874.84.16

ISRAEL
Praedicta
5 Shatner Street
P.O. Box 34030
Jerusalem 91430   Tel. (2) 52.84.90/1/2
Telefax: (2) 52.84.93

ITALY – ITALIE
Libreria Commissionaria Sansoni
Via Duca di Calabria 1/1
50125 Firenze   Tel. (055) 64.54.15
Telefax: (055) 64.12.57
Via Bartolini 29
20155 Milano   Tel. (02) 36.50.83
Editrice e Libreria Herder
Piazza Montecitorio 120
00186 Roma   Tel. 679.46.28
Telefax: 678.47.51
Libreria Hoepli
Via Hoepli 5
20121 Milano   Tel. (02) 86.54.46
Telefax: (02) 805.28.86
Libreria Scientifica
Dott. Lucio de Biasio 'Aeiou'
Via Coronelli, 6
20146 Milano   Tel. (02) 48.95.45.52
Telefax: (02) 48.95.45.48

JAPAN – JAPON
OECD Publications and Information Centre
Landic Akasaka Building
2-3-4 Akasaka, Minato-ku
Tokyo 107   Tel. (81.3) 3586.2016
Telefax: (81.3) 3584.7929

KOREA – CORÉE
Kyobo Book Centre Co. Ltd.
P.O. Box 1658, Kwang Hwa Moon
Seoul   Tel. 730.78.91
Telefax: 735.00.30

MALAYSIA – MALAISIE
Co-operative Bookshop Ltd.
University of Malaya
P.O. Box 1127, Jalan Pantai Baru
59700 Kuala Lumpur
Malaysia   Tel. 756.5000/756.5425
Telefax: 757.3661

MEXICO – MEXIQUE
Revistas y Periodicos Internacionales S.A. de C.V.
Florencia 57 - 1004
Mexico, D.F. 06600   Tel. 207.81.00
Telefax : 208.39.79

NETHERLANDS – PAYS-BAS
SDU Uitgeverij Plantijnstraat
Externe Fondsen
Postbus 20014
2500 EA's-Gravenhage   Tel. (070) 37.89.880
Voor bestellingen: Telefax: (070) 34.75.778

NEW ZEALAND
NOUVELLE-ZÉLANDE
Legislation Services
P.O. Box 12418
Thorndon, Wellington   Tel. (04) 496.5652
Telefax: (04) 496.5698

NORWAY – NORVÈGE
Narvesen Info Center – NIC
Bertrand Narvesens vei 2
P.O. Box 6125 Etterstad
0602 Oslo 6   Tel. (022) 57.33.00
     Telefax: (022) 68.19.01

PAKISTAN
Mirza Book Agency
65 Shahrah Quaid-E-Azam
Lahore 54000   Tel. (42) 353.601
     Telefax: (42) 231.730

PHILIPPINE – PHILIPPINES
International Book Center
5th Floor, Filipinas Life Bldg.
Ayala Avenue
Metro Manila   Tel. 81.96.76
     Telex 23312 RHP PH

PORTUGAL
Livraria Portugal
Rua do Carmo 70-74
Apart. 2681
1200 Lisboa   Tel.: (01) 347.49.82/5
     Telefax: (01) 347.02.64

SINGAPORE – SINGAPOUR
Gower Asia Pacific Pte Ltd.
Golden Wheel Building
41, Kallang Pudding Road, No. 04-03
Singapore 1334   Tel. 741.5166
     Telefax: 742.9356

SPAIN – ESPAGNE
Mundi-Prensa Libros S.A.
Castelló 37, Apartado 1223
Madrid 28001   Tel. (91) 431.33.99
     Telefax: (91) 575.39.98

Libreria Internacional AEDOS
Consejo de Ciento 391
08009 – Barcelona   Tel. (93) 488.30.09
     Telefax: (93) 487.76.59
Llibreria de la Generalitat
Palau Moja
Rambla dels Estudis, 118
08002 – Barcelona
     (Subscripcions) Tel. (93) 318.80.12
     (Publicacions) Tel. (93) 302.67.23
     Telefax: (93) 412.18.54

SRI LANKA
Centre for Policy Research
c/o Colombo Agencies Ltd.
No. 300-304, Galle Road
Colombo 3   Tel. (1) 574240, 573551-2
     Telefax: (1) 575394, 510711

SWEDEN – SUÈDE
Fritzes Information Center
Box 16356
Regeringsgatan 12
106 47 Stockholm   Tel. (08) 690.90.90
     Telefax: (08) 20.50.21
Subscription Agency/Agence d'abonnements :
Wennergren-Williams Info AB
P.O. Box 1305
171 25 Solna   Tel. (08) 705.97.50
     Téléfax : (08) 27.00.71

SWITZERLAND – SUISSE
Maditec S.A. (Books and Periodicals - Livres
et périodiques)
Chemin des Palettes 4
Case postale 266
1020 Renens   Tel. (021) 635.08.65
     Telefax: (021) 635.07.80

Librairie Payot S.A.
4, place Pépinet
CP 3212
1002 Lausanne   Tel. (021) 341.33.48
     Telefax: (021) 341.33.45

Librairie Unilivres
6, rue de Candolle
1205 Genève   Tel. (022) 320.26.23
     Telefax: (022) 329.73.18

Subscription Agency/Agence d'abonnements :
Dynapresse Marketing S.A.
38 avenue Vibert
1227 Carouge   Tel.: (022) 308.07.89
     Telefax : (022) 308.07.99

See also – Voir aussi :
OECD Publications and Information Centre
August-Bebel-Allee 6
D-53175 Bonn (Germany)   Tel. (0228) 959.120
     Telefax: (0228) 959.12.17

TAIWAN – FORMOSE
Good Faith Worldwide Int'l. Co. Ltd.
9th Floor, No. 118, Sec. 2
Chung Hsiao E. Road
Taipei   Tel. (02) 391.7396/391.7397
     Telefax: (02) 394.9176

THAILAND – THAÏLANDE
Suksit Siam Co. Ltd.
113, 115 Fuang Nakhon Rd.
Opp. Wat Rajbopith
Bangkok 10200   Tel. (662) 225.9531/2
     Telefax: (662) 222.5188

TURKEY – TURQUIE
Kültür Yayinlari Is-Türk Ltd. Sti.
Atatürk Bulvari No. 191/Kat 13
Kavaklidere/Ankara   Tel. 428.11.40 Ext. 2458
Dolmabahce Cad. No. 29
Besiktas/Istanbul   Tel. 260.71.88
     Telex: 43482B

UNITED KINGDOM – ROYAUME-UNI
HMSO
Gen. enquiries   Tel. (071) 873 0011
Postal orders only:
P.O. Box 276, London SW8 5DT
Personal Callers HMSO Bookshop
49 High Holborn, London WC1V 6HB
     Telefax: (071) 873 8200
Branches at: Belfast, Birmingham, Bristol, Edinburgh, Manchester

UNITED STATES – ÉTATS-UNIS
OECD Publications and Information Centre
2001 L Street N.W., Suite 700
Washington, D.C. 20036-4910 Tel. (202) 785.6323
     Telefax: (202) 785.0350

VENEZUELA
Libreria del Este
Avda F. Miranda 52, Aptdo. 60337
Edificio Galipán
Caracas 106   Tel. 951.1705/951.2307/951.1297
     Telegram: Libreste Caracas

Subscription to OECD periodicals may also be placed through main subscription agencies.

Les abonnements aux publications périodiques de l'OCDE peuvent être souscrits auprès des principales agences d'abonnement.

Orders and inquiries from countries where Distributors have not yet been appointed should be sent to: OECD Publications Service, 2 rue André-Pascal, 75775 Paris Cedex 16, France.

Les commandes provenant de pays où l'OCDE n'a pas encore désigné de distributeur devraient être adressées à : OCDE, Service des Publications, 2, rue André-Pascal, 75775 Paris Cedex 16, France.

6-1994

OECD PUBLICATIONS, 2 rue André-Pascal, 75775 PARIS CEDEX 16
PRINTED IN FRANCE
(96 94 04 1) ISBN 92-64-14211-8 - No. 47441 1994